The Private Lives of
Victorian Women

The Private Lives of Victorian Women

autobiography in nineteenth-century England

Valerie Sanders

Lecturer in English Literature
University of Buckingham

St. Martin's Press
New York

© 1989 Valerie Sanders

All rights reserved. For information, write:
Scholarly and Reference Division,
St. Martin's Press, Inc., 175 Fifth Avenue, New York, NY 10010

First published in the United States of America in 1989

Printed in Great Britain

ISBN 0-312-00961-5

Full CIP data are available from the publisher

For Paul and Rosemary

Contents

Preface

Soon after her marriage, when she had gone to live at Craigenputtoch, Jane Welsh Carlyle was sitting up at night, waiting for a loaf of bread to bake. Unused to doing anything so housewifely, she waited in intense solitude, her heart 'aching with a sense of forlornness and *degradation*'. Then she thought of the autobiographer Benvenuto Cellini, watching his statue of Perseus baking in the oven:

> The man's determined will, his energy, his patience, his resource, were the really admirable things, of which the statue of Perseus was the mere chance expression. If he had been a woman living at Craigenputtoch with a dyspeptic husband, sixteen miles from a baker, *and he a bad one*, all these same qualities would have come out most fitting in a *good* loaf of bread!
> I cannot express what consolation this germ of an idea spread over an uncongenial life, during five years we lived at that savage place.[1]

Had Jane Carlyle been a man, she would probably have written an autobiography herself; being a woman, she wrote autobiographical letters, and allowed the inspiration she had derived from Cellini to take a domestic and practical form. The purpose of this study is to see why so few Victorian women wrote autobiographies that fit the generally accepted definitions, and how those whose work approximated to this ideal were driven into a variety of rhetorical strategies which fulfilled their need to speak out, while preserving their aura of reserve and selflessness. The main emphasis is therefore literary, paying close attention to the language used by women in their attempts to reproduce their experiences and opinions within the constraints of a genre that has never been regarded as their rightful territory. The question of what each autobiographer decides to omit or stress, her artistic shaping of her own life, is a central concern, as are the consequent evasiveness of her self-portraiture and the existence of an undeciphered sub-text. It is always difficult, in a study of this kind, to decide how much to accept at face-value, and how much to 'read between the lines'. In some cases it is genuinely impossible to tell whether an autobiographer has internalised the values of a dominant male culture and really believes what she says about her own inferiority. In others, where a margin of doubt exists, I have tried to penetrate below the surface and work out what kind of debate may be going on under cover of conventional disavowals. The result may be tantalisingly inconclusive, but it further proves the wealth of this body of material, largely overlooked by critics of Victorian autobiography.

Certainly, autobiography cannot be treated purely as a literary phenomenon, as my choice of texts will demonstrate. The autobiographers I discuss were achieving women, writing in England between 1818 and 1930. Margaret Fuller Ossoli and Isadora Duncan, who were both Americans, are included because of their prominence in English cultural life and because of a certain rootless quality in their lives which made them less purely American than, for example, Elizabeth Cady Stanton. I have also omitted privately printed autobiographies, on the grounds that they are less widely accessible to the general reader, and working-class autobiographies, which belong to a separate (if related) tradition of their own. The autobiographies discussed here are essentially middle-class and professional, though their authors range from the fourteen-year-old child poet and prodigy, Elizabeth Barrett, to the Prime Minister's wife and society hostess, Margot Asquith. The way in which they are grouped, according to theme, profession, and, to some extent, chronology, risks levelling out the differences between them, but draws attention to the existence of a very real and tangible tradition of autobiographical writing by Victorian women. In Chapter 2, this tradition is given some context by a general survey of women's autobiography before the nineteenth century; and the final chapter ends with women born in the 1850s and 1860s, writing in the 1920s, beyond which point the notion of a 'Victorian' tradition becomes less easy to substantiate.

The study of autobiography is no longer the 'Cinderella' of literary criticism, as it was a few years ago. Particularly during the 1980s in the USA, perceptive readings of the genre have appeared fairly frequently; but there is still a shortage of full-length studies specifically of autobiography by women. The most useful collection of essays remains Estelle C. Jelinek's *Women's Autobiography: Essays in Criticism* (Bloomington and London: Indiana University Press, 1980), and to this I am chiefly indebted for inspiration and ideas. A 'Northern Network' seminar at the University of Hull in February 1988 gave me a much appreciated opportunity to discuss my work with a stimulating audience, and the editorial staff of Harvester Wheatsheaf helped me to formulate the initial plan and scope of the book. Jackie Jones and an anonymous, but constructive outside reader, gave valued assistance in the later stages. I am also grateful to Dr Kenneth Sanders for his comments on Kleinian psychoanalysis and to Philip Dodd, Editor of *Prose Studies*, for publishing an earlier version of my work on professionally successful Victorian women and their consciousness of a critical audience.

Finally, as autobiographers, in their self-obsession, rarely say much about their siblings, this book is dedicated to my brother and sister.

Notes

1. *I Too Am Here: Selections from the Letters of Jane Welsh Carlyle*, ed. Alan and Mary McQueen Simpson (Cambridge: Cambridge University Press, 1977), pp. 200–1.

Chapter 1

Hidden Lives

the problems of women's autobiography

Oh if I might write my own biography from beginning to end – without reservation or false colouring – it would be an invaluable document for my countrywomen in more than one particular – but '*decency forbids*'!

Jane Welsh Carlyle, 1843[1]

It was impossible for her to write an autobiography, but she wished that somebody else could do it, it might be useful – or that she could do it herself. She could do it better than any one else, because she could do it impartially, judging herself, and showing how wrong *she* was.

Emily Davies on George Eliot, 1869[2]

Jane Welsh Carlyle insisted that 'looking back was not intended by nature . . . from the fact that our eyes are in our faces and not in our hind heads'.[3] Perhaps few Victorian women would have accepted this bizarre physiological explanation, but most evidently agreed that to write one's own biography 'without reservation' savoured of egotism as well as indecency. It was an impossible task, which none of the major nineteenth-century women novelists attempted. Elizabeth Gaskell wrote a biography of her friend Charlotte Brontë; Brontë herself transmuted her memories into fiction; Emily Brontë wrote short diary papers on her birthdays, but no formal autobiography; George Eliot thought about it from time to time, but found the idea repellent, preferring to fictionalise her experiences, or commemorate important events in occasional journal entries. Among the poets, Elizabeth Barrett Browning wrote two autobiographical sketches in childhood but ultimately combined fact and fantasy (with a good deal else) in *Aurora Leigh*, while Christina Rossetti, in *Time Flies*, concealed her more personal thoughts among the leaves of an Anglican reading diary. For autobiography to compare with Anthony Trollope's, John Stuart Mill's, John Henry Newman's, or John Ruskin's, one must turn to the minor women novelists, such as Margaret Oliphant and Elizabeth Missing Sewell, or the social reformers and theorists, such as Harriet Martineau and Frances Power Cobbe. Not until the final quarter of the nineteenth century did a significant number of women who enjoyed professional success in any field publish formal autobiography, and even then it often dwindles into chatty reminiscences of old friends and extracts from their correspondence.

Perhaps, then, we should feel no surprise that so many recent studies of Victorian autobiography have treated the genre as though it were dominated entirely by men: a rugged terrain inhabited by the four 'giants', Mill, Carlyle, Newman and Ruskin, occasionally supplemented with studies of Gosse and Trollope. Linda Peterson admits Harriet Martineau to her band of hermeneutic autobiographers; George P. Landow and James Olney include, in their collections of essays, one or two studies of female autobiography; and Jerome Hamilton Buckley openly acknowledges 'the virtual absence of women' from his general argument. While conceding that several women have written cogently of their careers and special interests, he concludes that 'the more private subjective impulse in women writers seems for the most part to have been better satisfied in autobiographical fiction.'[4] Susanna Egan, in the same year as Buckley, confesses that some critics 'took umbrage' at her omission of female autobiographers. Again, she sees the novel as a richer area of autobiographical activity by Victorian women, adding that others, specifically Harriet Martineau and Beatrice Webb, were 'so "manly" in explanation of their hard-won dignity, purpose, and achievement that they do not lend themselves to a study of what is essentially Romantic autobiography'.[5] This accusation of excessive 'manliness' surely raises more questions than it answers and should make us query the implied identification of the 'Romantic' with the 'womanly'. Susanna Egan does suggest that the evolution of female autobiography deserves a study of its own, but so far there has been only one book specifically devoted to the subject: Estelle Jelinek's *Women's Autobiography* (1980). This, however, makes no pretensions to trace such an evolution. The book is a collection of essays, some historical, some theoretical, on individual writers or groups of writers, who are seen in some way as landmarks along the road taken by women who have attempted to retell their own lives.

Yet, as many critics have acknowledged, whether directly or by implication, there is no lack of self-writing by Victorian women to be considered. The great mass of diaries, journals, autobiographical fiction, travel books and memoirs written by women in the nineteenth century testifies to a widespread preoccupation with individual experience, and a desire to communicate it, if only privately, or in a disguised form. Increasingly, women felt that what had happened to them, whether at home or abroad, whether commonplace or extraordinary, deserved retelling, especially to other women, who could find it 'useful'. Both Jane Carlyle and George Eliot, in the passages quoted, hint momentously at the effect of their hypothetical disclosures; Jane specifically has in mind her fellow 'countrywomen'. When there were things she wished to say about Mr Carlyle, she told them humorously in letters to her friends, and morbidly in journals to herself. On special occasions, such as her journey of 1849 to her birthplace at Haddington, she opened a fresh journal to record a series of emotional reunions, closing it again when the temporary state of unreality was over. At the end of her Haddington journal, Jane takes a self-conscious farewell of herself, as if she were a character in a novel:

> And now having brought myself to Edinburgh and under the little protecting wing of Jeannie [a cousin], I bid myself adieu and 'wave my lily hand' – I was back into the Present! and it is only in connection with the Past that I can get up a sentiment for myself. The Present Mrs Carlyle is what shall I say? – *detestable* – upon *my* honour.[6]

Jane Carlyle was not alone in finding her past self more compelling, even more sympathetic, than her present. Charlotte Brontë's present, in the empty parsonage of the 1850s, often sounds more hollow and monotonous than the rich days of her Angrian romances. George Eliot, though much happier with Lewes in London than with her father in Coventry, recurs to the vanished past as a time of strong instinctual memories. Occasionally, in her adult life, she felt the need to commemorate an important event, to record, for example, how she came to write fiction, or what she remembered of her 'Aunt Samuel' who had provided the germ of Hetty's story in *Adam Bede*.[7] Emily and Anne Brontë, in their birthday diary papers, attempted to crystallise the essence of their present lives, as a way of shoring up fragments against time; and in the process, wrapped up small parcels of autobiography to be opened and read by themselves at stated intervals. This is perhaps the most complex autobiographical instinct among Victorian women writers. The sisters' diary papers combine both a summary of the last few years and a continuous narrative of the present, recording what everyone was doing at that precise moment, and any dialogue that interrupted their writing:

> Taby said just now Come Anne pilloputate [i.e. pill a potato] Aunt has come into the kitchin just now and said Where are your feet Anne Anne answered On the floor Aunt. Papa opened the parlour door and gave Branwell a letter saying Here Branwell read this and show it to your Aunt and Charlotte. The Gondals are discovering the interior of Gaaldine. Sally Mosley is washing in the back kitchin.[8]

The narrative veers not only, as has been noticed, from the real to the imaginary and back again, but also from the recent past ('just now') to the continuous present ('The Gondals are discovering . . . Sally Mosley is washing.'). In their more mature papers Emily and Anne select important events from the past few years, offering a longer retrospect than in this record of 1834. One by one, the opened diary-narratives formed a series of highlighted moments in the Brontës' lives, linking past, present and future, and personal aspiration with collective family history. Random, spontaneous and flexible, they were intended only for ceremonial reading within the family. Part of no recognisable genre, indeed unique to the Brontës, can they in any sense be called autobiography? Can Jane Carlyle's retrospective accounts of herself? Or George Eliot's commemorative notes of new eras in her life?

Definition of autobiography has always been difficult. Although the Oxford English Dictionary states plainly enough that autobiography is 'the writing of one's own history; the story of one's life written by himself', and every literate person knows the difference between this and biography, nevertheless, as a definition, it is riddled with ambiguities. Is autobiography a story or a history? Would a series of facts placed end to end, without interpretation or commentary, be considered autobiography? These ambiguities are typical of the vagueness that blurs the distinctions between texts that most critics would accept unequivocally as 'true' autobiography, part of the recognised canon, and those that many would reject, or banish to the margins. This seems to be especially true of self-writing by women. While few critics would question the right of Mill and Trollope to call their works autobiographies, most would be uneasy about including the Brontës' diary-papers or even Mrs Humphry Ward's recollections of her family and friends. For the purists, autobiography implies selection, order, shaping; a complex interplay between the present self and the self as recalled at various stages of the recorded life-story. Autobiography must do more than report: it must explore the meaning of a person's life, and interpret it, so that both writer and reader are enlightened by the study of an individual's growth to philosophical, as well as physical maturity. Jerome Hamilton Buckley suggests that the ideal autobiography 'presents a retrospect of some length on the writer's life and character, in which the actual events matter far less than the truth and depth of his experience'.[9]

Those who prefer a broader definition of the genre maintain that autobiography is identifiable by 'some evidence that the writer's self is either the primary subject or the principal object of the verbal action'.[10] A writer's collected works might be regarded as autobiography, if they trace the development of an individual, or if his identity is somehow inseparable from his writing, as one may feel with Tolstoy, T. S. Eliot, James Joyce or D. H. Lawrence. George Eliot certainly found this view congenial. 'It seems to me that just my works and the order in which they have appeared is what the part of the public which cares about me may most usefully know,' she argued against the craze for contemporary biography.[11] James Olney goes further still, suggesting first that 'a theology, a philosophy, a physics or a metaphysics', may all be treated as forms of autobiography; and then that definition of the genre seems to him 'virtually impossible, because the definition must either include so much as to be no definition, or exclude so much as to deprive us of the most relevant texts'.[12] This is the impasse that has been reached by much recent study of the forms of self-writing.

Most Victorian women saw autobiography as a forbidden area, and deliberately situated themselves outside its formal parameters. Significantly, the first recorded uses of the term, both critically and in the title of a work, are attributed to men.[13] Even those women who did set out to write formal autobiography tended to shy away from the generic term. Coleridge's daughter Sara called her unfinished work *Recollections of the Early Life of Sara Coleridge, Written by Herself* (1851); a modest title echoed by Mary Russell Mitford in her *Recollections of A Literary Life* (1852) whose subtitle, *Books, Places, and People*, deflected still further any pretensions to egotistical self-examination. In each of these cases, the writer proffers no more than a portion of her history, an area about which she feels no personal qualms ('Early Life', 'Literary Life') for public consumption. Fanny Kemble's *Record of a Girlhood* (1878) was originally serialised in the *Atlantic Monthly* as 'Old Woman's Gossip', though Kemble herself preferred 'Elderly Female Twaddle'. In the book version, the word 'gossip' occurs three times in the opening paragraph, varied by 'personal recollections' and 'reminiscences'. Her *Record* was designed primarily to amuse, and also to anticipate the efforts of biographers to tell her story for her. Faced with this unwelcome prospect, Kemble decided it was better to gather the 'lightest of leaves' on her own behalf.[14]

Mary Somerville, the mathematician and scientist who was universally admired for her domesticity, also chose the term *Personal Recollections* (1873) and her daughter Martha, who edited the work, warned her readers to adjust their expectations:

> The life of a woman entirely devoted to her family duties and to scientific pursuits affords little scope for a biography. There are in it neither stirring events nor brilliant deeds to record; and as my Mother was strongly averse to gossip, and to revelations of private life or of intimate correspondence, nothing of the kind will be found in the following pages.[15]

Using 'biography' and dropping the egotistical prefix, Martha Somerville implies that the genre is normally gripping and gossipy, and as such, somewhat disreputable for a woman. Her mother is prepared to write only on her own terms; though one cannot help suspecting the daughter of over-zealous policing. The adjective 'Personal' also serves a steadying purpose, in that the book is not offered as a record of Mrs Somerville's professional life. Mrs Humphry Ward, on the other hand, minimised the personal – another form of authorial self-defence – by calling her work *A Writer's Recollections* (1918). True to its title, the text meanders fairly randomly through a series of anecdotal portraits and descriptions.

The generic label 'Recollections' seems to have been especially attractive to women memoirists. Like 'Reminiscences', it suggests something casual, easy, unstructured, resembling family stories at the fireside. Everybody has 'recollections', and even the humblest have their share of interest. Moreover, they are usually about other people. The speaker is often no more than a reporter of outmoded practices, funny experiences, or impressions of the great and famous, and her audience's attention is focused on the told, rather than on the teller. 'Recollections', too, follow their own process of association, an inner logic that need not be justified or explained. 'All my little recollections are like pictures to which the meaning, naturally, is put long afterwards,' wrote Margaret Oliphan. one of the few who did actually call her work an 'autobiography'.[16] Elizabeth Wordsworth, who called hers only *Glimpses of the Past* (1912), explained that her 'recollections' would not be a 'continued account of years and days, but more like a collection of photographs, strung together by a very slight thread of narrative'.[17] Two of her chapter headings are simply 'Miscellaneous Extracts' and 'Various Letters'. Anne Thackeray Ritchie preferred the image of the witches' cauldron containing 'heterogeneous scraps . . . nothing more valuable than odds and ends happily harmless enough'.[18]

Those who were bold enough to call their work 'autobiography' were generally women who had already flouted convention, and drawn attention to themselves by their participation in controversial campaigns. Harriet Martineau and Annie Besant are the best examples, though the religious novelist, Elizabeth Missing Sewell, whose *Autobiography* was published in 1907, also accepts the more professional appellation. But by this time, the term was in more regular use. Critics wrote frequently about autobiography as a genre, just as Mrs Oliphant had done for *Blackwood's* in the 1880s, and some of the old stigmas were beginning to disappear.

Autobiography is traditionally an apologetic mode, both for men and for women. Even those male writers who called their works 'autobiography' (John Stuart Mill and Anthony Trollope, for example) felt the need to apologise for obtruding themselves and their concerns on the public; but the public, on the whole, was more ready to accept these obtrusions from famous men than from famous women. Annie Besant was sharply reprimanded by the critics for her vanity and conceit. The *Spectator* complained that there were many forms of egotism: 'few more insidious than that which besets Mrs Besant'; while the *Athenaeum* claimed her vanity was 'conspicuous on every page'.[19] Mrs Somerville and Fanny Kemble got a better press because they emphasised the pleasant and entertaining aspects of their lives, and seemed surprised to find themselves in a position of public interest. An aura of freshness and innocence was essential to the success of any autobiography by a Victorian woman. Once she appeared hardened and defiant, or too full of her own convictions, she risked hostility from her own sex, as well as from the other.[20]

The reasons for this are not far to seek. Every advice book and domestic manual since Hannah More reminds young women that their demeanour in the family should be modest and submissive, self-sacrificing and gentle. Advancing claims on other people, or attracting public notice were alike inimical to the womanly ideal. According to Ruskin in 'Of Queens' Gardens' (1865), a woman must be infallibly wise 'not for self-development, but for self-renunciation'; while the whole burden of Mrs Ellis's *Women of England* series is that consideration for others was the most important lesson that a girl could learn. Mrs Ellis, in fact, insists that a woman without domestic and family ties is an anomaly:

> Women, considered in their distinct and abstract nature, as isolated beings, must lose more than half their worth. They are, in fact, from their own constitution, and from the station they occupy in the world, strictly speaking, relative creatures. If, therefore, they are endowed only with such faculties as render them striking and distinguished in themselves, without the faculty of instrumentality, they are only as dead letters in the volume of human life, filling what would otherwise be a blank space, but doing nothing more.

Paradoxically, the more individual and 'striking' a woman is in herself, the more Mrs Ellis would deny her substance as a living being. An isolated woman who lives only for herself and her achievements is a hollow woman, living a fruitless existence. Her greatest role, for which she is 'most valued, admired, and beloved' is, quite simply, 'disinterested kindness'.[21]

Such theories as Mrs Ellis's assume that every middle-class woman lives in a state of comfortable ease in the midst of a large family of parents, siblings, children and husband, and that her sphere of activity will be limited, selfless and domestic. A sound education makes a woman rational, and a good companion for her husband, rather than encouraging her to pursue a career of her own. Clearly, everything about Mrs Ellis's womanly ideal is the direct opposite of the qualities needed to initiate an act of self-writing, or indeed to see oneself as a separate being, detached and motivated, claiming an audience in one's own right. The theory of 'separate spheres', upheld especially by Ruskin and Mrs Ellis, was at its most influential between about 1837 and 1865: significantly a time when there was very little formal autobiography by women.

Even in the second half of the century, when collections of exemplary female biographies enjoyed a popular revival, editors were uneasy about the self-evident contradiction between feminine modesty and distinction. 'In writing the Lives of Women, it is impossible not to feel one special source of difficulty,' admits one of Charlotte M. Yonge's contributors to her *Biographies of Good Women*((1862):

> Nearly all women, who have been renowned enough to come under the notice of history, (even of those more quiet histories which dwell the least on political changes, and the most on domestic life,) have been so by the sacrifice of something more or less womanly: they have done or said something to be talked of. Most of all does this strike us when we have to speak of learned women.[22]

W. H. Davenport Adams, who published a volume called the *Child-Life and Girlhood of Remarkable Women* (1883), felt bound to warn his impressionable young readers against some of the negative examples in his collection, particularly Harriet Martineau. Accusing her of 'stupendous egotism', he concluded that she 'had none of that exquisite tenderness and sympathetic power which we find in the greater minds'.[23] Adams attempts to show that achievement is not necessarily incompatible with a pleasant temperament, but he underlines the moral dangers of intellectual confidence.

Most commentators simply assumed that the female mind was wrongly constituted for the writing of autobiography. As Linda Peterson has recently shown, educational theorists, from the end of the sixteenth century onwards, regarded women's mental capacities as fundamentally limited and unsuited to the process of synthesis and analysis that is indispensable to true autobiographical writing.[24] Peterson concentrates on the example of Hannah More, but similar theories were held well into the nineteenth century. Again, Ruskin is the chief propagandist. He sees women as being graceful, tender, intuitive, potentially brimming with empathy, and unlike the male historian, able to 'trace the hidden equities of divine reward, and catch sight, through the darkness, of the fateful threads of woven fire that connect error with retribution'.[25]

While Ruskin contrasts woman's special intuitive powers with the historian's techniques of analysis and organisation, an earlier theoriser, M. A. Stodart, in her *Female Writers: Thoughts on Their Proper Sphere, and on Their Powers of Usefulness* (1842), states quite categorically that women ought not to be historians because their feelings interfere with their judgement. Their mental characteristics are sensitivity, delicacy, tact and sympathy, but they cannot reason. Whatever may be their talents, she decides, 'they must be shaded by sweetness, veiled by modesty'. She even warns her readers against the dangers of excessive letter-writing, as 'very dangerous to the moral character. When we speak of ourselves, we are standing on the edge of a precipice, and it is well if we escape a heavy fall.' Concluding with some dark warnings as to the risks run by literary women, she insists that 'publicity can, to a woman, never be a native element; she may be forced into it by circumstances, but the secret sigh of every truly feminine heart will be for the retirement of private life.'[26] 'Man excels in imagination, woman in fancy,' argued another critic, William Landels, in *Woman: Her Position and Power* (1870):

> He reflects profoundly on facts and principles, laboriously manipulating them, and marshalling and remarshalling, that he may arrive safely at generalisations which he can turn to practical account; she, on the other hand, using her quick perception, brings it immediately to bear on the details of practical life, and, without stopping to reason about them, uses her fine tact in applying to others the things which she knows.[27]

A supporter of women's property reform, and even the suffrage, Landels makes man sound slow and clumsy, woman deft and quick, but this fails to compensate for his conclusion that man's study is ultimately more profound and successful, while woman is better suited to being a 'charming and agreeable companion'. However much mid-century theorists urged women to become more rational, there was always a sense that biology would prevail and prevent women from achieving any real distinction in areas other than novel-writing. Quickness and intuition alone were flimsy equipment for the mighty task of compiling an autobiography of the philosophical type, like John Stuart Mill's, or the professional, like Anthony Trollope's, or the theological, like John Henry Newman's. There is a sense, too, that male commentators on the whole preferred it that way.

John A. Kempe, who edited the *Autobiography of Anna Eliza Bray* (1884), prefaces the work with a lengthy apology for his relative's inability to shape and compress her anecdotal memories. Anna Eliza Bray (1789–1883) was a minor literary figure; a friend of Southey, and author of journals, notebooks and undemanding historical works such as

Courtenay of Walreddon (1844), *Joan of Arc* (1874) and *Good St. Louis* (1870). 'The faculty which was wanting in her,' Kempe argues, 'and for the want of which her genius fell short of the first rank, was that of selection and condensation.' She was surrounded by appreciative friends, subjected to little criticism, and endowed with 'defective logical judgement', which Kempe attributes to her 'nervousness, a constitutional weakness which accompanied her, and had its effect upon her fortunes throughout life'. For Kempe, the image of Anna Eliza Bray is inseparable from a certain cabinet in her sitting-room, which contained all the precious memorials of her career: 'there is great order, but no method'.[28] Kempe's criticism is accurate enough, in view of Bray's 'loose baggy monster' of a narrative, but his tone is patronising and discouraging. He clearly relegates her to the quiet backwaters of her vicarage drawing-room, where she could nurse her 'nervousness' in unregarded tranquillity.

In fact, many Victorian women were only too well aware of the dangers inherent in any serious form of self-writing. 'To be one's own chronicler is a task generally dictated by exteme vanity,' Elizabeth Barrett confessed at the age of fourteen; and although she was intrigued by the process, she recurred uneasily to the accusations of egotism that she felt might, with some justice, be levelled at her. She wondered, too, whether she might be guilty of too much feeling and too little argument: 'Perhaps there is too much of sentiment in my disposition and too little rational reflection.'[29] Jane Carlyle felt guilty about keeping even a journal, in case she was tempted to let her emotions run away with her. As a sharp warning, she retold herself Charles Buller's maxim, 'What could a poor fellow do with a wife who kept a journal but murder her?' and accepted that there was a certain truth in it: 'Your journal all about feelings aggravates whatever is factitious and morbid in you'; so henceforth she would keep only a record of 'the fact of things'.[30] This, combined with her sense of decency, served to keep in check any latent autobiographical instincts.

Among those who did write formal autobiography, there was a perpetual feeling of awkwardness, a nervous looking over the shoulder at an accusing audience. Even Annie Besant, whom most reviewers regarded as quite brazen in her outspokenness, admits in the Preface to her *Autobiography* (1893) that, at the best, telling the story of one's own life 'has a savour of vanity, and the only excuse for the proceeding is that the life, being an average one, reflects many others, and in troublous times like ours may give the experience of many rather than of one.' Autobiography, which most people would regard supremely as the narrative of an individual life, and the growth of an individual consciousness, became, for some Victorian women, the story of a generation, a slice of representative life in a specific period. This was certainly one way of minimising the egotistical impulses behind their writing. Annie Besant argued, improbably enough in her case, that since we all have the same anxieties and hopes, 'it may well be that the tale of one soul that went out alone into the darkness and on the other side found light . . . may bring some ray of light and of peace into the darkness and the storm of other lives.'[31] Frances Power Cobbe, too, saw her life as representing more than her own personal aspirations and achievements: 'the joys, sorrows and interests, the powers and limitations of one of my sex and class in the era which is now drawing to a close.' Perhaps the best known example of this representative consciousness, though outside the Victorian period, is Vera Brittain, who regarded her story in *Testament of Youth* (1933), as 'typical' of a whole generation's tragic experiences.[32]

For most male autobiographers, by contrast, the expected format was along the lines of 'a history of my life and opinions', the pattern followed most notably by John Stuart Mill and J. H. Newman. Where the author had undergone several changes of belief, a stage-by-stage account of his philosophical evolution formed an essential part of his public act of self-justification, as it did for a small number of women, especially Harriet Martineau; but there is a sense too, that male autobiographers felt they owed their audiences a special insight into the way their careers developed and their books were written. Perhaps the most extreme example is the psychologist and logician Alexander Bain (1818–1903) whose *Autobiography* (1904) is divided into regular chronological episodes ('Winter Session 1836–37', 'Summer Recess 1837') reflecting with minute exactitude every degree of his intellectual progress. Among his 'objects in writing' Bain lists his wish to 'indicate the stages of mental growth, under the circumstances of the time', and 'to present a con-secutive view of my published writings and pass a judgement upon each, so that the latest positions may be indicated'.[33] A similar pattern informs Trollope's readers of his mature judgement on his novels, both good and bad, and gives his *Autobiography* a firm chronological structure.

That few Victorian women felt at home with this tradition is proved by their unwillingness to engage in long, consistent examinations of all their achievements. More commonly, those who wanted, in some way, to narrate their experiences, adapted other forms to their uses. If the more formal and regular kinds of autobiography, which depicted the growth of a mind or the development of a career, were alien and inappropriate, because women were not encouraged to view themselves in those terms, there were other modes that could be made both congenial to the writer and acceptable to the reader. If, on one side, autobiography was related to history and philosophy, on the other it had clear links with the diary and letter, the travel memoir and the novel. These four modes were pre-eminently the province of women in the nineteenth century, and for readily discernible reasons.

The diary, unlike the autobiography, is private and unstructured. It registers the smallest changes of feeling, and is written blindly, without foreknowledge of the future. Its range is entirely a matter of choice for the writer. She can use her diary to monitor her spiritual progress, as many Evangelicals did; or she can confine herself to bald facts, a straight record of what was done when. Essentially, the diary requires only brief spurts of attention, and is the ideal outlet for a woman who is likely to be interrupted, or who dreads publicity. Queen Victoria herself sanctioned the practice in 1868, by publishing her *Leaves from the Journal of Our Life in the Highlands*. From the domestic journal, it was only a short step to the journal kept on a foreign tour, which often formed the basis for a modest publication on the diarist's return. The travel-journal was clearly more public than the private diary, but by the middle of the century women had claimed it as their special field. Lady Eastlake, for one, was convinced that women wrote better travel books than men. There was 'an advantage in the very nature of a book of travels peculiarly favourable to a woman's feelings – the almost total absence of responsibility. It is merely the editorship of her own journal.' Nevertheless, she cautioned, the writer's personality was one of its most important ingredients. 'But though the lady tourist has her modesty thus far screened and sheltered, it is equally certain that there is no department of writing through which her own individual character is more visible.'[34]

Her character was visible, but it need not be tainted with vanity and egotism. The woman traveller went abroad as a reporter of strange customs or breathtaking views, which it was her task to relay home with an appropriate sense of the picturesque. She need hardly mention herself and still less anything beyond the most conventional feelings. The letter-form was especially attractive to women travel-writers, with its assurance that the recipient was a friend, real or invented, the initial audience, at least, carefully circumscribed. Fanny Kemble's *Journal of A Residence on a Georgian Plantation in 1838–1839* (1863) is dedicated to her friend Elizabeth Dwight Sedgwick, with the inscription that the journal was kept originally for her. Although the Preface describes it as a 'diary', the book is composed of letters to 'My dear E.', but they are specially fabricated letters that were never posted. None the less, Kemble evidently felt at home with this mode of presentation, especially since many of her observations concerned the controversial issue of slavery on her former husband's estate.

Anna Jameson's travel books are even more personal. Her *Diary of an*

Ennuyée (1826), based on journals written during a tour of France and Italy when Jameson was a governess, purports to be the diary of a melancholy twenty-six-year-old, whose death at the end is gently announced by the 'editor'; but the writer's sorrows and ills represent Jameson's own, after the temporary breaking off of her engagement. Its fragmentary nature is indicated by asterisks marking 'the places where one or more leaves had been torn away by the writer, and where there may sometimes appear a want of continuity'.[35] In *Winter Studies and Summer Rambles in Canada* (1838), the act of writing is seen as therapeutic, and yet unselfishly motivated:

> If it were not for this journalizing, I should fall into a lethargy – as it is I could envy a marmot or a dormouse; and if it were not for my promise to you, I should even abandon this daily noting of daily nothings, of which I begin to be thoroughly ashamed.[36]

Anna Jameson is one of several women writers who combine the diary and letter forms in their autobiographical writing. Since the eighteenth century, as Ruth Perry has pointed out, 'letters were the one sort of writing women were supposed to be able to do well'.[37] Like the diary form, the letter evades formal patterning. The writer can use it to discuss anything or nothing as the mood takes her; she can interrupt herself or be interrupted without necessarily damaging the coherence of what she has written. Again, the recipient is known and trusted; the form as nearly as possible reproducing the conditions of a confidential talk between friends. Both altruistic and self-indulgent, the letter form may be used to solace others or provide an outlet, as in Jane Carlyle's case, for the relief of oppressive feelings about her husband and family. Victorian women autobiographers use letters in two main ways. Actual letters are inserted at crucial points in the work, partly to increase its authenticity and give a flavour of the times, but often to record spontaneous praise for their achievements by an incidental or indirect method; while fabricated letters that were never posted or received, but give the author the illusion that she is addressing someone, other than the impersonal public, form the basis, not only of travel-books, but also of memoirs, collections of essays and even spiritual autobiography.

For many nineteenth-century women, the illusion of writing letters to a sympathetic friend was the only enabling entry into autobiographical discourse. The letters, in such cases, do not form a genuine correspondence between two people, but a one-sided narrative, regularly broken off, and written in response to an imagined request for information about the writer's life. Urged to tell all, the writer can hardly refuse: her story is then retold as an act of kindness to an implied friend, rather than from an unwomanly desire for attention and admiration. Few men found it necessary to invent such elaborate subterfuges as that revealed by the Evangelical novelist, 'Charlotte Elizabeth' (Mrs Tonna) in her *Personal Recollections* (1841), which she begins with the declaration: 'I have given my best consideration to the arguments by which you support the demand for a few notices of events connected with my personal recollections of the past'; the word 'demand' contributing an urgency she can hardly ignore.[38] In Mrs Tonna's case, the unselfish motives were fuelled by an Evangelical compulsion to offer spiritual testimony to the discipline she had received from God. Another minor writer and auto-biographer, Mary Sewell, mother of Anna Sewell who wrote *Black Beauty*, constructed her unfinished autobiography as a letter to her grandchildren. Her opening lines both domesticate her readership, and reduce it to the family circle. 'My dear Grandchildren,' she begins com-fortably, as if introducing a fireside story, '– I entirely sympathise with your wish to know all I can tell you of your ancestors on the Wright side.' Although she was born 'about the time of the great French Revolution – and from that time to this includes the grand march of commerce, science, and invention', she intends telling nothing 'but family scraps – odds and ends'. The focus of interest is frequently directed away from herself. 'I want to try to immortalise my father in the memory of his descendants.'[39] Mrs Sewell was a Quaker, and her seventy-six-page autobiography is reminiscent of the seventeenth-century family memoir. Her editor, Mrs Bayly, willingly reinforces the impression of a quiet, unobtrusive life given by the autobiographical narrative, and suggests that it represents the experience of the undistin-guished majority.

As late as 1942, and in entirely different circumstances, the diarist Anne Frank also felt that the illusion of writing to a friendly correspond-ent, whom she calls 'Kitty', was more congenial than communing only with herself. Because Kitty is not herself, she begins with a sketch of her own and her family's history, something that would be irrelevant if the diary lacked an implied audience. Virginia Woolf addressed the 'Reminiscences' she began around 1907 to her nephew Julian Bell. In this way, many women have externalised and objectified their desire to write about themselves, against the assumed prohibitions of a disapproving society, and at the same time made their act of self-writing essentially a private gesture.

Of course, men as well as women deposit fragments of autobiography in unlikely places. As David DeLaura has shown, Victorian men often used the medium of the essay to explore aspects of their own lives, 'shaping and reshaping their past experience for present purposes, while ostensibly talking about something else: society, literature or religion.'[40]

It has always been difficult to draw a firm dividing line between the end of a personal reminiscence and the beginning of autobiography: most writers, after all, draw on their own knowledge and comprehension of human emotion and society. But most of the male essayists, such as Mill, Ruskin and Newman, also wrote formal autobiography and did not depend on the essay as a means of filtering personal experience.

Self-writing by Victorian women frequently turns up on the fringes of apparently altruistic projects. Mrs Gaskell's friend, Susanna Winkworth, tells much of her own story in the life of her sister Catherine, having been 'asked by many friends, whether she could not write some slight memorial of her'.[41] Henry James, admittedly, does much the same in *A Small Boy and Others* (1913), which professes to be about his brother William, but the confident and leisurely pace of James's narrative suggests an autobiographer more at ease with the form, and the encouragement to introspection. Lady Martin (formerly the actress Helen Faucit) allows herself only snatches of autobiography in her survey of Shakespeare's heroines: a book presented as a series of letters to friends who have asked her to write down the substance of their conversations. The fact that most of Lady Martin's friends were dying when they made their requests further intensified the need. 'My friend lived to see only two of them,' she reported of Geraldine Jewsbury, 'but after reading these, she asked me to promise her that I would have them printed, at least for circulation among my friends.' Viewed in these terms, Lady Martin's task was obligatory; but she used the opportunity of writing about Ophelia to describe the daydreams and delicate health of her childhood days alone by the sea.[42]

Both Anna Jameson and Harriet Martineau insert childhood memories into what are ostensibly domestic manuals. Under cover of advising parents how to deal humanely with nervous children, both authors reveal the traumas of their own upbringings, especially the fears which they were afraid to confess and the reveries they indulged.[43] Repeatedly in writing by Victorian women, the intimate is marginalised, pushed to the very edge of their text, or restricted to incidental or fragmented expression in works purporting to be about something else. As if they felt their own experiences were an unpardonable intrusion, they held them back from all but occasional expression, using themselves more as case-histories than as unique examples of personality and achievement.

Finally, there remains the problem of autobiographical novels. Why did so many women prefer to transmute their lives into fiction, instead of making a direct plea for the understanding of their audiences? The two writers with the strongest autobiographical impulse were Charlotte Brontë and George Eliot, whose writing is generally a refraction of their

own emotional experiences. Charlotte Brontë uses the first-person narrator in every novel except *Shirley*, while George Eliot, in her early tales
and novels often depicts herself as a nostalgic wanderer in the landscape
of her childhood. Both draw on a recognised body of autobiographical
material, which has been too well documented by other critics to need
further elaboration here. Both, however, seem to have been tempera-
mentally resistant to any form of openly autobiographical writing; and
to this temperamental reluctance were added further social and personal
disincentives raised by their private lives. From the start, both were determined to conceal their true identities: neither novelist had the slightest
inclination to gratify the public with a candid account of her innermost
feelings and development as a writer.

On the positive side, there were many good reasons for fictionalising
their experiences, rather than recounting them in formal autobiography.
One might argue, in any case, that even the formally autobiographical
self remains a fictional construct, since nobody can reproduce exactly
what happened at any one time and bridge the inevitable gap between the
lived life and the written.[44] This being the case, the step towards
autobiographical fiction is only a small one, with numerous additional
advantages.

Foremost of these must be freedom from the severe linear chronology
of formal autobiography. Fiction of this kind is more selective than its
non-fictional counterpart, and the writer is also free to make adjustments
in her heroine's family circumstances to bring out the sense of emotional
isolation which is nearly always a characteristic of women's autobiography, whether fictional or formal. Then, whereas formal autobiography
usually peters to a half-hearted conclusion, as the author loses interest in
herself and waits for death, a fictional story can be ended at a contrived
or conclusive moment: the symbolic drowning of Tom and Maggie in
each other's arms, the death of Lucy Snowe's delusive hopes in M. Paul's
shipwreck, or Jane Eyre's painfully happy reunion with the maimed and
chastened Mr Rochester. Art, inevitably, is tidier than life. It allows a
cathartic shaping, and is therefore more successful in laying ghosts.

The stylistic freedom of fiction over formal autobiography is another
attraction. The formal autobiographers tend to adopt a conservative
style, combining self-mockery with earnestness, in the accepted mode,
whereas the surreal element in Brontë, for example, constitutes a new
way of exploring the anarchic potential of female passion: something no
decent Victorian woman autobiographer would directly acknowledge.
Of course, many women autobiographers do describe their irrational
emotions, their fears of strange lights or the dark, but these are normally
confined to the period of childhood. On the other hand, *Villette*'s (1853)

rich symbolic structures, its series of buried treasures and identities, its succession of enclosed rooms and fevered escapes, release a more radical psychological truth than generally can be found in the 'scientific' step-by-step method of non-fictional self-writing. An imaginative, or poetic reconstruction of a life, with its opportunity to explore new experiences that were not available to the author, or even to play multiple parts in one story, enabled writers such as Charlotte Brontë to broaden the dimensions of autobiography in a profound, yet protected format.

Unlike Charlotte Brontë, George Eliot rarely uses the first-person narrator as the central consciousness of the novel, and when she does, as in *The Lifted Veil* (1859) or *Impressions of Theophrastus Such* (1879), the speaker is always male. However closely she identified with her heroines, especially Maggie Tulliver and Dorothea Brooke, she was apparently never tempted to write their lives as a first-person narrative. Except perhaps in *Middlemarch*, the omniscient narrator's voice, with its nostalgic references to the slow and sleepy days before the railways, is also generally masculine, especially in the early novels. Perhaps this appeared to give her writing more detachment and authority, or even, occasionally, a worldly humour that would relieve the dour atmosphere of her memories. 'Looking back on my past, it seems to me so full of errors and failures, that any testimony to happy memories of me cherished by those with whom I used to be in frequent contact, is exceedingly precious to me,' she told a friend in 1868.[45] The male narrative persona arises logically enough from the male pseudonym, which has survived the passage of time far more durably than 'Currer Bell', but it also provides a more impenetrable disguise than anything afforded by a female voice. After reading Harriet Martineau's *Autobiography* (1877), George Eliot was filled with a renewed sense of horror at the indignities of self-exposure, especially where close personal relationships were concerned. Martineau's comments on her own works filled Eliot with 'shuddering vexation' with herself that she had 'ever said a word to anybody about either compliments or injuries' in relation to her own doings:

> I confess, that the more I think of the book and all connected with it, the more it deepens my repugnance – or rather creates a new repugnance in me – to autobiography, unless it can be so written as to involve neither self-glorification nor impeachment of others. I like that 'He, being dead, yet speaketh,' should have quite another meaning than that.[46]

What she did admire in the *Autobiography* was its depiction of Martineau's childhood, and its omission of any references to the quarrel between Harriet and her brother James, which was as severely divisive as that between Marian and Isaac Evans. When the *Autobiography* appeared, George Eliot told Cara Bray that she 'rejoiced profoundly in the conquest of right feeling which determined her to leave the great, sad breach with her once beloved brother in almost total silence'.[47] What seemed impossible to recount in conventional autobiography she clearly felt the need to exorcise in some other form, and nearly all the autobiographical references in her novels refer to the sorrows and ephemeral joys of childhood. However close her identification with Maggie, George Eliot's separation from her heroine is reinforced by the use of an omniscient adult narrator, whose maturity and wisdom are ultimately greater than that of the adult autobiographer looking back at his or her younger and sillier self. In a formal autobiography, it would have been impossible for her to effect such a break between the self-as-character then, and the self-as-commentator now, even though, as many critics have noticed, the break in the novel is by no means as clean as the artistic integrity of the work requires.

She also resisted the strict patterning that she felt would be imposed by the task of retracing her own life in chronological order. In the section on 'Story-telling' in *Leaves from a Note-Book* (1913), her jottings for *Theophrastus Such*, she suggests that memory revives certain incidents which made a strong impact in the past. Images and pictures have a superior mastery in grasping the attention; afterwards, in adult life, comes the desire for orderly narration, to trace the antecedent facts behind the image. She describes 'our earliest, strongest impressions, our most intimate convictions', as 'simply images added to more or less of sensation', and goes on to relate this to autobiography:

> The only stories life presents to us in an orderly way are those of our autobiography, or the career of our companions from our childhood upwards, or perhaps of our own children. But it is a great art to make a connected strictly relevant narrative of such careers as we can recount from the beginning. In these cases the sequence of associations is almost sure to overmaster the sense of proportion.[48]

This helps to explain the imbalance of *The Mill on the Floss* (1860), but also posits an almost Joycean kind of autobiography, where the author follows an 'associative' stream of ideas with an inner and personal, rather than an external logic.

As it is, Avrom Fleishman regards *The Mill* as 'at once an autobiographical novel and a critique of the entire canon of autobiographical writing as it descended into (George Eliot's) own time.'[49] Autobiography, especially as written by Victorian men, usually celebrates a triumph over adverse circumstances, an emergence from a troubled childhood to a successful maturity, whereas according to Fleishman *The Mill's* tragic sense of life marks it out from the generality of self-satisfied retrospects. In fact, its writing was interrupted by the production of a far darker piece of fictional autobiography, *The Lifted Veil* (1859), whose first-person narrator foretells his own date of death, and, unlike Maggie, becomes his brother's rival. Like Theophrastus Such and Lucy Snowe, Latimer is presented as an isolated eccentric, morbid and introspective, craving understanding but unlikely to meet it. Whenever Charlotte Brontë and George Eliot use the autobiographical mode in their fiction, they seem to be challenging their readers to feel compassion for an unprepossessing or apparently unimportant individual: a friendless teacher, a brown-skinned, dark-haired schoolgirl, a clairvoyant of 'diseased consciousness', and a man who, in old age, finds himself 'uncared for and alone'.[50] Yet each of these pseudo-autobiographies makes a valid claim for its protagonist. Each of these neglected people deserves understanding from his invisible audience; the audience itself, George Eliot suggests, must learn to foster sympathy for the ordinary and ugly. In this respect, many Victorian women make an important contribution to the development of autobiography in the nineteenth century, proving that the hidden, or unremarkable life has as much right to be told and understood as the lives of great leaders and statesmen.

As her career developed, George Eliot became less interested in imagining scenes in which she was 'chief actress', and more aware of the fundamental similarities between people. 'We are all apt to forget how little there is about us that is unique, and how very strongly we resemble many other insignificant people who have lived before us,' she told John Blackwood when speculation about her identity was at its height. In 1870, Lewes gave her 'a Lock-up book for her Autobio[raphy]', but in the end it was left to her young widower, John Cross, to gather up her memorabilia and compile 'an *autobiography* (if the term may be permitted) of George Eliot. The life has been allowed to write itself in extracts from her letters and journals.'[51]

In fact, George Eliot's personal memories are diffused widely through all her writing, and defy any neat parcelling up into packets of retrospect. She is typical of the vast majority of Victorian women who needed to tell their own story, but evaded direct confrontation with their former selves. Throughout the nineteenth century, women are found pushing the retrospective impulse to one side of their writing lives: concealing it in travel memoirs, disguising it in autobiographical fiction, releasing fragmented memories into manuals or essays that profess to be about Shakespeare or household management, confining themselves to the private and short-term retrospect of diaries and letters, weaving together their more public letters into 'recollections', mostly of other people, or assuming the character of reclusive men whose surly manner has cost them all but a few close friends. For most women, formal modes of autobiography, the 'stage-by-stage' professional or intellectual pattern of growth, were alien and inappropriate. 'What has a woman to do with dates?' asked Lady Morgan, rejecting the 'cold, false, erroneous, chronological' approach that George Eliot also found uncongenial. 'Her poetical idiosyncrasy calculated by epochs, would make the most natural points of reference in woman's autobiography.'[52]

* * *

The critic of Victorian women's autobiography has a bewildering choice of analytical equipment to assist in the process of deciding whether there is a separate tradition of women's self-writing. Lady Morgan's protest, for example, seems to anticipate some of the most avant-garde thinking of French feminist theory, particularly Julia Kristeva's essay 'Women's Time', first published in 1979. Kristeva here contrasts the cyclical and 'monumental' notions of time that she associates with female subjectivity, with the linear time of history: 'time as project, teleology, linear and prospective unfolding: time as departure, progression and arrival.' This is also the time of language, considered as the structure and enunciation of sentences. Referring to Freud's *Studies on Hysteria* (1895), she adds that 'the hysteric (either male or female) who suffers from reminiscences would, rather, recognise his or her self in the anterior temporal modalities: cyclical or monumental.'[53] Kristeva's insight into women's apparent alienation from notions of linear time might seem to argue a case for approaching the problems of autobiography by Victorian women through the linguistic and psychoanalytic methods of French feminist theory. Certainly, recent studies in this field have powerfully affirmed the 'foreignness' of the social order to women, and encouraged critics to observe the ways in which this consciousness of difference, of marginality, reveals itself in their writing. In an interview of 1974, Julia Kristeva argued that 'women generally write in order to tell their own family story ... Freud's statement "the hysteric suffers from reminiscence" sums up the large majority of novels produced by women.'[54] Kristeva also recognises that while women have the potential to explode social codes, they tend to identify with a power after having rejected it. This is very much the case with the majority of Victorian women novelists and even some of the ambivalent feminists, such as Harriet Martineau.

French feminist theory emphasises the problematic nature of women's relationship to language. 'In women's writing,' says Kristeva, 'language seems to be seen from a foreign land.'[55] At the same time, it urges women to develop a fluid, semiotic language of their own, and assert their identity in what Hélène Cixous calls 'a *new insurgent* writing'.[56] Entry into any form of public discourse in seen as a kind of triumphant agony. 'Every woman has known the torment of getting up to speak,' Hélène Cixous argues. 'Her heart racing, at times entirely lost for words, ground and language slipping away – that's how daring a feat, how great a transgression it is for a woman to speak – even just open her mouth in public.'[57] This offers a useful gloss on a recurrent symbolic scene in Victorian women's autobiography: a speech-making experience, in which the autobiographer recalls her first liberating attempt to speak aloud in an empty room, listening to the miraculous sound of her own voice reverberating around her. Jane Eyre undergoes a similar experience when she turns on Mrs Reed, and upbraids her for telling lies to Mr Brocklehurst. Yet the moment of verbal release is generally followed by an overwhelming sense of shame and self-censorship, akin to the consciousness of 'transgression' mentioned by Cixous. Discussion of Victorian women's autobiography will inevitably keep returning to the assertion-negation pattern of much female self-writing.[58]

Where French feminist theory proves disappointing in a project based on the close study of nineteenth-century texts is in its argument that 'the female body is seen as direct source of female writing'.[59] If Victorian women were sometimes uneasy about their relationship to dominant forms of autobiographical writing, fixed chronologies and mental history, there is no evidence that they escaped into a distinctively feminine '*jouissance*' or in any way celebrated female sexuality. If anything, they see it as a disruptive and unwelcome force, the source of tragic passions and unwanted babies. Moreover, sexual crises in autobiography, such as courtship, marriage, and the birth of children, are given relatively little attention in the nineteenth century. 'Conventionally female moments are not assigned privileged status', as Nancy K. Miller puts it in a recent study of women's autobiography in France. The really meaningful trajectory, as she explains, is not marriage and childbearing, but 'the transcendence of the feminine condition through writing'.[60] Since a significant number of Victorian women autobiographers were childless, single, and sexually inactive, Cixous' celebration of the gestation drive seems not only irrelevant, but a disturbing revival of Victorian male medical theory, propounded by doctors such as William Acton, who saw 'woman's sphere' as concerned entirely with the welfare of children. Not all women wish to be mothers, nor do all have the opportunity. The notion that all women are the same in their response to the 'gestation drive' (assuming that such a force exists, which is questionable) seriously underestimates the psychological differences which have always marked out the 'career woman' from the wife and mother who feels fulfilled in her biological and familial role. Whereas autobiography affirms individual identity, biological determinism denies it, making the two theories mutually contradictory, and therefore unhelpful in a study such as this. The formative influence of social conditions, whether derived from family background or literary milieu, is perhaps the single most important factor in the writing of any autobiography, especially in the nineteenth century, when most women felt unable to offer more than passive resistance to the pressures of their position. Harriet Martineau's Norwich is quite different from Sara Coleridge's Lake District and Frances Cobbe's Ireland; and any theory of autobiography that overlooks these vital social and cultural divergences, preferring instead to assume the existence of shared libidinal drives behind their writing, is surely imposing an anachronistic viewpoint that, in the process, discards a great deal of useful material. Besides, the French feminists themselves write openly of women's oppression by centuries of Western civilisation: why not consider this in detail alongside the individual responses to it in women's autobiography?

Nor is *écriture féminine* always appropriate as a way into understanding the dynamics of nineteenth-century women's writing. The notion of fluidity and diffusion may apply more accurately to a male writer, such as James Joyce, than to women such as Frances Cobbe or Harriet Martineau. As Virginia Woolf noticed long ago, Victorian women used the ponderous Victorian sentence, however awkwardly, much as men did.[61] The *content* of autobiography by Victorian women is certainly different from that of their male contemporaries, but that is because entirely different expectations conditioned their lives from the very beginning, and made their life-crises and decisions essentially peculiar to the social situations in which they lived. Their language may be volcanic and subversive in the autobiographical novel, *Jane Eyre* and *Villette* particularly, but in formal acts of self-writing before 1900, there is little sign of 'flying' or 'airborne swimming' as Cixous has characterised the feminine text. Julia Kristeva admires the fluid writing of Joyce, Artaud, and other male avant-garde artists, but overlooks the very different kinds of rhetorical significance to be found in texts by Victorian women: the passive constructions, self-contradictions and tortuous sentences that try to erase the impression of egotism by internalising the values of the dominant male culture and appplying them to undercut the effect of their own writing. There are certainly moments in Victorian women's autobiography where a fluid, semiotic language – what Margaret Oliphant calls her 'sing-song, guided by no sort of law, but my ear' – momentarily takes command, but these occasions are rare and usually short-lived.[62] The interest lies in seeing when they occur (often, significantly, when a woman celebrates her new-found powers of speech), rather than in expecting them to occur all the time.

It may be that French feminists are more interested in late twentieth-century writing and political issues, but this necessarily reduces their usefulness to the Victorian specialist, who will often find their theories askew from the temper and character of nineteenth-century thinking. Cixous' ideas especially risk exiling women too far into the wild, relegating them to camps of the incoherent and unconscious, stationed on the edges of.male discourse, like the witches in *Macbeth*. Disturbing too is Kristeva's notion that women's role in the continuing process of social revolution must be negative: the rejection of 'everything finite, definite, structured, loaded with meaning, in the existing state of society'.[63] This seems only to confirm centuries of male assertion that women are illogical, rely on their powers of intuition when they are ignorant of the facts and are incapable of arguing their case systematically. These skills may be seen as unattractive by French feminists, but they are still indispensable in certain fields of activity. Many women autobiographers, such as Annie Besant, Frances Cobbe and Harriet Martineau were experienced campaigners who frequently wrote and spoke in support of their own causes. Their language had to be clear, cogent and logical. At this stage of women's history, they were still working with society's established rhetorical equipment, rather than inventing new and individual tools of their own.

The language used by some French feminist writers tends to be either breathless and mystical, like Cixous', or riddled with a semiotic jargon like Kristeva's, that inhibits understanding by all but an elite group of initiates. This again seems to reduce the effectiveness and general accessibility of their ideas, which mostly need to be approached via a combined study of linguistics and psychoanalysis, semiotics and philosophy, Lacan and Derrida. While accepting that literary criticism should be pitched higher than the understanding of the average undergraduate or the old lady in the railway carriage, my chosen approach attempts to challenge the increasing unintelligibility of much recent critical writing, its growing elitism, and its reliance on a purely technical vocabulary that dehumanises the subject of its study.

These trends are particularly inimical to the analysis of autobiography, which is, essentially, the story of an individual life. Any methodology that negates the importance of the individual, that, in this case, suggests that all women are equally assertive of physical experience and sexual pleasure, is, to a large extent, merely inverting the Victorian theory that *no* women were supposed to enjoy sex, except as a way of pleasing their husbands. Both theories deny the existence of important social and psychological variations, and are equally in danger of parcelling women into an easily badged and categorised subgroup of human society.

Ultimately, the Anglo-American tradition of feminist criticism offers a more helpful approach to non-modernist texts, though always with the door left open for dialogue with the French feminists. As Elaine Showalter has suggested, a theory based on a model of women's culture can provide 'a more complete and satisfying way to talk about the specificity and difference of women's writing than theories based in biology, linguistics, or psychoanalysis'. In the end, 'no theory, however suggestive, can be a substitute for the close and extensive knowledge of women's texts.'[64] Whereas French feminist theorists often avoid this kind of close textual analysis, critics of the Anglo-American school have been largely instrumental in salvaging forgotten, but influential Victorian novelists for the general as well as the specialist and educated modern reader, and making us read more familiar texts with a new understanding of the silences and omissions, the symbols and patterns that constitute their response to society. In the nineteenth century, the notion of a 'women's culture' is well supported by evidence of close friendships between female writers, mutual encouragement of their work, reviews of women's texts by other women and generally a heightened awareness of what other women were writing and saying about the novel and about autobiography. Counteracting this productive tradition was a more discouraging assumption that the implied audience was at worst hostile, and at best on its guard: akin perhaps to the 'religious reader' or 'stern sage' mentioned by Lucy Snowe, or the 'judicious reader putting on his spectacles to look for the moral' at the end of *Shirley*.[65] In the relationship between these two cultural forces, and the underlying prohibition, for women, against the violation of their privacy by all but the most neutral forms of self-writing, seems to lie a more fruitful approach to the dynamics of Victorian women's autobiography.

As for the vexed question of a final working definition of the generic term 'autobiography', this is perhaps best left open. It will be necessary to redefine the term from time to time, and question the definitions that have so far excluded some of the most intriguing self-writing. The main purpose of this exercise is to recover that lost ground surrounding the great upsurge of women's autobiographical writing in the modern age; to establish terms by which this writing can be taken seriously; and to judge it from a fresh and flexible perspective.

Notes

1. *I Too Am Here*, p. 74.
2. *The George Eliot Letters*, ed. Gordon S. Haight (New Haven and London: Yale University Press, 9 vols, 1954–78), III, 465.
3. *I Too Am Here*, p. 235.
4. Linda H. Peterson, *Victorian Autobiography: The Tradition of Self-Interpretation* (New Haven and London: Yale University Press, 1986); *Approaches to Victorian Autobiography*, ed. George P. Landow (Athens: Ohio University Press, 1979) includes essays on Mrs Oliphant and Elizabeth Sewell; *Autobiography: Essays Theoretical and Critical*, ed. James Olney (Princeton, NJ: Princeton University Press, 1980) includes a general essay on women's autobiography; Jerome Hamilton Buckley, *The Turning Key: Autobiography and the Subjective Impulse Since 1800* (Cambridge, Mass., and London: Harvard University Press, 1984), p. ix.
5. Susanna Egan, *Patterns of Experience in Autobiography* (Chapel Hill and London: University of North Carolina Press, 1984), p. x.
6. *I Too Am Here*, p. 197.
7. *The George Eliot Letters*, II, 406–10; 502–4. cf. Mary Shelley's autobiographical preface to *Frankenstein* (1818; Author's Introduction, 1831).
8. *The Brontës: Their Lives, Friendships and Correspondence*, ed. T. J. Wise and J. A. Symington (Oxford: Basil Blackwell, 4 vols, 1932), I, 124.
9. Buckley, p. 39.
10. William C. Spengemann, *The Forms of Autobiography: Episodes in the History of a Literary Genre* (New Haven and London: Yale University Press, 1980), p. xvi.
11. *The George Eliot Letters*, VI, 67.
12. James Olney, *Metaphors of Self: The Meaning of Autobiography* (Princeton, NJ: Princeton University Press, 1972), pp. 38–9.
13. Robert Southey was the first to use the term critically, predicting an 'epidemical rage for auto-biography', *Quarterly Review* I (May 1809), p. 386; the first title was W. P. Scargill's *Autobiography of a Dissenting Minister* (London: Smith Elder & Co., 1834).
14. Frances Ann Kemble, *Record of a Girlhood* (London: Richard Bentley and Son, 3 vols, 1878), I, 1–2.
15. *Personal Recollections, from Early Life to Old Age, of Mary Somerville. With selections from her correspondence. By her daughter, Martha Somerville* (London: John Murray, 1873; p. 1.
16. *The Autobiography and Letters of Mrs. M. O. W. Oliphant*, ed. Mrs Harry Coghill (London and Edinburgh: William Blackwood & Sons, 1899), p. 11.
17. Elizabeth Wordsworth, *Glimpses of the Past* (London and Oxford: A. R. Mowbray & Co., 1912), p. 1.
18. Anne Thackeray Ritchie, *Chapters from Some Memoirs* (London and New York: Macmillan, 1894), p. 67.
19. 'Mrs. Besant's autobiography', *Spectator* (3 March 1894), p. 309; 'Annie Besant', *Athenaeum* 103 (3 February 1894), p. 146.
20. For example, Mrs Oliphant's hostile review of Harriet Martineau's *Autobiography*, *Blackwood's* 121 (April 1877), pp. 472–96.
21. *The Works of John Ruskin*, ed. E. T. Cook and Alexander Wedderburn (London: George Allen, 39 vols, 1903–12), XVIII, 123; Mrs Ellis, *The Women of England* (London: Fisher, 1839), p. 155; p. 63.

22. *Biographies of Good Women, Chiefly by Contributors to 'The Monthly Packet'* [ed. Charlotte M. Yonge] (London: J. & C. Mozley, 1862), p. 1.
23. W. H. Davenport Adams, *Child-Life and Girlhood of Remarkable Women* (London: W. Swan Sonnenschein, 1883), p. 14; p. 16.
24. Peterson, pp. 126–8.
25. *Works of John Ruskin*, p. 126.
26. M. A. Stodart, *Female Writers: Thoughts on Their Proper Sphere, and on Their Powers of Usefulness* (London: R. B. Seeley & W. Burnside, 1842), p. 127; p. 117; p. 190.
27. William Landels, *Woman: Her Position and Power* (London and New York: Cassell, Petter, and Galpin, 1870), pp. 69–70.
28. *Autobiography of Anna Eliza Bray*, ed. John A. Kempe (London: Chapman & Hall, 1884), pp. 5–6; p. 17.
29. 'Two autobiographical essays by Elizabeth Barrett', *Browning Institute Studies*, II (New York, 1974), ed. William S. Peterson, p. 130.
30. *I Too Am Here*, p. 233.
31. Annie Besant, *An Autobiography* (London: T. Fisher Unwin, 1893), pp. 5–6.
32. *Life of Frances Power Cobbe. By Herself* (London: Richard Bentley and Son, 2 vols 1894), I, iv–v; Vera Brittain, *Testament of Youth: An Autobiographical Study of the Years 1900–1925* (1933; London: Virago, 1978), p. 12.
33. Alexander Bain, *Autobiography* (London: Longmans, Green, 1904), pp. v–vi.
34. 'Lady travellers', *Quarterly Review* 76 (June 1845), p. 100.
35. [Anna Jameson] *Diary of an Ennuyée* (London: H. Colburn, 1826; repr. Philadelphia: E. Littell, 1826), p. 1.
36. Anna Jameson, *Winter Studies and Summer Rambles in Canada* (1838; ed. Clara Thomas; Toronto: McClelland and Stewart, 1965), p. 68.
37. Ruth Perry, *Women, Letters, and the Novel* (New York: AMS Press, 1980), p. 68.
38. 'Charlotte Elizabeth', *Personal Recollections* (London: R. B. Seeley & W. Burnside, 1841), p. 1.
39. *The Life and Letters of Mrs. Sewell by Mrs. Bayly* (4th edition, London: James Nisbet, 1889), pp. 1–2.
40. David J. DeLaura, 'The allegory of life: the autobiographical impulse in Victorian prose', in *Approaches to Victorian Autobiography*, p. 351.
41. *Memorials of Two Sisters, Susanna and Catherine Winkworth*, ed. Margaret J. Shaen (London: Longmans, Green, 1908), p. vii.
42. Helena Faucit, Lady Martin, *On Some of Shakespeare's Female Characters* (London and Edinburgh: William Blackwood & Sons, 1885), pp. vii–viii; p. 5.
43. 'A revelation of childhood', in Mrs Jameson's *A Commonplace Book of Thoughts, Memories, and Fancies, Original and Selected* (London: Longman, Brown, Green & Longmans, 1854); Harriet Martineau, *Household Education* (London: Edward Moxon, 1849).
44. Linda Anderson, 'At the threshold of the self: women and autobiography', in *Women's Writing: A Challenge to Theory*, ed. Moira Monteith (Hemel Hempstead: Harvester Wheatsheaf, 1986), p. 59.
45. *The George Eliot Letters*, IV, 437.
46. *Ibid.*, VI, 371.
47. *Ibid.*, VI, 353.
48. 'Story-telling', in *Essays and Leaves from a Note-Book* (Illustrated Copyright Edition, London: Virtue & Co., 1913), pp. 299–300.

49. Avrom Fleishman, *Figures of Autobiography: The Language of Self-Writing in Victorian and Modern England* (Berkeley, Los Angeles and London: University of California Press, 1983), p. 236.

50. The clairvoyant is Latimer in *The Lifted Veil*; the old man is Theophrastus Such.

51. *The George Eliot Letters*, V, 123; *George Eliot's Life as Related in Her Letters and Journals*, ed. J. W. Cross (New York: Harper Bros., 3 vols, 1885), I, v.

52. *Lady Morgan's Memoirs: Autobiography, Diaries and Correspondence*, ed. W. Hepworth Dixon (London: William H. Allen, 2 vols, 1862), I, 6–7.

53. *The Kristeva Reader*, ed. Toril Moi (Oxford: Basil Blackwell, 1986), pp. 191–2.

54. *New French Feminisms: An Anthology*, ed. Elaine Marks and Isabelle de Courtivron (Hemel Hempstead: Harvester Wheatsheaf, 1981), p. 166.

55. *Ibid.*, p. 166.

56. *Ibid.*, p. 250.

57. *Ibid.*, p. 251.

58. See the sections on 'speech-making experiences' in the work of Fanny Kemble and Annie Besant, ch. 5.

59. Ann Rosalind Jones, 'Writing the body: toward an understanding of l'écriture féminine', in *The New Feminist Criticism*, ed. Elaine Showalter (London: Virago, 1985), p. 366.

60. Nancy K. Miller, 'Women's autobiography in France: for a dialectics of identification', in *Women and Language in Literature and Society* (New York: Praeger Publishers, 1980), p. 263.

61. Virginia Woolf, *A Room of One's Own* (1929; St Albans: Granada, 1977), p. 73.

62. Oliphant, *Autobiography*, p. 86.

63. *New French Feminisms*, p. 166.

64. Elaine Showalter, 'Feminist criticism in the wilderness', in *The New Feminist Criticism*, p. 259, p. 266.

65. Charlotte Brontë, *Villette* (1853; ed. Tony Tanner, Harmondsworth: Penguin, 1979), p. 228; *Shirley* (1849; ed. Andrew and Judith Hook, Harmondsworth: Penguin, 1974), p. 599.

Since this book went to press, a further two important collections of essays have been published: *The Female Autograph: Theory and Practice of Autobiography from the Tenth to the Twentieth Century* (Chicago and London: University of Chicago Press, 1987), ed. Domna C. Stanton; and *The Private Self: Theory and Practice of Women's Autobiographical Writings* (London: Routledge, 1988), ed. Shari Benstock. Neither, however, gives much space to discussion of Victorian women's autobiography.

Chapter 2

Fragments, Apologies, Memoirs, True Relations

women's autobiography before 1800

The first important date in the history of women's autobiography is 1413, when Margery Kempe, aged forty, from Kings Lynn, and mother of fourteen children, met Julian of Norwich, aged seventy, a mystic and anchoress. They talked about the younger woman's visions and dramatic bursts of weeping, and Julian assured her that 'any creature that hath these tokens may steadfastly believe that the Holy Ghost dwelleth in his soul.'[1] If we are searching for evidence of a female subculture in the evolution of autobiographical writing, this is the earliest sign that women with shared interests felt there was something to be gained from comparing their experiences and seeking validation from within the ranks of their own sex. According to Margery's account of their meeting, however, they said nothing about recording their visions for others to read, and neither would have regarded her writing as autobiographical in the modern sense. Both wrote to communicate a mystical awakening; Margery hoped to comfort 'sinful wretches' and Julian proved that the profoundest 'showing' could be witnessed by 'a symple creature unlettyrde leving in deadly flesh'.[2] Can we therefore regard Margery and Julian as the mothers of women's autobiography? Or should the title be offered to Margaret, Duchess of Newcastle? Or, as some critics have suggested, should all claims be frozen until the eighteenth century?[3] The problem of definition arises as soon as any attempt is made to order the fragments of such a scattered tradition.

Most recent critics agree that to qualify as an autobiography a narrative must be told in the first person by the man or woman whose life is being recounted; it must be told retrospectively, not diurnally, though not necessarily in old age, or at one sitting; the author should be the central character, though he is usually seen interacting with other people and the conditions of contemporary society; and the narrative should discern some pattern or meaning to the life, rather than tumble out randomly and without purpose. In mapping a history of women's autobiography, we may also want to ask whether there is a continuing and coherent tradition of female self-writing, and when women first developed a professional sense of themselves as writers. If we accept the notion that an autobiography must confer 'meaning' or shape on a life, we may want to know whether this criterion was alien to women living disjointedly as wives and mothers without a significant achievement to buttress, or even establish their identity. We may also want to consider their relationship with the implied audience. Autobiography need not be written for other people to read, but an attempt to set down the important experiences of a life generally indicates a desire for sympathetic attention: not necessarily a reasonable claim in a 'relative creature', whose prime allegiance was to her husband or father. Between the standard definition of autobiography (at least the lowest common denominator of accepted characteristics) and the additional qualifications or questions that may have to be asked of women's autobiography, therefore, are gaps and pitfalls yawning for the critic with a sack of simple generic labels. The history of female self-writing progresses along roughly the same steeps and flats as that of male autobiography (which is itself a broken tradition, especially in the nineteenth century), but its emphases are different; its permutations follow other patterns; and right from the beginning, the subject-matter of women's autobiography and the manner of telling are distinctly divergent from the contemporary male practice.

Margery Kempe's claims to be considered the first English female autobiographer are probably stronger than Julian of Norwich's. Although Julian sets her visions in an autobiographical context, describing the circumstances of her illness and miraculous recovery, neither the short nor the long text of her *A Book of Showings* (1978) is a sustained attempt to delineate the shape of her life or the growth of her personality. On the other hand, to criticise Julian's work on these grounds may be to impose anachronistic expectations (the only model available to women at this time was the saint's life), and to apply the very standards of evaluation that I have suggested seemed foreign to women. Certainly, the Augustinian model, with its oratorical survey of a whole life and division into narrative and expository books, never seems to have held much appeal for them, either in the Middle Ages or beyond. If life, for Julian, acquired meaning only through an active relationship with God, and an enlarged understanding of the unity and harmony of things, then her *Showings* should perhaps be regarded as an autobiographical prototype: the first known example of a woman's attempt to write about herself and her life in whatever form was meaningful to her. Perhaps the most profitable way of approaching the history of women's autobiography is to see what aspects of themselves the authors chose to foreground.

With Margery Kempe, autobiography assumes a more 'modern' quality. Although she says nothing about her childhood, or how she came to be married, she does combine her inner and outer experiences in a narrative that arises from a spiritual awakening after the birth of her first child. For many critics, Margery Kempe is in fact the first English autobiographer. Margaret Bottrall, Mary G. Mason and Clarissa Atkinson agree that hers is 'the first full autobiography in English by anyone, male or female'.[4] More than the majority of spiritual autobiographies, it transmits a strong sense of Margery's personality, seen both from within and from the irritated perspective of her fellow pilgrims and her defeated husband (who, after fourteen children, reluctantly agreed to end the sexual side of their marriage). Having flaunted about in slashed cloaks 'with divers colours between the slashes, so that they should be the more staring to men's sight, and herself the more worshipped', Margery became so fanatically spiritual on her overseas tours that she incurred the lasting enmity of her table companions:

> And they were most displeased with her because she wept so much and spoke always of the love and goodness of Our Lord, as much at the table as in other places. And therefore shamefully they reproved her, and severely chid her, and said they would not put up with her as her husband did when she was at home and in England. (p. 79)

In the authentic ring of that last phrase, especially, Margery's narrative has the stamp of realism and particularity; as does her account of an unresolved discussion with her husband when 'they went forth towards Bridlington in right hot weather, the creature having great sorrow and dread for her chastity' (p. 31). She emphasises in her preface that people specifically encouraged her to write down her 'feelings', which she does, in conjunction with reported dialogues (a recurrent feature of autobiography by women) and accounts of her mystical experiences. She also has a strong sense of herself as a writer, recalling moments when the book was going well and she felt 'a flame of fire about her breast, full hot and delectable'. Even her scribe was moved to tears; while for Margery, writing had distinctly therapeutic effects, as it was to have for many of her successors:

> And she was many times sick while this treatise was in writing, and, as soon as she would go about the writing of this treatise, she was hale and whole suddenly, in a manner; and often she was commanded to make herself ready in all haste. (p. 288)

It seems a significant coincidence that the history of women's autobiography begins with two experiences of dangerous illness, one a form of post-natal depression perhaps suggesting the 'dis-ease' that was often symptomatic of women's dissatisfaction with their role in society. The writing of autobiography, for many, provided a way of reconstructing the self and recovering from various forms of 'dis-ease', whether physical, emotional or social. Margery Kempe was the first to express how this felt.

Her *Book*, however, presents other generic difficulties. For a start, Margery was illiterate and employed two scribes to write at her dictation. The first died after composing Book One, and when the second took over, he thought his predecessor had made such a poor job of it that he offered to rewrite the first part before going on with the second. Margery herself is always referred to as 'this creature'; which for James Osborn, must exclude her *Book* from the genre. 'Because the narrative was written by others, and not by the person herself, I submit that Margery's *Book* should not be considered an autobiography.' He sees it instead as 'the life of a would-be saint', wandering between hagiography and autobiography as we now know it.[5] The hybrid classification is certainly attractive, especially if the *Book* is regarded as an autobiographical travel memoir, like many produced in the nineteenth century. Before her conversion, Margery bears more than a passing resemblance to Chaucer's Wife of Bath, another oral autobiographer, with a taste for travel and outlandish clothes. Both are surging individuals whose confident sense of selfhood amply qualifies them for the role of autobiographer; their similarity as intrusive female pilgrims demonstrating the close relationship between fiction and autobiography that persists throughout literary history. If Margery's *Book* evades generic expectations, it does, at least, establish an important precedent, and set a pattern for subsequent female autobiographers who were more attracted to the hybrid rather than the 'pure' form of autobiographical narrative.

The first English male autobiographer is now thought to be a composer, Thomas Whythorne, who was writing around 1576, but during the fifteenth and sixteenth centuries the introspective impulse seems to have been at an exceptionally low ebb. 'It was not until the late seventeenth century that the autobiography commonly became both secular and introspective, a record of personal emotions rather than of external events or religious experiences,' Lawrence Stone has argued, suggesting that at this time there was 'clear iconographic and literary evidence for a new interest in the self, and for recognition of the uniqueness of the individual.'[6] Dramatic shifts of consciousness are always difficult for the historian to explain, and are often over-emphasised, but there was undoubtedly a great upsurge of autobiographical writing at the time of the English Civil War. It may be that in times of unprecedented instability people feel the need to relocate their certainties; to write down what they know of themselves and their families, partly to pass on to their descendants but also to fix an enduring sense of selfhood. It is certainly the case that the two most important bursts of autobiographical writing before the present age, occurred in the seventeenth and nineteenth centuries, both times when radical uncertainties about the social fabric and religious faith preoccupied the thoughts of most literate people.

In the seventeenth century autobiography splits into the secular and the spiritual, though some forms combine elements of both. Spiritual autobiographies were written by Puritans and Quakers, who were also encouraged to keep diaries and examine their own motives and spiritual progress. Biographies immortalised exemplary lives, such as: *The Life and Death of Mrs. Margaret Andrews*, a fourteen-year-old girl who died in 1680; Richard Baxter's wife Margaret, whose *Breviate* appeared in 1681; and the 'true and exact narrative' of 'the most Virtuous Lady', Alice, Duchess of Dudley (1669). For the first time, in any significant showing, there was a new interest in the experiences of apparently obscure individuals, as well as in the lives of great military leaders. Male autobiographies of the seventeenth century tend to be either spiritual or professional, ranging from Bunyan's *Grace Abounding to the Chief of Sinners* (1666) to Clarendon's *Life* (1668–71) and the lawyer Roger North's *Autobiography* (1887). The lives of women were still largely hidden, offering little justification for separate attention. Indeed, two seventeenth-century women who did write fragmentary autobiographies, Margaret, Duchess of Newcastle, and Lucy Hutchinson, are better known for writing their husbands' lives, which they clearly saw as being more important than their own. For both these women, however, the need to commemorate themselves, especially their own singularity as individuals, finally overcame any inhibitions on the score of vanity and egotism.

The Duchess's *True Relation of my Birth, Breeding, and Life*, which first appeared in 1656, and was subsequently appended to her *Life of William Cavendish, Duke of Newcastle* (1886), was written partly to refute accusations that her works were not her own, and therefore to clear her reputation. In this respect, it anticipates the direction of most eighteenth-century autobiographies by women, who were prolific in their own defence against calumny. At the same time, there is no false humility in the Duchess's writing. She says frankly that she delights in her singularity, is ambitious, and has written her *True Relation* for her own sake and not for that of her readers.[7] More than any other seventeenth-century female autobiographer (and many men, for that matter), she is unashamedly fascinated by herself as an individual. She explores the contradictions of her personality in sentences that seem to feel round corners and discover concealed passages in her mind. She notes that she behaves differently in company from when she is alone with her husband, and that her eccentricities are perfectly compatible with a natural 'bashfulness', or rather 'fear', that she tries to understand. She is equally aware of her difficulties as a writer, observing her need to tell stories aloud before writing them down:

> But my letters seem rather as a ragged rout than a well armed body, for the brain being quicker in creating than the hand in writing or the memory in retaining, many fancies are lost, by reason they ofttimes outrun the pen, where I, to keep speed in the race, write so fast as I stay not so long as to write my letters plain, insomuch as some have taken my handwriting for some strange character . . . (p. 307)

Her sentence accordingly runs on in a race against itself, breathless and increasingly incoherent, as she tries to catch up with her own ideas. Like Margery's account of the exhilaration she found in writing, the Duchess's analysis of the gap between the conception of a thing and the writing of it shows an unusually sharp awareness of herself as a writer. The Duchess is also aware of herself specifically as a *woman* writer. While her husband, she says, 'recreates himself with his pen, writing what his wit dictates to him,' (a sentence that is itself relaxed and confident, like her husband's writing), she herself passes her time 'rather with scribbling than writing, with words than wit' (p. 306). She repeatedly associates women with confused or incoherent self-expression, cautioning them against jostling for pre-eminence: 'words rushing against words, thwarting and crossing each other, and pulling with reproaches, striking to throw each other down with disgrace, thinking to advance themselves thereby' (p. 299). Her headlong sentences imply that whereas men are at home with language, women are still crashing against themselves, using words like unfamiliar weapons. Her observations are perhaps the most perceptive of any autobiographer writing at this time, combining narrative of her life with detailed analysis of her personality. She recognises, too, that she has had to select: 'for should I write every particular, as my childish sports and the like, it would be ridiculous and tedious' (p. 310).

With the Duchess of Newcastle and Lucy Hutchinson arrives an interest in childhood and the perplexities of falling in love. The Duchess's love for her husband was 'not amorous love,' she explains, but though I did dread marriage, and shunned men's company as much as I could, yet I could not, nor had not the power to refuse him, by reason my affections were fixed on him, and he was the only person I ever was in love with. Neither was I ashamed to own it, but gloried therein. (p. 288)

Lucy Hutchinson also held out against marriage, though she acknowledges this aggressive stance not in her autobiographical fragment but in the *Memoirs of the Life of Colonel Hutchinson* (1806), to which it is appended. Having abandoned her autobiography, significantly at the birth of a sister who ousted her from the position of family pet, Lucy retells the story of her courtship from her husband's viewpoint, so that all praise of her intelligence and manner comes as if from him rather than from herself. As Cynthia Pomerleau has shown in her survey of women's autobiography in the seventeenth and eighteenth centuries, male autobiographers at that time rarely mentioned their personal lives. 'One can thumb through index after index in works by men and find only the most cursory references, if any, to wife and children.'[8] For men, their public or professional life was their reason for writing; for women who wanted to write, the choice was between commemorating their husbands' achievements, or recounting their domestic experiences, unless, like the Duchess of Newcastle, they had acquired notoriety in their own right.

Lucy Hutchinson defines her adult self entirely in relation to her husband: 'as his shaddow, she waited on him every where', and when he died, 'she vanisht into nothing'. Nevertheless, as a child she was precocious and like the young Mary Ann Evans 300 years later, preferred the company of adults to that of other children.[9]

play among other children I despis'd, and when I was forc'd to entertaine such as came to visitt me, I tir'd them with more grave instructions than their mothers, and pluckt all their babies [dolls] to pieces, and kept the children in such awe that they were glad when I entertain'd myselfe with elder company, to whom I was very acceptable. (p. 288)

This rare piece of child analysis appears in what purports to be mainly a spiritual autobiography. Like Margaret Cavendish's *True Relation*, Lucy Hutchinson's fragment communicates overall an inviolable sense of self, and taken with her *Memoirs* of Colonel Hutchinson does it largely through resistance to the usual pattern of a woman's life. In each narrative the woman is reluctant to marry, having developed a strong sense of independence, which made submission to a man unwelcome. Even those who professed to be thankful for everything in their lives recalled a time of psychological disturbance caused by prospective marriage plans or quarrels over lovers. Mary Rich, Countess of Warwick, first had 'an aversion to marriage' ('living so much at my ease that I was unwilling to change my condition'), then fell in love with a man she thought her father would reject because of his relative poverty. Although her marriage was happy, she was anxious not to have too many children: 'out of a proud conceit I had, that if I childed so thick it would spoil what my great vanity then made me to fancy was tolerable (at least in my person)'. She had preferred to spend her time reading romances and 'minding nothing but curious dressing and fine and rich clothes'.[10]

The motif of 'curious dressing' recurs with significant frequency in the earliest autobiographical writing by women. Not just a symbol of frivolity, it was clearly the route to self-assertiveness and marking oneself out as different. The Duchess of Newcastle invented her own fashions, and resented imitators (p. 312). In the eighteenth century, the clothes theme resurfaces more outrageously in Charlotte Charke's references to wearing breeches and passing herself off as a man.[11] By the nineteenth century, most women had either become less bold about their dress or had found other ways of expressing their individuality, chiefly through the novel.

Another seventeenth-century autobiographer with an enduring sense of self was Anne, Lady Halkett, who remained unmarried until she was thirty-three. Her *Memoirs* (1875) constitute a distinctively female version of the English Civil War, in which she was a staunch supporter of the Royalist cause and self-confident bargainer with enemy soldiers. Dialogues are narrated in full, as they tend to be more frequently in women's autobiographies than in men's: perhaps because of the greater interest in personalities and the details of daily living, which occupied many women in place of a career. Her scorn is also more often vented on men than on women, as in her altercations with a 'Mr. N.', who had compromised her reputation. 'I lifted up my eyes and hands to heaven and said, "Good God, hath this man the confidence to say this?"'[12] Yet Anne Murray, the skilled intermediary, is only half the composite persona presented by the *Memoirs*. The other is a proud, but vulnerable girl with an unfortunate tendency to fall in love with inaccessible men. The first, Thomas Howard, an impoverished nobleman, was chased off by parental opposition; the second, Colonel Joseph Bampfield, turned out to be married already. Anne's emotions were frequently driven inward by hostility from her family, or sheer perplexity and isolation. When she heard that Howard was married, she wrestled with her feelings of hurt pride and disappointment:

> I was alone in my sister's chamber when I read the letter, and flinging my selfe downe upon her bed, I said, 'Is this the man for whom I have sufred so much? Since hee hath made himselfe unworthy my love, hee is unworthy my anger or concerne.' And rising, immediately I wentt outt into the next roome to my super as unconcernedly as if I had never had an interest in him, nor had ever lost itt. (p. 22)

This split between the public persona and the tormented inner life becomes a recurrent feature of female autobiography in the eighteenth and nineteenth centuries, as it does in the novel, to which autobiography bears an increasing resemblance. Jane Austen's heroines retire to their rooms to meditate or recover from a disturbing experience. So do Charlotte Brontë's and George Eliot's. An unrestrained display of emotion in company seems to have been shunned by all self-respecting women who wrote either fiction or autobiography, with the notable exception of Margery Kempe. Even Margery, however, writes of herself as unusually emotional, and highly unpopular as a result.

Lady Halkett's densely written dialogues of misunderstanding between 'Mr. N.', 'Sir Ch.', 'Lady H.', and herself, which occur before the more serious concerns of wartime parleys, look ahead to the novels of Samuel Richardson, especially *Clarissa*, where every nuance is noted and weighed in its context. Male autobiographers of this period lack such an interest in what might be called the 'dailiness' of their lives, the different shades assumed by visits to great houses, and the interaction of personalities. To Lady Halkett, they were important because they were the substance of her life during her formative years; and in her *Memoirs* she demonstrates the validity of her experiences.

Female self-writing of the seventeenth century divides not only into the spiritual and the secular (of which the secular is the more assertive and individual), but also into the domestic and the tale of travel or confrontation. Lady Halkett's *Memoirs* combine both the latter varieties, as does Ann, Lady Fanshawe's, another Royalist autobiography written in the 1670s. Lady Fanshawe, however, locates herself firmly in family rather than personal history. Her *Memoirs* are written for her son, Richard, to inform him of his antecedents, and the text generally refers to her husband as 'your father'. Richard's father is treated as the most important figure in her tale; she herself tags along behind, grateful for his company and loth to complain of her numerous pregnancies often borne in acutely uncomfortable conditions. In her opening address, she announces her subject-matter as 'the most remarkable actions and accidents of your family, as well as those of more eminent ones of your father and my life': placing herself last in her proposed table of contents.[13] Her narrative is anecdotal, circumstantial, a series of vivid episodes put together without much structure or artistry, although they never lose sight of the central figures, herself and her husband. They rarely see themselves as separate individuals: Lady Ann is always by his side, often alone with him in marital discussion, but determined to live her own life to the full.

The most notable aspect of her work is its attention to detail, her way of swamping the reader in the felt texture of her life. After the premature birth of a child, for example, she recalls having had '2 fits everyday':

> That brought me so weake that I was like an anatomy. I never stirr'd out of my bed in 7 months, nor during that time eat flesh, or fish, or bread, but sack, posett drink, and pancake or eggs, or now and then a turnip or carrot. Your father was likewise very ill, but he rose out of his bed some houres dayly and had such a greedyness upon him that he would eat and drink more than ordinary persons that eat most, though he could not stand upright without being held, and in perpetual sweats, and that so violently that it ran down like water day and night. (p. 137)

From Margery Kempe onwards, women's autobiography has had a raciness, which marks it out from the more solemn tones of self-writing by men with a stately reputation to preserve. A distinctive speaking voice can often be heard through the narrative, reflecting the author's irony or humour, as in the passage just quoted; and frequently the irony is directed against men. On another occasion, when they were at sea, she bribed a cabin-boy to lend her his clothes so that she could go on deck (p. 128): another example of the way the clothes motif functions as a symbol of female singularity and determination to transcend the limitations of a conventional role.

Whether or not secular self-writing by women in the seventeenth century really qualifies as autobiography is difficult to determine. The main exponents of the form undoubtedly see themselves as distinct from the mass of conventional women who never step out of their appointed roles: indeed the very writing of autobiography at this stage seems to presuppose some degree of nonconformity, whether unusual courage, resistance to marriage, or a preference for writing and solitude over sociality. The danger with this form of self-assertion is that the writer rarely does more than explore her own uniqueness, without attempting to site it in a process of maturation and development. Childhood is still accorded relatively little importance, except by Lucy Hutchinson, whose memoirs are incomplete. All seventeenth-century autobiographies by women are fairly short, and often break down without formal completion. Consequently, they lack the structure or pattern, what Georges Gusdorf calls 'the effort of a creator to give the meaning of his own mythic tale', that many recent critics see as an essential component of true autobiography. It was easier for the spiritual autobiographers to view their lives in this way. Alice Thornton of York, for example, organises her recollections round a remarkable series of deliverances from fires, shipwrecks and other disasters; though she, too, changes direction half way through, and assumes the more worldly task of defending her own good name against charges of improvidence and financial misdealing.[14]

Nevertheless, traditions are established by seventeenth-century women that were to make the way easier for their successors. The Duchess of Newcastle tackles the issue of egotism, and defends her freedom to write as she wishes; Lady Halkett demonstrates the intrinsic interest of domestic and emotional detail; Lady Fanshawe continues Margery Kempe's style of personal travelogue; and Lucy Hutchinson validates the psychological significance of childhood behaviour in a study of the self. All four were happily married, aristocratic and reasonably free; their autobiographies celebrate the variety and happiness of their lives, reliving a past that is largely a pleasure to recall. In the eighteenth century, however, the picture is very different.

The typical eighteenth-century female autobiographer is down on her luck, more or less disreputable, and strident in her claims for justice. Colley Cibber's daughter, Charlotte Charke, at one time earned a living selling sausages; then tried her hand as pastrycook, waiter, 'hog-merchant' and strolling player; Letitia Pilkington opened a pamphlet shop, and openly called herself 'a lady of adventure'; the notorious Mrs 'Con' Phillips informs her readers that 'the House she lives in was Yesterday surrounded with 13 Constables, in order to seize upon, and carry her to *Newgate*.'[15] Defoe's *Moll Flanders* (1722) often seems no more than a slight exaggeration of the way in which many contemporary women were living, and writing about their lives. Clearly, their role in society had undergone a dramatic change since the time of the Civil War.

The reasons for this were largely economic. As the middle class developed, women were pushed into an increasingly domestic role as wives and mothers and discouraged from going out to work. In any case, men were taking over industries such as brewing and weaving, that had been the province of women; and, as Ruth Perry has argued, since 'women's function in society diminished to the obviously reproductive one, they were increasingly thought of in exclusively sexual terms.'[16] The pressure to marry was overwhelming, the alternative being not only economic self-dependence, which was always difficult, but also loss of status and redundancy as a spinster. 'To be sure, I thought it gave me an Air of my Consequence to be call'd Mrs. *Charke*, than Miss *Charlotte*,' Charlotte Charke recalls in the tragi-comic narrative of her life.[17] Most eighteenth-century female autobiographers build into their memoirs a warning to all their women readers to beware of the dangers that ruined them. George Anne Bellamy, the actress, wrote 'to warn the young and thoughtless of my own sex from the syren shore of vanity, dissipation, and illicit pleasures, of which remorse and misery, as I too sensibly feel, are the sure attendants'; while Letitia Pilkington proposed herself 'not as an Example, but a Warning', to the 'Female Part' of her readers.[18] In other narratives, it is difficult to see what the author could have done to avoid her unhappy marriage. Mary Granville was pressurised, as a girl of seventeen, to marry the sixty-year-old wealthy landowner, Alexander Pendarves, in consideration of her father's 'unhappy circumstances', her own want of fortune, and her small prospect of happiness if she disobliged her family in the matter.[19] Clearly, her uncle wanted her off his hands and safely married to a man who would not only maintain her, but also die within a few years and leave her a comfortable income.

Eighteenth-century autobiographies also indicate a shift of activity from the countryside to London. The capital was the place to go fortune-hunting, and most female autobiographers finished up there when their marriages had collapsed and their families declined to take them back. Although Lawrence Stone has argued for the growth of companionate marriages and the closed, domesticated nuclear family during the eighteenth century, the parents of women autobiographers seem to have been particularly heartless towards their daughters and taken scant care of them. Cruel stepmothers abound, with new young families and a policy of protecting their own. Loss of repectability was the inevitable consequence of a hand-to-mouth existence in dirty London lodging-houses, fuelling the self-defensive autobiographical urge in many women who felt they had been misunderstood and badly done by. Perhaps most of them wrote for the reason that they *were* unhappy and needed to affirm their real selves in writing: a very different motive from that of their seventeenth-century predecessors. Even the more 'respectable' women, such as Hester Thrale Piozzi, wrote out of a sense of being undervalued, or valued for the wrong reasons. Jealous of her first husband's sentimental attachment to Sophia Streatfield, Mrs Thrale declares bitterly: 'No one who visited us missed seeing his preference of her to me', especially as she was, at the time, 'exceedingly oppressed by pregnancy'.[20] The mother of twelve children in fourteen years, she evidently gained some relief from pouring out the accumulated wrongs of her exhausting married life.

The world of women's autobiography in the eighteenth century is strikingly like that of Defoe's novels, especially *Roxana* (1724) and *Moll Flanders*, where women are thrown on their own wits and the financial resources of their lovers. Although most of the autobiographers stop short of prostitution, they soon discover a fundamental conflict between their needs as individuals and the self-righteous standards of respectable society. Few female autobiographers of this time were happily married, and many would have agreed with Roxana's disillusioned outburst against marriage: 'I had no Inclination to be a Wife again, I had had such bad Luck with my first Husband, I hated the Thoughts of it; I found, that a Wife is treated with Indifference, a Mistress with a strong Passion'.

Roxana insists that a woman is freer on her own: 'that while a Woman was single, she was a Masculine in her politick Capacity; that she had then the full Command of what she had, and the full Direction of what she did; that she was a Man in her separated Capacity'.[21] On the other hand, the spinster's lot was far from enviable, and because there was a surplus of single women on the market, competition for a man was all the more desperate.[22] Yet, once married, a woman relinquished control of her property to her husband; and divorce was only possible by a private Act of Parliament. Roxana argues that 'a Woman gave herself entirely away from herself, in Marriage, and capitulated only to be, at best, but an *Upper-Servant*' (p. 187).

Both eighteenth-century autobiographies and novels reflect the de-valuation of women into sex-objects in a society that none the less set great store by chastity for women. Mary Delarivière Manley was quick to publicise the double standard. 'If she had been a Man, she had been without Fault,' she wrote in her disguised autobiography, *The History of Rivella* (1714): 'But the Charter of that Sex being much more confin'd than ours, what is not a Crime in Men is scandalous and unpardonable in Woman.'[23] Mary Astell had already urged women to cultivate their 'souls' as well as their bodies, and value themselves for something other than fine dressing. Men, she argued, saw them as 'cheap and contempt-ible': 'Women are from their very Infancy debar'd those Advantages, with the want of which they are afterwards reproached, and nursed up in those Vices which will hereafter be upbraided to them.'[24] Although women had more say in their choice of partner than in the previous century, fathers still exerted a powerful right of veto, and, if necessary, locked their daughters away from undesirable suitors. Catherine Jemmat recalls being penned up for two months because she was being wooed by a gentleman her father disliked.[25] Like Richardson's Clarissa, Lady Mary Wortley Montagu was offered a suitor chosen by her father, and wrote desperate letters to her friends, devising means of escape. Lady Mary's would-be husband, Clotworthy Skeffington, is the equivalent of Clarissa's Mr Solmes, and her hasty, frequent letters, scribbled on 'Friday Night' and 'Satterday Morning' communicate a similar mood of terror and excitement to that of Clarissa's correspondence with Anna Howe. 'I tremble for what we are doing', Lady Mary wrote to Wortley as their plans reached a crisis. 'Are you sure you will love me for ever? Shall we never repent.'[26] Evidence suggests too that those who left home young and chose their own marriage partners entered their new state with higher expectations and found their subsequent disappointment all the more bitter.[27]

Even in novels written by men, the sympathetic protagonists are usually women, and generally women on their own, round whom develops a mythology of victimisation. In an age where the popular vogue was for 'personal histories', whether in novels, biographies, or scurrilous confessions, women who had already lost their respectability tried either to recover it in narratives of their undeserved suffering, or else exploited the freedom of speech (having nothing more to lose) in libellous attacks on those who had injured them. Mrs Manley and Mrs Phillips were perhaps the most notorious in this respect, but Letitia Pilkington uses her *Memoirs* (1749) as a stalking-horse for sneers against clergymen.[28] As in much eighteenth-century poetry, especially Pope's and Dryden's, the issue of personalities is paramount. Mrs Manley assisted her readers with a 'key' at the back of her *New Atalantis* (1709) and *Rivella* (1714) but initiates usually knew who was meant. Catherine Jemmat insisted that a real-life history should be at least as interesting as a fictitious account of a woman's misfortunes:

> But why may not the true story of Catherine Yeo, who absolutely does exist, divert as much, allowing for the different abilities of the authors, as those of Miss Pamela Andrews, or Miss Clarissa Harlowe, who never had any local habitation except in the happy fancy of their admirable author, whose characters of virtue and constancy are the native children of his truly benevolent soul? (Jemmat, *Memoirs*, I, 115)

From protests such as this emerge signs that female autobiographers were beginning to think consciously about the artistic value of their writing, and of the implied audience who would read it. Certainly in an age of improved literacy, a wider reading public and a taste for tales of individual lives, the incentives to write autobiography were stronger than they had ever been. Printers ensured that books came out quickly, and often published controversial correspondence prefixed to later editions of a work, so that readers felt they were participating in an ongoing debate. Margaret Cavendish is perhaps the first female auto-biographer to write with a strong sense of audience, which made her both defensive and defiant. This sometimes prickly marriage of moods lends an additional self-consciousness to eighteenth-century women's writing. Letitia Pilkington, for example, often looks over her shoulder at a reader impatient with her digressions. This was particularly serious when some of the readers were known to be subscribers, with their names printed inside the book. Letitia Pilkington promises hers 'a key to whatever secrets I have been obliged to lock up,' and warns them that they have reached the 'mournfulest' half of her book. 'My readers will, I hope, acknowledge I deal candidly with them when I not only acquaint them with my actions but reveal to them even the inmost recesses of my soul as freely as to Heaven,' she adds in a later authorial comment.[29] Against the reader's assumed intolerance of digressions, she explodes in a final, conclusive burst of self-defence:

> Well now, Mrs Pilkington, says, perhaps, my reader, what in the name of wonder have we to do with all this.
>   Why, truly, no more, I think, than with a buff jerkin, or mine hostess at St Albans; but I am no Methodist either in writing or religion. Sometimes irregularities please; shapeless rock, or hanging precipice, present to the poetic imagination more inspiring dreams than could the finest garden. (III, 359)

Whereas the Duchess of Newcastle seemed to regret her 'ragged rout' of handwriting, Mrs Pilkington boasts of her 'irregularities', and looks beyond the handwriting itself to the 'poetic imagination' and the form (or formlessness) of her work. 'I am, in short, an heteroclite, or irregular verb, which can never be declined or conjugated,' she declares triumphantly (p. 359), a vaunt that few nineteenth-century women would dare to make.

Her audience is sometimes assumed to be male, sometimes female, sometimes her husband, sometimes her subscribers. The presence of barbed addresses to each of these, and self-conscious discussions of her style and method give Mrs Pilkington's *Memoirs* an instability typical of much autobiographical writing by women in the eighteenth century. Charlotte Charke writes in a similar way, with an equally strong sense of audience. The youngest child of Colley Cibber, she was estranged from her father, and hoped to be reconciled with him in the course of her writing. Her audience is promised an update on the affair, should anything interesting happen, and is occasionally involved in 'tragical occurrences', which happened 'but last Week'. Mrs Charke's closeness to her audience was facilitated by serial publication: very different circumstances from the strictly private conditions that fostered the writing of most seventeenth-century autobiography, and clearly they produce a more exhibitionist style of self-presentation on the part of the writer. Unlike their seventeenth-century predecessors, most eighteenth-century women wrote for money, and to attract support and sympathy. Mrs Pilkington and Mrs Charke also laid themselves out to be entertaining, an intention that often conflicted with the facts of their lives and led to disjunctions in their work between the humorous early part, and the sour, accusatory tone of the later sections.

Most eighteenth-century autobiographers address their readers openly and directly, if only because they wanted to clear their own good names, but there are some examples of the evasionary methods that became more widely used in the nineteenth century. Both Mrs Manley and Mrs Phillips write in the third person, and invent elaborate machinery for their concealment; while the actress, George Anne Bellamy, employs another autobiographical mode, the letter form, which was to become so popular with the Victorians. Addressing her instalments 'Madam,' she hopes that through their recipient, 'the extenuations which occur may be diffused through that circle whose good opinion I am anxious to regain.'[30] In each of these three examples, the writer conceals herself behind a more respectable spokesman, who will act as her mediator with the public.

The subject-matter of much eighteenth-century autobiography by women is a debased version of the previous century's love-stories. There is still little interest in childhood as evincing important psychological influence on the events of adult life, except perhaps in the case of Charlotte Charke, who dressed herself up in her father's clothes (she was later to find work as a waiter) and was 'deem'd an Alien' from her family (p. 24). Mrs Phillips passes over her childhood, 'which is in no way material to this Narrative', and little is said anywhere about mothers and siblings or even children. The two important relationships for eighteenth-century women in their accounts of themselves, are with fathers and husbands, and in both roles men are shown as mercenary and often predatory.

The tone is set by a conversation between Lovemore and D'Aumont at the beginning of Mrs Manley's *Rivella*. 'How are Her Teeth and Lips, spoke the Chevalier? Forgive me, dear Lovemore, for breaking in so often upon your Discourse; but Kissing being the sweetest leading Pleasure, 'tis impossible a Woman can charm without a good Mouth' (p. 9). Lovemore replies that until she grew fat, 'there was not I believe any Defect to be found in her Body': indeed 'Her Hands and Arms have been publickly celebrated' (p. 10). Their meaty appreciation of Rivella is typical of the male response to women as recorded by the women themselves. For most, sexual maturity came early, at least in terms of male pursuit, and is viewed as the cause of their undoing. Catherine Jemmat was hounded by enthusiastic 'sparks', and hidden away by her father; Mrs Phillips was raped in her early teens; Mary Granville was married at seventeen to a man old enough to be her grandfather; Mrs Manley was trapped into a bigamous marriage; Lady Vane was first introduced into the world as a woman at the age of thirteen, and instantly surrounded by admirers. Most protest their innocent intentions, and portray themselves as victims. Even the notorious Mrs Phillips becomes a Clarissa, 'absolutely inconsolable' after her rape:

> Never was a poor Creature's Mind torn by such a Tempest of Troubles: She made a thousand different Resolutions in a Moment, without being able to fix on one; and to hear her relate the melancholy Scene, even at this Distance of Time, one is scarce able to refrain from Tears. (Phillips, *An Apology*, I, 39)

Subsequently rejected by her husband, Mr Muilman (like Tess of the d'Urbervilles, because of her soiled history), Mrs Phillips protests that she would have made a good wife, 'from the Sweetness and Affability of her Temper', besides her great 'Fortitude', if she had only been given a fair chance (I, 253–4). The marriages of Mrs Pilkington, Catherine Jemmat and Charlotte Charke also broke down, leaving each of them with at least one child. When this happened, a woman was thrown upon her own resources, which, in the cases of Pilkington and Charke, meant a shaky existence in the shadow of the debtors' prison. Both embody Defoe's concept of economic individualism, picking up friends here and there, but largely surviving on what Charlotte Charke calls the workings of her 'projecting Brain' (p. 133). For Mrs Pilkington, at least, this was not altogether an unpleasant way of life:

> I am sure, I ought to thank my loving husband for the opportunity he has afforded me of seeing the world from the palace to the prison; for, had he but permitted me to be what nature certainly intended me for, a harmless household dove, in all human probability I should have rested contented with my humble situation, and, instead of using a pen, been employed with a needle, to work for the little ones we might by this time have had. (p. 289)

Her language is certainly equivocal: should she have followed her 'nature' or not? Her image of the household dove sewing baby-clothes seems more ironical than wistful, and her opposition of pen and needle becomes a popular symbol for many other writing women. Mrs Jemmat, for instance, speaks of 'resigning the needle for the pen' (I, 3), as did Margaret Oliphant and Harriet Martineau in the following century.[31] All communicate a sense of having unsexed themselves by their exchange of weapon, though the pen, as a rule, is the key to liberty. Mrs Pilkington actively 'uses' the pen (perhaps exploits its possibilities), but might have 'been employed' (perhaps exploited) by a needle. For Charlotte Charke, indeed, the pen grew into a prop: her work became 'the Staff of my Life' (p. 87), with a suggestion of therapeutic, as well as economic necessity. Both Mrs Charke and Mrs Thrale say they were drawn into a fuller exposition of their lives than they originally intended. Mrs Thrale's was written at the request of Sir James Fellowes, whom she occasionally addresses directly from within her narrative. 'But you make me an egotist,' she accuses him, 'and force me to remember scenes and ideas I never dreamed of communicating.'[32] In the eighteenth century autobiographers we begin to see something of the process of association which gives their work its idiosyncratic structure. Lacking the orderliness of their male contemporaries, David Hume and Edward Gibbon (whose autobiographies are shaped by their professional activities), female autobiographers of this time allow their writing to wander diffusely over the past, spilling over into accusation and digression as the mood takes them. The shape of their writing reflects the random, almost vagabond lifestyle of their precarious existence in London, and, as a result, lacks the essential meaning or pattern that most critics now regard as a quality of true autobiography.

No eighteenth-century woman explores her own personality with the wonder and delight of the Duchess of Newcastle, or, to a lesser extent, Lucy Hutchinson. Few had the leisure or contentment to do so, quite apart from the interest, which seems to have been lacking, perhaps because there was little to celebrate in their disordered lives. The contemplation of one's own personality is best practised in unhurried circumstances, and by one who has a strong consciousness of her own uniqueness. Most eighteenth-century women cast themselves as conventional victims, and though most survive because of their overwhelming determination to do so, they rarely stop to analyse what it was exactly that made them go on. Letitia Pilkington, in fact, refers to 'so often running away from myself' (p. 91), instead of concentrating on her own history; though she does recount a dream of being locked inside Westminster Abbey, and, like Macbeth, watching a show of crowned heads parading past her (pp. 293–4). Catherine Jemmat also recalls a dream with explicit Freudian symbolism. She was coming from church, when she met an old gentleman, who showed her a coffin containing the body of one of her suitors, 'Mr. B.'. 'I was contemplating the body with earnestness, when suddenly a snake jumped from it, twisted round my arm, and stung me; upon this I shrieked out and awoke' (I, 108–9). She later records her experiences of 'hypochondriac symptoms', when she imagined monsters coming to devour her, and 'my father all in a rage with his sword drawn coming to put me to death', her stepmother powerless in a corner (II, p. 3). These are, however, unusual occurrences in memoirs generally devoted to the external events in their authors' lives.

Now that autobiographies were being published during their writers' lifetimes, and exciting public controversy, eighteenth century women were aware of one another's work in a way that was uncommon in the seventeenth century. Lady Mary Wortley Montagu devoured the memoirs of Lady Vane (in Smollett's *Peregrine Pickle*), Mrs Phillips, and Charlotte Charke. 'Her History, rightly consider'd, would be more instructive to young Women than any Sermon I know,' she said of Lady Vane's, which reminded her of Mrs Phillips's.[33] Fanny Burney and Mrs Thrale mixed freely in professional literary circles; Letitia Pilkington was a protegée of Swift; Fielding referred, in *Amelia*, to 'the Apologies with which certain gay Ladies have lately been pleased to oblige the World'; Lady Vane paid Smollett to include her memoirs in *Peregrine Pickle*; and satirical jibes at female memoirists became part of the popular versifier's stock-in-trade:

> Without a blush behold each nymph advance,
> The luscious heroine of her own romance;
> Each harlot triumphs in her loss of fame,
> And boldly prints and publishes her shame.[34]

The writing of women's autobiography peaked around the middle of the eighteenth century, and then seems to have declined until the second half of the nineteenth. Perhaps it had simply become too scandalous, as in the case of Harriette Wilson, who opened her *Memoirs of Herself and Others* (1825) with the notorious lines: 'I shall not say when and how I became, at the age of fifteen, the mistress of the Earl of Craven.'[35] Or perhaps late-eighteenth-century women were more interested in the novel, which had opened up new possibilities for their enjoyment of intrigue, sentiment and female adventure. Those who still liked to study themselves were more attracted to the private journal; and it is with the diaries of Fanny Burney and Dorothy Wordsworth, the one unashamedly worldly and bubbling with gossip, the other faithfully recording walks and washing and the ups and downs of her brother's health, that the eighteenth-century tradition of women's autobiographical writing regained some of its lost balance and respectability.

Nineteenth-century practitioners of autobiography seem to have had a three-way choice. They could draw on the example of the seventeenth-century tradition, the largely contented memoir of family and some individual history; or on the eighteenth-century tradition of recrimination and scandal; or they could start anew, bringing in material which had not been used by men or women in the previous centuries. Nevertheless, the history of women's autobiographical writing before the nineteenth century is not as disjointed as it may appear. Although there are dramatic contrasts between the seventeenth- and eighteenth-century traditions, they share certain likenesses that mark them out from the male mainstream. Whereas men concentrate on their careers and write, for the most part, in a stately prose style without rancour, women focus on the vicissitudes of their private lives and tell stories of endurance and survival in a society where they had no prominence and few claims.

The starkest example of the differences between male and female self-writing in the eighteenth century can be seen in a comparison between David Hume's fourteen-page *Life* (1777) and Letitia Pilkington's gossipy, diffuse, self-referential three-volume *Memoirs*. Whereas Hume declares: 'It is difficult to be more detached from life than I am at present', and recognises that almost all his life has been spent 'in literary pursuits and occupations', Mrs Pilkington frequently begs pardon for a 'rambling digression' and describes herself as 'a lady of adventure'.[36] But less extreme comparisons suggest a similar conclusion: that from the beginnings of an autobiographical tradition in England, women favoured a more personal, more detailed, more colloquial style than men, and allowed their memories to follow an unstructured process of 'free association', rather than conform to a framework based on the assumption of a drive to success or the development of a career. The memoirs of Charlotte Charke and Letitia Pilkington, especially, record many false starts, setbacks and changes of direction, which undermine the notion that autobiography records a steady triumph over adversity, or the imposition of a coherent pattern on the messiness of real life.

On the other hand, the didacticism implicit in women's autobiography since Julian of Norwich ensures that it offers at least some endorsement of the *status quo*. Women are warned against foolish behaviour, and the autobiographers themselves seek approval from the respectable reading public. None questions the importance attached to a woman's reputation. What is perhaps disappointing about their approach is their unwillingness to launch a fuller attack on their society's response to the upbringing and expectations of its women. Certainly, there are protests, particularly against an inadequate education or an over-hasty marriage, and their depiction of men as lustful and rapacious condemns male sexual behaviour. But as female writers, their tone is distinctly apologetic. They know they will have to fight for every inch of ground regained. Charlotte Charke published with such low expectations of success, that she begged for her book's having the 'common Chance of a Criminal, at least to be properly examin'd, before it is condemn'd' (p. 11).

All female autobiographies before the nineteenth century testify even more than men's to the writer's exceptional sense of selfhood. To survive at all as a middle-class woman was a feat of will; to write about that act of survival was a further defiance of convention, and remained so for the Victorians. As the vocabulary of the brothel, constabulary and criminal court slipped out of women's autobiography, together with the 'lady of adventure', the question of what to put in its place, and how to express it, became acute. Victorian women lost no time in fumigating the eighteenth-century tradition, and creating a form of self-writing that would accommodate the contradictions of their position. Whereas Wordsworth felt 'it was a reasonable thing that he should take a review of his own mind', Victorian women had still to prove that they had minds, and that the reading public might want to know about them.[37]

Notes

1. *The Book of Margery Kempe: A Modern Version*, ed. W. Butler Bowdon (London and Toronto: Oxford University Press, 1952), p. 55.

2. Kempe, p. 345; *A Book of Showings to the Anchoress Julian of Norwich*, ed. Edmund Colledge and James Walsh (Toronto: Pontifical Institute of Medieval Studies: 2 vols, 1978), II, 285.

3. Dean Ebner, *Autobiography in Seventeenth-Century England: Theology and the Self* (The Hague, Paris: Mouton, 1971) suggests that 'Autobiography as a distinct literary genre was virtually nonexistent in England (or elsewhere) prior to the seventeenth century' (p. 14); Paul Delany, *British Autobiography in the Seventeenth Century* (London: Routledge and Kegan Paul, 1969) says that outside the religious sects 'no substantial literary tradition of autobiography existed in Britain until well into the eighteenth century' (p. 170); Karl J. Weintraub, 'Autobiography and Historical Consciousness', *Critical Inquiry*, vol. I, no. 4 (June 1975) says that 'only since 1800 has Western Man placed a premium on autobiography' (p. 821).

4. Margaret Bottrall, *Every Man A Phoenix: Studies in Seventeenth-Century Autobiography* (London: John Murray, 1958), p. 1; Mary G. Mason, 'The Other Voice: Autobiographies of Women Writers', in *Autobiography: Essays Theoretical and Critical*, ed. James Olney, p. 209; Clarissa W. Atkinson, *Mystic and Pilgrim: The Book and the World of Margery Kempe* (Ithaca and London: Cornell University Press, 1983), p. 18.

5. James M. Osborn, *The Beginnings of Autobiography in England* (Los Angeles: University of California, 1960), p. 7.

6. Lawrence Stone, *The Family, Sex and Marriage in England 1500–1800* (1977) (Abridged Edition, Harmondsworth: Peregrine Books, 1982), p. 153.

7. *The Life of William Cavendish, Duke of Newcastle to which is added The True Relation of My Birth, Breeding, and Life by Margaret, Duchess of Newcastle*, ed. C. H. Firth (London: John C. Nimmo, 1886), pp. 317–18.

8. Cynthia S. Pomerleau, 'The Emergence of Women's Autobiography in England', in *Women's Autobiography: Essays in Criticism*, ed. Estelle C. Jelinek (Bloomington and London: Indiana University Press, 1980), p. 26.

9. Lucy Hutchinson, *Memoirs of the Life of Colonel Hutchinson, with the fragment of an autobiography of Mrs. Hutchinson* (1806; ed. James Sutherland, London and New York: Oxford University Press, 1973), p. 33; *The George Eliot Letters*, I, 41.

10. *Some Specialities in the Life of M. Warwicke*, ed. T. Crofton Croker (London: Percy Society, 1848), p. 4, pp. 32–3; p. 21.

11. *A Narrative of the Life of Mrs. Charlotte Charke, Written by Herself* (London: W. Reeve, 1755), p. 139; p. 136.

12. *The Memoirs of Anne, Lady Halkett, and Ann, Lady Fanshawe*, ed. John Loftis (Oxford: Clarendon Press, 1979), p. 45.

13. *Ibid.*, p. 101.

14. Georges Gusdorf, 'Conditions and Limits of Autobiography', in *Autobiography*, ed. James Olney, p. 48; *The Autobiography of Mrs. Alice Thornton, of East Newton, Co. York* (Edinburgh: Surtees Society, 1875).

15. *An Apology for the Conduct of Mrs. Teresia Constantia Phillips* (Printed for the Author, 3 vols, 1748), I: 'To the candid and impartial Reader' (no page number).

16. Perry, p. 50.

17. Charke, p. 52.

18. *An Apology for the Life of George Anne Bellamy, Late of Covent-Garden Theatre. Written by Herself* (2nd edition, 2 vols, Dublin: Moncrieffe, 1785), I, 2; *Memoirs of Mrs. Letitia Pilkington, Wife to the Rev. Mr. Matthew*

Pilkington. Written by Herself (3 vols, Dublin, 1749; ed. Iris Barry, London: Routledge and Kegan Paul, 1928, p. 25).

19. *The Autobiography and Correspondence of Mary Granville, Mrs. Delany: with interesting reminiscences of King George the Third and Queen Charlotte*, ed. Lady Llanover (London: Richard Bentley and Sons, 3 vols, 1861), I, 27.

20. *Autobiography, Letters and Literary Remains of Mrs. Piozzi (Thrale)*, ed. A. Hayward (London: Longman, Green, Longman & Roberts, 2 vols, 1861), I, 297.

21. Daniel Defoe, *Roxana: The Fortunate Mistress* (1724) (ed. David Blewett, Harmondsworth: Penguin, 1982), p. 170; p. 188.

22. Roxana declares that an Old Maid is 'the worst of Nature's Curses' (p. 40); on surplus of women, see Pomerleau, p. 30; Stone, pp. 243–4; Peter Earle, *The World of Defoe* (Newton Abbot: Readers Union Group of Book Clubs, 1977), p. 250; on the importance of marriage, see E. A. Wrigley, 'The growth of population in eighteenth-century England: a conundrum resolved', *Past and Present* (February 1983), pp. 121–50. I am grateful to Dr Jane Ridley for drawing my attention to this article.

23. *Mrs. Manley's History of Her Own Life and Times, Published from Her Original Manuscript* (1725), incorporating *The History of Rivella* (1714), p. 7.

24. *A Serious Proposal to the Ladies, for the Advancement of their True and Greatest Interest*, by a Lover of her Sex [Mary Astell] (3rd edition, 1696), p. 4; p. 18.

25. *The Memoirs of Mrs. Catherine Jemmat, Daughter of the late Admiral Yeo of Plymouth. Written by Herself* (2 vols, 2nd edition, 1772), II, 52. Though note the full title, and the prominence given to her relationship with her father.

26. *The Complete Letters of Lady Mary Wortley Montagu*, ed. Robert Halsband (Oxford: Oxford University Press, 3 vols, 1967), I, 159.

27. Stone, p., 191.

28. Pilkington, *Memoirs*, p. 83.

29. *Ibid.*, p. 105, p. 110, p. 242; Catherine Jemmat's subscribers, listed in her book, include Queen Charlotte, the Duke of Gloucester, Charles James Fox, Edmund Burke and the Duke of Marlborough.

30. Bellamy, *Apology*, I, 2.

31. Oliphant, *Autobiography*, p. 16; *Harriet Martineau's Autobiography* (1877; ed. Gaby Weiner, London: Virago, 2 vols, 1983), I, 142.

32. Piozzi (Thrale), *Autobiography*, I, 262.

33. Tobias Smollett, *The Adventures of Peregrine Pickle in which are included Memoirs of a Lady of Quality* (1751; ed. James L. Clifford, London and New York: Oxford University Press, 1964), Introduction, p. xviii.

34. *Ibid.*, p. xviii.

35. Harriette Wilson, *Memoirs of Herself and Others* (1825; ed. James Laver, London: Peter Davies, 1929), p. 1.

36. *The Life of David Hume, Esq., Written by Himself* (London: W. Strahan and T. Cadell, 1777), p. 13; Pilkington, *Memoirs*, p. 320.

37. *William Wordsworth: Poetical Works*, ed. Thomas Hutchinson; new edition revised by Ernest De Selincourt (Oxford and New York: Oxford University Press, 1984), p. 494.

Chapter 3

'At five I supposed myself a heroine'

autobiographies of childhood

'What do we know of that which lies in the minds of children? we know only what we put there,' declared Anna Jameson in the middle of the nineteenth century. The mystery of childhood, its 'world of instincts, perceptions, experiences, pleasures, and pains', often mute and unexpressed, was, she felt, entirely unknown to adult theorists, although they had once been children themselves. 'We do not sufficiently consider that our life is not made up of separate parts, but is *one* – is a progressive whole,' she insisted. 'When we talk of leaving our childhood behind us, we might as well say that the river flowing onward to the sea had left the fountain behind.'[1] Employing a popular image for the growth towards maturity, Anna Jameson echoes the philosophy of Jean-Jacques Rousseau, nearly a century before, in his study of the ideal childhood, *Emile* (1762). 'We know nothing of childhood,' Rousseau had said, pleading, like Mrs Jameson, for a reverent treatment of the state.[2] For both, the notion of individual human life as 'a progressive whole' is perfectly compatible with the treatment of childhood as a distinct stage, characterised by its own ways of thinking and seeing. What is important is that educators should acknowledge the fundamental differences between adult and child psychology and not expect children to behave with the considered rationality of their parents. The difficulty was that before the nineteenth century, childhood experiences were not well documented, or considered important in themselves. Children were generally regarded as small adults, to be hurried out of an inconvenient stage as quickly as possible.[3] Few autobiographers since Augustine had paid much attention to their childhood adventures, or considered them in any way formative in the development of their adult personalities. The 'Childhood', as a distinctive autobiographical genre, according to

Richard N. Coe's definition, came late to Western literature, with Stendhal's *Vie de Henri Brulard* (1835); while Peter Coveney argues that 'until the last decades of the eighteenth century the child did not exist as an important and continuous theme in English literature.'[4]

The catalysing agents in the growth of a child-aware consciousness were, apart from Rousseau himself, the German Romanticists, especially Goethe; and Blake, Wordsworth and Coleridge among the English Romantic poets. More disturbing in their psychological findings were the Romantic prose writers, especially Lamb and De Quincey, who emphasised the loneliness and emotional suffering of imaginative children living constantly on the edge of fear. De Quincey's childhood life was inextricably linked with death, and his sleeping and waking dreams haunted by visions of dead little sisters; and both Lamb and De Quincey drew attention to the child's susceptibility to night terrors: 'that power in the eye of many children by which in darkness they project a vast theatre of phantasmagorical figures moving forwards or backwards between their bed-curtains and the chamber walls.'[5] More than any other aspect of childhood experience, the Romantic prose writers stressed the irrational contours of psychic suffering, establishing their validity in mental history, and their intimate connection with adult personality.

Situated half way between the Romantic discovery of childhood, and the Freudian, Victorian autobiographers occupy a transitional ground of crucial importance. As it was, Victorian theorists were undecided in their response to the state. Either the child was born an Original Sinner, to be systematically repressed for his own good, or he was essentially innocent and vulnerable, a source of hope, to be protected and carefully nurtured. Another view, propounded by John Locke in his *Some Thoughts Upon Education* (1693), the *'tabula rasa'* theory, argued that the newborn child was neither good nor bad, but a blank sheet receptive to whatever imprint his environment provided. Whereas the second and third theories seemed to have gained ground in the eighteenth century, the first enjoyed something of a comeback in the nineteenth century, with the Evangelical revival. This, in turn, generated a heightened anxiety about the future, an overwhelming feeling of insecurity, especially in early life. Among the novelists, Charles Kingsley in *Alton Locke*, Charlotte Brontë in *Jane Eyre* and Dickens in *Great Expectations*, testify to the disapproval and suspicion of children on religious grounds, that made their first ten years a series of uncomfortable moral sores. Among the autobiographers, Edmund Gosse, in *Father and Son*, offers the most detailed tragi-comic account of a Calvinistic upbringing overshadowed by an unresting watchfulness for lapse.

LuAnn Walther has argued convincingly that this cultural ambivalence about childhood produced two main impulses in Victorian selfwriting: on the one hand, an emphasis on adversity and suffering, and on the other, the presentation of childhood as a blissful, Edenic state.[6] In any case, the tendency to mythologise childhood has long been recognised by critics. Biblical typology, and the recurrence of narrative patterns based on paradisal or confessional models gave shape, throughout the nineteenth century, to autobiographical reconstructions of childhood and the often painful growth to maturity.[7] Once established, the tradition quickly gained wide appeal, though it was not until the twentieth century that 'the Childhood', as Richard Coe calls the narrative of child life as distinct from full-length autobiography, became a prominent genre.

George Eliot found the childhood sections of contemporary autobiography the most successful part of an otherwise intrusive mode. 'The account of her childhood and early youth is most pathetic and interesting,' she commented on Harriet Martineau's *Autobiography*, 'but as in all books of the kind the charm departs as the life advances, and the writer has to tell of her own triumphs.' She felt much the same about John Stuart Mill's *Autobiography*. 'The account of his early education and the presentation of his Father are admirable, but there are some pages in the latter half that one would have liked to be different.'[8] Her response emphasises the appeal of childhood reminiscence, as against the more egotistical or vindictive direction taken by the narrative of professional success. Every account of childhood draws, to some extent, on universal experiences, while maintaining the specificity of an individual, often idiosyncratic consciousness. The reader, in turn, recognises points where the writer's anxieties or pleasures cross with his own, and others where he can only marvel at the difference between one child's extraordinarily good or bad fortune and the more humdrum normality of another's middling experiences. Throughout the reading process, an instinctive weaving of cross-references and comparisons in the reader's mind intensifies the emotional appeal of the genre, and stamps its validity. Along with the truth of a childhood experience, the reader willingly swallows any fictional embellishment.

As Anna Jameson was quick to point out, the mystery of childhood largely derives from a lack of self-writing *by* children. 'The child lives, and does not contemplate its own life,' she wrote in her 'Revelation of Childhood'. 'It can give no account of that inward, busy, perpetual activity of the growing faculties and feelings which it is of so much importance that we should know' (p. 119). Hence the discovery by Melanie Klein that one can understand far more of a child's anxieties by watching his play, or studying his drawings. The autobiographer of childhood can rarely recapture the daily lived quality of his early life, but must step from island to island of significant reminiscence. This in itself gives the childhood a shape, a distinctive pattern, and encloses it in a pool of memory, essentially static and unchanging. At the same time, this fragmentary structure brings the childhood autobiography close to the broken narrative cited by Freud in the opening of 'Dora's' case history, as characteristic of the hysteric's account of her early life.[9] Since many of the female autobiographers of childhood describe distinctly neurotic symptoms, the Freudian case history supplies a useful analogue to the consideration of pre-Freudian women's evocation of their early lives.

As Richard Coe has pointed out, almost all autobiographers of childhood, men and women, were, as children, solitary, alienated or exceptional.[10] Among male autobiographers of the nineteenth century, however, there is less interest in the psychological nuances of common-place experience. The most extreme example is Mark Pattison, whose *Memoirs* begin with his coming up to Oxford in 1832: 'for I have really no history but a mental history.' He deliberately left his 'boyish years for a later book of reminiscences', but this was never written. Similarly, Thomas Henry Huxley states baldly: 'I have next to nothing to say about my childhood.'[11] John Henry Newman records mainly what he read, and the effect his reading had on his imagination and religious conviction; while John Stuart Mill's childhood recollections are an exhausting catalogue of texts read, learned and inwardly digested, digested again by the narrative that recounts them. Charles Darwin has slightly more to say about his earliest memories, but several of them are retailed at second hand. 'I have been told that I was much slower in learning than my younger sister Catherine,' he observes; and later, 'I have heard my father and elder sister say that I had, as a very young boy, a strong taste for solitary walks; but what I thought about I know not.' He is often vague and non-committal about remembered details. His earliest recollection was of going to 'near Abergele for sea-bathing', when he was slightly over four years old: 'and I recollect some events and places there with some little precision.' Yet the events and places are not repeated now. Contrast Harriet Martineau, whose earliest memories are sharply visual and impressionistic: she remembered large holes in the planking of Yarmouth jetty and 'great tufts of green weed' swaying below.[12] With Trollope, Ruskin, Carlyle, and Gosse, the male reconstruction of child-hood acquires more introspective complexity; though Trollope's account of his painful school life occupies only a few pages of an autobiography largely devoted to what he 'and perhaps others' round him 'have done in literature'.[13]

Most male autobiographies are shaped from the beginning by

foreknowledge of a professionally successful adult life. Darwin, for example, notes early instances of his interest in botany; Ruskin of his attention to minute detail; Newman of his susceptibility to dreams of saints and angels, and superstitious practices. There is a tendency to see their lives moving purposefully in a specific direction, and childhood as a kind of antechamber to the proper business of adult life. Only Ruskin and Gosse linger over small, significant details; and by the time Ruskin was writing his *Praeterita* his mind was begining to break down. Gosse, in any case, wrote with a distinct didactic aim: to show the conflict between father and son, and old and new philosophies. His semi-fictionalised account of his childhood is not an exploration of early psychological experience for its own sake, of the kind to be found in a Dickens novel. In fact, the best autobiographical evocations of nineteenth-century boyhood, in its full imaginative complexity, are to be found in *David Copperfield* and *Great Expectations*.

From the point where women first began to write about themselves, they showed a greater interest than men in the 'unofficial' side of their lives. Before the nineteenth century, of course, few had a professional life anyway; but even afterwards, the home was their legitimate sphere of action, the 'mother of a family' a sacred office.[14] Childhood was also an enclosed, safely distant period of the past, and less controversial than the present. Whereas hostile readers might criticise a woman for overstressing her professional commitments, they would see nothing wrong in her studying the problems of childhood, provided she took care not to implicate her own parents in any critique of contemporary child-rearing practices. 'We are each of us bound to reticence by the piety we owe to those who have been nearest to us and have had a mingled influence over our lives,' wrote George Eliot in *Theophrastus Such*.[15] Charlotte Mary Yonge discouraged anyone from writing a biography of her during her lifetime because 'her mother would not have liked such a thing to be done.'[16] Fraught with dangers as it was, the writing of childhood reminiscences nevertheless provided Victorian women with an opportunity to protest against the values and priorities of their society. Full-length autobiographies, such as those by 'Charlotte Elizabeth', Frances Power Cobbe, Annie Besant and Harriet Martineau, include a detailed account of their early years; while another group of nineteenth-century women wrote only about their childhood, without producing an account of their adult lives. In the latter group are Elizabeth Barrett (before her marriage to Robert Browning), Sara Coleridge (only daughter of the poet), Anna Jameson, Charlotte Mary Yonge, the Brontë sisters in their diary papers, and the American philosophical writer, Margaret Fuller Ossoli. George Eliot also remained preoccupied by childhood experience throughout her career, though especially in her first novels, where the tenacity of early memory and its association with childhood landscape are treated with detached irony and painful nostalgia.

Elizabeth Barrett and the Brontës were the only ones to write about childhood when they were still children, and this gives their writing a special interest lacking in autobiography by their male contemporaries. Elizabeth Barrett wrote two Autobiographical Essays: the first, 'My Own Character' in 1818, when she was twelve, and the second, and more important, 'Glimpses into My Own Life and Literary Character', in 1820, when she was fourteen. Opening with a quotation from Locke's *Essay Concerning Human Understanding*, the first essay, as William Peterson has suggested, is, in effect, 'a product of the Evangelical tradition of spiritual self-examination', circling back to Locke at the end, with a discussion of his theory that there is 'no innate principle in the human breast'.[17] Gesturing towards the psychoanalytic concept of the super-ego, she refers to the infant's knowledge of right and wrong, which grows as he grows, and the development of conscience. By the time she is twelve, Elizabeth Barrett is already entangled in the anxiety of authorship, especially when its products are distinctly autobiographical. She refers to this twice in her first half page, torn between her vivid sense of self and the knowledge that any celebration of special qualities smacks of vanity. 'The investigation of oneself is an anxious employment,' she declares:

> The heart may appear corrupted by vanity, exalted by pride, soured by ill temper, & then that brilliant phantom, so dear to every soul, self estimation, fades for ever, & those shining clouds, on which you have soared so often to fame, sink under self-debasement – but shall such weaknesses prevent us from looking into ourselves? No. – I am not vain, but I have some tincture of pride about me, which I fear not to own, on the contrary which I like to boast of – (pp. 119–20).

Her self-analysis swings back and forth between delight in her singularity (like the Duchess of Newcastle's), and inbuilt inhibition, which makes her undercut every flourish with a reminder of her limitations. Her image of the fading phantom and the sinking clouds aptly reproduces the dawning of self-criticism, the realisation that she might be reproached by external standards for her 'tincture of pride' and susceptibility to flattery. Her responses are mostly extreme and absolute. She 'hates' needlework, 'detests' exaggerated flattery, 'dreads' being 'despised' as vain and 'abhors' music (p. 120), all, incidentally, conventional feminine accomplishments or attributes. Through all its Evangelical seriousness, Elizabeth Barrett's writing emerges as tough and determined, her sense of self irrepressible. As she herself puts it, 'I am not in the least obstinate, but I am always decided in what I think right' (p. 120).

The second Essay begins with an ambivalent response to the autobiographical impulse: 'TO BE ONE'S OWN chronicler is a task generally dictated by extreme vanity and often by that instinctive feeling which prompts the soul of man to snatch the records of his life from the dim and misty ocean of oblivion –' (p. 121). Her first three paragraphs suggest that nothing can be more appalling than total extinction, even to the sage. 'Is it not dreadful to descend into the damp grave unseen unmourned unwept for and forgotten?' (p. 122). The reader assumes her accordance with this string of doleful negatives, but she instantly denies it. 'But no feeling of this kind has influenced me or prompted me to write my own life. I am of too little consequence' she insists (p. 122). Yet the rest of the Essay is an extended affirmation of an enduring self in conflict with social custom and turbulent emotion. Shelleyan imagery of clouds, mist, light, stars, floating barks and veils of loneliness emphasises both her own intensely poetic and passionate nature, and the ephemeral quality of human life, which can only be counteracted by the achievement of success and fame. From an early age, she established a position of superiority. At three, she remembers 'reigning in the Nursery', and at six, still enjoying her 'triumph to a great degree over the inhabitants of the Nursery, there being no UPSTART to dispute my authority' (p. 123). This Adlerian urge to retain a position of vantage took different forms as she grew up. 'At five I supposed myself a heroine,' she reports (p. 123), but at six she is more excited by her father's calling her the 'Poet Laureat of Hope End'. At twelve, she 'enjoyed a literary life in all its pleasures', and 'was in great danger of becoming the founder of a religion of my own' (p. 126). Then suddenly, at thirteen, the start of adolescence, she has taught herself '"to throw away ambition" and to feel that pride & self conceit can only bring in self degradation on awaking from the splendid dream of vanity & folly!' (p. 127). From now, the vocabulary of restraint increases, as she tries to subdue her wilder emotions:

> I am now fourteen and since those days of my tenderest infancy my character has not changed – It is still as proud as wilful as impatient of controul as impetuous but thanks be to God it is restrained. I have acquired a command of my self which has become so habitual that my disposition appears to my friends to have undergone a revolution – But to myself it is well known that the same violent inclinations are in my inmost heart and that altho' habitual restraint has become almost a part of myself yet were I once to loose the rigid rein I might again be hurled with Phaeton far away from every thing human . . . every thing reasonable! (pp. 127–8).

Straining against the bounds of language, the subversive, tumultuous nature of her writing finally splits her identity into two selves: the outwardly controlled, which her friends see, and the inwardly anarchic, which feels an affinity with the imaginative and the irrational. Protesting that she is 'not so much influenced by exterior forces as by internal reflection and impetuosity', she dreads inactivity as a sign of nullity, 'for if that exertion be wanting, I should indeed appear to myself a dreary void!' (p. 128). By the end of the Essay, she has established her own values, in defiance of those upheld by society; yet she never entirely breaks free from convention. The most revealing comments come towards the end of the Essay, when she declares: 'My mind is naturally independant [sic] and spurns that subserviency of opinion which is generally considered necessary to feminine softness.' Finally, she struggles to explain and justify her principles:

> Better oh how much better to be the ridicule of mankind, the scoff of society [,] than lose that self respect which tho' this heart were bursting would elevate me above misery – above wretchedness & above abasement!!! These principles are irrevocable! It is not [–] I feel it is not vanity that dictates them! it is not [–] I know it is not an encroachment on masculine prerogative but it is a proud sentiment which will never allow me to be humbled in my own eyes!!! (p. 131)

The near-breakdown of coherency in her protests against imagined charges of vanity and 'encroachment on masculine prerogative' shows Elizabeth Barrett already enmeshed in the contradictions of her position. It is almost impossible for her to justify her stance without in some way overturning contemporary gender expectations, and deserving the accusations of vanity which trouble her throughout the Essay. If she spurns feminine softness and subserviency, she must, to some extent, be 'encroaching on masculine prerogative'.

The Essay rehearses some of the problems Elizabeth Barrett was to investigate further in her autobiographical poem *Aurora Leigh* (1857). Here, too, childhood ends at thirteen (this time because her father dies), and constricted by her aunt's curriculum of 'accomplishments' Aurora is again forced into the practice of a double life:

> I kept the life thrust on me, on the outside
> Of the inner life with all its ample room
> For heart and lungs, for will and intellect,
> Inviolable by conventions.[18]

More patient than Elizabeth, 'a meek and manageable child' initially, Aurora, like her creator, reads and writes and nurses her ambitions, all the time anticipating criticism. Even the birthday self-crowning with ivy leaves is accompanied by deflationary excuses:

> What, therefore, if I crown myself to-day
> In sport, not pride, to learn the feel of it – (2: 33–4)

External conditioning, unwillingly internalised, enforces the split, in both Aurora and Elizabeth, between outward conformity and inward fantasy life.

Freud and Breuer discovered a similar split in the case history of 'Anna O', an intelligent girl who escaped from her monotonous outward life into 'systematic day-dreaming, which she described as her "private theatre"'. Breuer concluded that 'her monotonous family life and the absence of adequate intellectual occupation left her with an unemployed surplus of mental liveliness and energy, and this found an outlet in the constant activity of her imagination.'[19] Her daydream life developed into an hysterical state of what Breuer calls 'alienation', though this existed, throughout her illness, alongside a perfectly normal psychic state. Fifty years earlier, the conduct-book writer, Sarah Ellis, had noticed a 'musing, listless tendency' in girls, and advised the 'Mothers of England' to guard against it. 'The musing, quiet, listless little girl,' warned Mrs Ellis, 'though possibly she may in her early life be more gentle and ladylike than the other [the 'romping' kind], seldom grows up to be so useful and valuable a character.'[20]

In fact, many women autobiographers in the nineteenth century recalled having lived a dual life in their childhood and adolescence, preserving the imaginative or ambitious daydream world from the knowledge of sceptical adults. 'I can truly say that, from ten years old to fourteen or fifteen, I lived a double existence,' wrote Anna Jameson; 'one outward, linking me with the external sensible world, the other inward, creating a world to and for itself, conscious to itself only. I carried on for whole years a series of actions, scenes, and adventures.' While Elizabeth Barrett pored over 'fairy phenomenons and the actions of necromancers', playing the daydream role of 'a forlorn damsel in distress rescued by some noble knight', Anna Jameson was herself

> a princess-heroine in the disguise of a knight, a sort of Clorinda or Britomart, going about to redress the wrongs of the poor, fight giants, and kill dragons; or founding a society in some far-off solitude or desolate island, which would have rivalled that of Gonsalez, where there were to be no tears, no tasks, and no laws – except those which I made myself, – no caged birds nor tormented kittens.[21]

Like Mrs Ellis, Anna Jameson suggests that girls with a weakness for airy visions should be given more practical things to do, such as cooking and medicine. As Deborah Epstein Nord has shown in her study of Beatrice Webb, female memoirists generally express guilt about their early fantasies of success, whereas for men 'daydreams represented an acceptable sign of healthy aspiration'.[22] Herbert Spencer comments specifically on the assumed detrimental effect of what he calls 'castle-building', a term also used frequently by his friend and pupil, Beatrice Webb. 'In moderation,' argues Spencer, 'I regard it as beneficial. It is a play of the constructive imagination, and without constructive imagination there can be no high achievement.' He believed that this early love for 'castle-building' arose from 'the spontaneous activity of powers which in future life became instrumental to higher things'.[23] For women, the only acceptable outlet for fervent reverie was religious enthusiasm, and even this, sooner or later, was supposed to be channelled towards practical ends.

'Charlotte Elizabeth', the Evangelical novelist, and Annie Besant, the social reformer, both discovered a religious outlet for their daydreams, and fantasised about martyrdom. Annie Besant's masochistic visions were of standing before Roman judges and Dominican inquisitors, being 'flung to lions, tortured on the rack, burned at the stake'. The more she read of the Early Christian fathers, the stronger grew her 'hidden life'; while for Charlotte Elizabeth, reality became 'insipid, almost hateful', as she imagined herself the heroine of 'all the foolish, improbable adventures' she met with.[24] Early readings of Shakespeare often triggered a tendency to egotistical fantasy, and preceded a later religious fanaticism, as in the cases of Charlotte Elizabeth and Harriet Martineau. Whatever the route to the 'hidden life', however, those who travelled it felt both superior to the duller, more earthbound members of their families, and secure in a world of their own making. At the same time, most record some twinges of guilt or doubt at the long-term validity of what they were doing. The return to reality is as inevitable as the recall of Shakespeare's courtly characters from the country to their kingdoms. The only female dreamers to remain uninhibited about their fantasy-world, at least until they became novelists, were the three Brontë sisters, whose autobiographical notes pass so unselfconsciously from the real to the private and hidden worlds of their imagination. Charlotte's 'History of the Year' (1829) summarises both the activities and reading habits of everyone at Haworth Parsonage, and the established 'plays' of the four children, with their origins. Sixteen years later, when Emily and Anne were well into their twenties, Emily described an excursion to York and Keighley, when she and her sister 'were, Ronald Macalgin, Henry Angora, Juliet Angusteena, Rosabella Esmaldan, Ella and Julian Egremont, Catharine Navarre, and Cordelia Fitzaphnold, escaping from the palaces of instruction to join the Royalists who are hard driven at present by the victorious Republicans.'[25] Unlike Elizabeth Barrett, the Brontës were not apparently interested in their own immortality. Their diary papers say nothing about wanting to be famous; but the real world clearly takes second place to the hidden. Tabby fussing about the potatoes, or 'Aunt' about correct posture, are dismissed by sixteen-year-old Emily as comic and bothersome, compared with the serious doings of the Gondals.

The counterpart of triumphant fantasy by day was, for many Victorian girls, uncontrollable terror by night. Almost every female autobiographer recalls a fear of the dark, and of the spectres projected by her imagination. Much of Sara Coleridge's brief childhood memoir reconstructs a series of frights and accidents, and she remembers proclaiming to her aunt 'I'se miseral.' During a visit to Grasmere, she was frightened of the dark, but not yet of:

> the whole host of night-agitators, ghosts, goblins, demons, burglars, elves, and witches. Horrid ghastly tales and ballads, of which crowds afterwards came in my way, had not yet cast their shadows over my mind. And yet I was terrified in the dark, and used to think of lions, the only form of terror which my dark-engendered agitation would take. My next bugbear was the Ghost in Hamlet. Then the picture of Death at Hell Gate in an old edition of Paradise Lost, the delight of my girlhood. Last and worst came my Uncle Southey's ballad horrors, above all the Old Woman of Berkeley. Oh, the agonies I have endured between nine and twelve at night, before mama joined me in bed, in presence of that hideous assemblage of horrors, the horse with eyes of flame.[26]

Melanie Klein has argued that 'there is probably not a single child who has not suffered from *pavor nocturnus* [night terrors], and we are probably justified in saying that in all human beings at some time or other neurotic anxiety has been present in a greater or lesser degree.'[27] In the writing of autobiography, more women than men admit to this intensity of fear. Ruskin, for example, declared that he was never afraid of anything, 'either ghosts, thunder, or beasts', and wanted to play with the lion cubs in Wombwell's Menagerie. Male autobiographers who confessed their fear of darkness belong mainly to the Romantic Movement: Lamb, De Quincey, and Leigh Hunt who called himself 'an ultra-sympathising and timid boy'.[28] Klein regards the night terrors suffered by two- to three-year-olds as being liberated in the first stage of repression of the Oedipus complex: a state that may, if unresolved, lead to hysteria or excessive fantasising. In fact, Sara Coleridge feared the most famous Oedipal Ghost of all, perhaps with reason, as she displaced each of her parents from their bed, and remained ambivalently disposed towards her father. When Wordsworth's children proved more demonstrative, she watched 'benumbed; for truly nothing does so freeze affection as the breath of jealousy' (Coleridge, *Memoir*, p. 18).

Coleridge clearly expected his daughter to conform to his ideas of femininity. 'My father liked me wearing a cap,' Sara Coleridge recalls. 'He thought it looked girlish and domestic' (p. 21). Having strong 'fancies about dress', he hated the scarlet socks worn by Sara and her cousin, and would reject a child if he disapproved of her clothes:

I remember going to him when mama had just dressed me in a new stuff frock. He took me up, and set me down again without a caress. I thought he disliked the dress; perhaps he was in an uneasy mood. He much liked everything feminine and domestic, pretty and becoming, but not fine-ladyish. (Coleridge, *Memoir*, p. 20)

Sara's reminiscences, begun eight months before her death, were intended to suggest a moral or maxim based on each section of her life, but in the event, she died before she could recount more than a few disturbed memories of rejection, fear and strained family relations. Virginia Woolf describes her as 'mixed in herself', divided between loyalty to her father, and a clinging relationship with her mother.[29] Her recollections were addressed to her daughter in a letter, as if she were talking privately to her, away from the public gaze, and could expect a friendly hearing, and her original plan was to divide her history into 'childhood, earlier and later, youth, earlier and later, wedded life, ditto, widowhood, ditto': a pattern clearly designed to represent the chief 'life-events', rather than the professional career, of a woman. As it was, her approaching death compressed her grand plan into a 'brief compendium', twenty-six pages breaking off with the tantalising words: 'On reviewing my earlier childhood, I find the predominant reflection –' (p. 26).

Anna Jameson, too, wrote her 'Revelation of Childhood' for didactic purposes. She regarded her childhood as representative, not exceptional ('No, certainly I was not an extraordinary child'), and its experiences, retold in simple factual detail from her own life, as potential teaching material: 'hints towards a theory of conduct' in parents (p. 122). She, too, suffered from secret terrors at night, which she kept to herself because she had heard other children being ridiculed for their fear. Like Sara Coleridge, she was afraid of the Ghost in *Hamlet*, and of other book illustrations, which seem to have exerted a particularly frightening influence on susceptible children. Anna Jameson describes the picture of Hamlet with his hair on end, and the Ghost encased in armour with nodding plumes:

O that spectre! for three years it followed me up and down the dark staircase, or stood by my bed: only the blessed light had power to exorcise it.... The figure of Apollyon looming over Christian, which I had found in an old edition of the "Pilgrim's Progress", was also a great torment. But worse, perhaps, were certain phantasms without shape, – things like the vision in Job ... and if not intelligible voices, there were strange unaccountable sounds filling the air around with a sort of mysterious life. (pp. 128–9).

These bookish terrors, which tormented her until she was nearly twelve years old, can be seen as the obverse of her equally bookish heroism during daylight, when she fought giants, killed dragons and played the Spenserian warrior-princess. As Erik Erikson has suggested, of rather younger children, 'the child indulges in fantasies of being a giant and a tiger but in his dreams he runs for dear life'.[30] One of the most perceptive child-theorists, Anna Jameson warned educators against insensitive experimentation on children, and showed them the complexities of the child's hidden fantasy life, again using herself as an example. At six, she says, she suffered from the fear of not being loved where she had attached herself: in Freud's view, a key determinant of anxiety in cases of hysteria.[31]

This was accompanied by jealousy directed against a rival, and a desire for vengeance on those who had injured her. She imagined herself rescuing her enemy from a burning house, deep water, or imprisonment; but, 'if this were magnanimity, it was not the less vengeance; for, observe, I always fancied evil, and shame, and humiliation to my adversary; to myself the *rôle* of superiority and gratified pride.' (p. 125).

Anna's fantasies were clearly her only way of recovering her dignity, of compensating for her insignificance, both as a small child, and, presumably, as a girl. The eldest of five daughters, she was likely to feel displaced by the arrival of younger children; hence, too, her tendency to exhibitionism, and the danger of 'becoming a precocious actress' (p. 146). Both the revenge-fantasies and the exhibitionism were eventually regulated by 'a growing sense of power and self-reliance' (p. 126) and by 'the recoil of resistance and resentment' excited in her mind (p. 146). In other words, she developed a conscience or super-ego, and learnt to repress instincts that were clearly anti-social; but her account of childhood aggression and the sense of inferiority that caused it, remains one of the most uninhibited autobiographical case histories before Freud's analyses of female hysterics.

Charlotte Mary Yonge's autobiography, like Sara Coleridge's, is unfinished, breaking off at the time of her confirmation, for which she was prepared by John Keble. Her editor, Christabel Coleridge, who interjects comments from time to time in the narrative, suggests that for Yonge the story of childhood is 'specially important': 'because the child was so entirely the mother of the woman; what she was at fifteen, that she was, with modifications, at fifty.'[32] This implies that much of Yonge's adult life was static, without significant experiences, while her childhood established both her strict religious principles, and her sense of family. It is hardly surprising that a novelist who placed her heroines in huge sprawling families riddled with neuroses and tubercular diseases, should be especially sensitive to the influences of family life, and the experiences of childhood. The first thirty-five pages of her memoir are devoted to collective family history, in the seventeenth-century tradition of autobiographers such as Ann Fanshawe, which Charlotte Yonge believed would throw some light on the formation of her character. This is followed by descriptions of Otterbourne Church, and of both her parents. 'I do not recollect so far back as some people do,' she admits. 'I have a hazy remembrance of a green spelling-book, and the room where I read a bit of it to some unaccustomed person' (p. 55):

> Mine was too happy and too uneventful a childhood to have many epochs, and it has only one sharp line of era in it, namely my brother's birth when I was six and a half. I can remember best by what happened before, and what happened after. (pp. 55–6)

Few autobiographers of either sex say much about their siblings, perhaps because as independent achievers they quickly developed a sense of self-sufficiency and separateness. Close relationships with sisters are rarely mentioned, except by Mary Howitt, and by Harriet Martineau in references to her youngest sister, Ellen. Closeness to brothers is recalled by Harriet Martineau, George Eliot and Charlotte Yonge; but the first two were estranged from them in adult life, and even the last recalls sensations of bewilderment and neglect at the time of her brother's birth. She was at first left in the dark in her crib, and then taken on a walk by her father, 'There was a deep snow, I had not been properly equipped to encounter it, and though he carried me part of the way I arrived with bitterly cold hands, and when brought to the fire knew the sensation of aching with cold.' (p. 73). Although she professes nothing but excitement and happiness at the birth of her brother, her account of his arrival obliquely suggests a contrary view: a subtext of dissent, which is not quite repressed. Her response carries more psychological conviction than Elizabeth Barrett's melodramatic declaration, in her second Autobiographical Essay, that if her brother were to 'stray from the path of honorable rectitude', she would wish to 'sleep in peace the cold sod reposing on my breast & deaf to the call of misery!' (p. 129).

Like the other Victorian women who wrote about their childhood, Charlotte Yonge lived a dual life, split, as before, between outward conformity (down to the eating of dry bread and milk) and a concealed imaginative life. Before her brother's birth, she invented a family of ten boys and eleven girls (the ratio is interesting) as outdoor companions, while indoors, her dolls were her children and her sisters (p. 59). Indeed her first longings were for a sister, not a brother, and she was later rebuked for walking about with her arms round her cousin Anne's waist (p. 83). From early childhood, she was perplexed about her appearance:

> I have since had reason to know that I was a very pretty and clever child, or at any rate that my mother thought me so, but I really never knew whether I was not ugly. I know I thought myself so, and I was haunted occasionally by

doubts whether I was not deficient, till I was nearly grown up. My mother said afterwards that I once asked her if I was pretty, and she replied that all young creatures were, i.e. the little pigs. (p. 56)

Simone de Beauvoir has argued that social conditions lead women more than men to devote themselves to their own persons, to find reality in their own immanence, rather than in external activities. 'For the child this dream is materialised in the doll; she sees herself in the doll more concretely than in her own body, because she and the doll are actually separated from each other.'[33] Charlotte Yonge, who never married, defined herself in childhood in terms of other female images: an imagined sister, a family of sisters, a girl cousin, a doll, an ideal of female beauty. The intricate web of negatives in her description ('I really never knew whether I was not ugly') mirrors the conflicting impulses of her narcissism, which was under constant siege from the self-denying practices of her religion. Another split occurs between her night fears and her common sense by day:

My only real trouble was terrors just like what other solitary or imaginative children have – horrors of darkness, fancies of wolves, one most gratuitous alarm recurring every night of being smothered like the Princes in the Tower, or blown up with gunpowder. In the daylight I knew it was nonsense, I would have spoken of it to no one, but the fears at night always came back. (p. 60)

This was despite an ignorance of ghosts: 'the nervous fright could not have been more even if I had been nurtured on them.' Writing before Freud, Charlotte Yonge uses imagery that suggests sexual repression or extinction of the personality. Religious fears aggravated her imaginative ones, particularly dread of the end of the world, with God as a bogeyman, coming to get her when everyone was asleep. In adolescence, her nervous susceptibilities were sublimated into a love of beauty, and she was warned against devoting herself to Church doctrine 'in a merely poetical tone' (p. 119).

Charlotte Yonge was educated at home by an exacting father, as was the American, Margaret Fuller, who records a similar catalogue of night terrors. Fuller felt her nerves had been unnaturally stimulated by too much late-night study. A youthful prodigy by day, she was by night 'a victim of spectral illusions, nightmare, and somnambulism', which later brought on headaches, weakness and 'nervous affections of all kinds'.[34] Margaret Fuller wrote her childhood memories in 1840, at the age of thirty, intending them 'as the introductory chapter to an autobiographical romance' (p. 4). As with Sara Coleridge and Anna Jameson, therefore, the impulse to tell her own story was partly cleansed of its purely egotistical motives. As a 'romance', her story was entitled to explore her morbid psychology, especially her preoccupation with death. Her first memory is, in fact, the death of a younger sister, another projection of her own image, as in Charlotte Yonge's childhood fantasies. The dead sister was an idealised version of herself. If she had lived, Fuller predicts, her character would have been 'soft, graceful, and lively' (in other words, a perfect feminine image), and it would have tempered her own 'to a gentler and more gradual course' (p. 7). This influence being removed, she fell victim to dreams of 'colossal faces advancing slowly towards her', and of horses trampling her to death, 'or, as she had just read in her Virgil, of being among trees that dripped with blood, where she walked and walked and could not get out, while the blood became a pool and splashed over her feet, and rose higher and higher, till soon she dreamed it would reach her lips.' (p. 10) In a dream more obviously related to her family structure, she saw herself 'following to the grave the body of her mother, as she had done that of her sister, and woke to find the pillow drenched in tears' (p. 11). Her mother was in reality often ill, and absorbed in the care of younger children. Fuller's dream suggests a stock repressed wish for her mother's death, accompanied by guilty mourning. Later, she was to develop an adolescent crush on an Englishwoman of 'thoroughbred *mille-fleur* beauty, the distilled result of ages of European culture' (p. 35), another idealised role-model to replace the near-perfect sister. For a long time before their meeting, real life had offered no attraction. Like Elizabeth Barrett, Anna Jameson and Breuer's 'Anna O', she inhabited a hidden world of her own invention:

> My own world sank deep within, away from the surface of my life; in what I did and said I learned to have reference to other minds. But my true life was only the dearer that it was secluded and veiled over by a thick curtain of available intellect, and that coarse, but wearable stuff woven by the ages, – Common Sense. (p. 13)

To nineteenth-century girls denied any acceptable outlet for their narcissistic fantasies, books offered escape from the monotonous and ladylike existence their families expected them to find satisfying. For most, the momentous authors were Shakespeare and Milton: significantly the authors whose images also gave them nightmares. Margaret Fuller's first Shakespeare play was *Romeo and Juliet*, which she discovered at the age of eight (p. 26); 'Charlotte Elizabeth's' *The Merchant of Venice*, read at seven, when she 'imbibed a thorough contempt for women, children, and household affairs', entrenching herself 'behind invisible barriers that few, very few, could pass' (p. 25). This contempt for her own sex was strengthened by an adoring relationship with her only brother, which gave her a 'habit of deference to man's judgement, and submission to man's authority', in accordance with God's wishes (p. 67). For Anna Jameson, the key plays were *The Tempest* and *Cymbeline* (p. 139); for the actress Helen Faucit, Juliet and Ophelia were the great heroines. Ophelia attracted her by 'the mystery of her madness', though she also admired Milton's Satan: 'His address to the council I have often declaimed to the waves, when sure of being unobserved.' Though her life was 'wrapped up' in fictitious characters, she never revealed the details to friends or family, not even to her only sister. As for the books themselves, 'they filled my young heart and mind with what fascinated me most – the gorgeous, the wonderful, the grand, the heroic, the self-denying, the self-devoting.'[35] The last two properties are sublimated versions of the Satanic heroics that she was not the only Victorian woman to enjoy. Annie Besant recalls that she 'liked to personify Satan, and to declaim the grand speeches of the hero-rebel' (p. 32). The chance to 'declaim', if only in another's language (and ironically that of a notorious misogynist) was clearly an opportunity to assert oneself in a specially dramatic manner; the obverse of this being a longing for martyrdom. Fanny Kemble suffered from 'every conceivable form of terror', yet she had a 'lingering desire for the distinction of a public execution by guillotine', perhaps for poisoning her sister.[36] Harriet Martineau, another nervous child who found consolation in Milton, indulged for years 'in exciting and vain-glorious dreams' after the amputation of a friend's leg: 'All manner of deaths at the stake and on the scaffold, I went through in imagination, in the low sense in which St Theresa craved martyrdom.'[37]

Sometimes the longing to be noticed took a more bizarre form, as when Fanny Kemble exhibited herself in 'a fool's cap of vast dimensions' that she had been made to wear as a punishment. Instead, she took the earliest opportunity of 'dancing down the carriage-drive to meet the postman, a great friend of mine, and attract his observation and admiration to my "helmet", which I called aloud upon all wayfarers also to contemplate, until removed from an elevated bank I had selected for this public exhibition of myself.'[38] Elizabeth Sewell, the religious novelist, who was known to her family as 'blighted Betty', because of her small size, recalled that even as very young child she 'liked to *dream* of being noticed'. She pretended she was walking along a tightrope: 'whilst in imagination I was displaying my feats before a large party which I had heard had assembled at Lord Yarborough's cottage at St. Lawrence to meet one of the Royal Dukes.' Yet, with other people, she shrank from 'being actually brought forward' and receiving praise, as if compensating in her public life for the egotistical fantasies of her private dreams.[39] While Fanny Kemble mocks her own childhood self-absorption and dismisses it with a laugh, Elizabeth Sewell obsessively apologises for hers, covering every oblique boast with twice as many denials or reproaches. Just as Charlotte Yonge found it hard to state directly that she was pretty, Elizabeth Sewell recoiled from stating that she was ambitious and intelligent. Elizabeth Barrett, who admitted to being both, and repeatedly identifies herself as exceptional, whether in ability or feeling, ended her second Autobiographical Essay with a self-consciously dramatic flourish. Her farewell to the imagined reader is like Rosalind's curtain speech at the end of *As You Like It*. Inspired by the disguised heroine's deflationary wit, Elizabeth Barrett closes her 'tragic Comedy' at the epoch of her fifteenth year: '& most stupid dramatis personae they have been!' 'And you my most patient auditors [,] as it may be requisite for dramatic effect to give you a little advice before the Curtain falls let me begs [*sic*] you if you wish to keep up your spirits never to write your own life.' (p. 133).

In precarious possession of their own identities, conditioned to define themselves in terms of others, many Victorian women writing about their childhood reveal their ambitions and sense of unique individuality through verbal disguise. Either they construct a stage on which to walk the tightrope, declaim grand speeches, or take witty curtain-calls; or they symbolically erase whatever act of self-assertion their unguarded prose may have performed. These evasionary tactics are especially notable in the autobiography of childhood, for there the identity is still in the making, and its adult owner particularly anxious to retain the reader's sympathy and approval. If the formation of an identity is difficult at the best of times, and always subject to external influences, not all of them beneficial, the crisis of self-discovery is a major problem for Victorian women. Even for Elizabeth Barrett, who was exceptionally confident of her abilities, and still adolescent when she recalled her childhood, external prohibitions against self-display produce a split between the desire to attract notice and a deep-seated consciousness that this is wrong and must be atoned for. In male autobiographers of the same period, no such split disrupts the harmony of their self-portraiture.

Simone de Beauvoir has suggested that 'Women more than men cling to childhood memories.' As children, they are more independent, more secure, and feel they have the potential to do anything; as women, they may be imprisoned as servants or objects.[40] Certainly, the adult potential of their lives, for many Victorian girls, seemed boundless. There are few who do not in some way allude to their cleverness as children, their literary ambitions, or their longing for distinction even passively as saints or martyrs; yet few recall their early life with much nostalgia or regret. Islands of happiness stand out here and there, but childhood as Eden is not, on the whole, a female myth. For many, it lacked the companionship of Eden; for others, the timeless contentment. 'I never will believe that our youngest days are our happiest,' George Eliot wrote when she was still in her twenties. To her, this seemed only logical:

> What a miserable augury for the progress of the race and the destination of the individual if the more matured and enlightened state is the less happy one. Childhood is only the beautiful and happy time in contemplation and retrospect – to the child it is full of deep sorrows, the meaning of which is unknown.

At this point in her letter, she tries to laugh off the serious implications of her argument:

> Witness colic and whooping-cough and dread of ghosts, to say nothing of hell and Satan, and an offended Deity in the sky who was angry when I wanted too much plum cake. Then the sorrows of older persons which children see but cannot understand are worse than all. All this dear Sara [Hennell] to prove that we are happier than when we were seven years old, and that we shall be happier when we are forty than we are now, which I call a comfortable doctrine and one worth trying to believe.[41]

That childhood is overshadowed by mysterious sorrows is a belief borne out by George Eliot's treatment of the subject in *The Mill on the Floss* fifteen years later. By then, she felt it was difficult for adults to recall and understand the poignancy of their early unhappiness. 'Is there any one who can recover the experience of his childhood,' she asks, 'not merely with a memory of what he did and what happened to him . . . but with an intimate penetration, a revived consciousness of what he felt then – when it was so long from one Midsummer to another?' Surely, she concludes, 'if we could recall that early bitterness, and the dim guesses, the strangely perspectiveless conception of life that gave the bitterness its intensity, we should not pooh-pooh the griefs of our children.'[42]

Most Victorian women autobiographers take these griefs seriously, and are glad to have escaped them. Sara Coleridge, who often thought about her childhood in the Lake District, regarded it as a 'lower stage of existence', which she had no wish to relive. 'Youth and childhood are indeed beautiful and interesting to look back upon,' she told Isabella Fenwick in 1848; 'but I feel as old Matthew did about the lovely child [in Wordsworth's poem 'The Two April Mornings'], *I do not wish them mine* – mine to go over again.'[43] Harriet Martineau, Beatrice Webb and Eliza Lynn Linton (in her novel *The Autobiography of Christopher Kirkland* (1885), which is a thinly disguised account of her own life), all view child-hood as predominantly a time of dissatisfaction and unhappiness. Even those whose childhoods were relatively happy, such as Frances Power Cobbe and Charlotte Yonge, often remembered themselves as solitary and self-sufficient, without many close companions. Relationships with parents were sometimes damaged by intensive teaching at home (Margaret Fuller and Charlotte Yonge were taught by strict fathers), or by the dominance of one parent: usually the father over a weak or ill mother. A greater sense of security seems to have surrounded those whose childhoods were dominated by the mother (for example, Margaret Oliphant and Annie Besant), but there are always important exceptions. Harriet Martineau's *Autobiography* records perhaps the coldest mother-daughter relations in Victorian family history, and sounds the most strident note of accusation. For Martineau, at least, the 'golden gates' of childhood, as George Eliot calls them in *The Mill on the Floss* slam shut with a distinctly tarnished clang.

Hardly any Victorian women autobiographers recall a consistently sociable childhood; and if we were to identify one single theme that unites all the major autobiographical texts, including novels, written by women in the nineteenth century, it would be consciousness of solitude. 'My childhood, though a singularly happy, was an unusually lonely one,' wrote Frances Power Cobbe, who thus became 'rather a solitary mortal', never depressed by living alone. The youngest of five children, and the only daughter, she had an invalid mother, to whom she felt exceptionally close. 'She was the only being in the world whom I truly loved through all the passionate years of growth and early womanhood,' Cobbe recalled; 'the only one who really loved me'.[44] As she describes the self-sufficiency of her childhood, there seems to be a direct link between the independence she acquired as a girl and the sense of self that enabled her to lead bold campaigns, and subsequently to write a two-volume auto-biography. In the second half of the nineteenth century, when more women were publishing their lives, readers and writers alike delightedly recognised their own experiences of solitude in the works of other female contemporaries. Margaret Oliphant, for example, expressed herself 'enchanted' with Mary Somerville's *Personal Recollections*: 'which recalls to me my mother and even my own recluse childhood in the most delightful way'; while nearly thirty years earlier, Harriet Martineau and Charlotte Brontë had each recognised their childhood selves in writing by the other.[45] What had appeared to be a uniquely unhappy experience gradually emerged as commonplace and familiar, although evocations of how it felt continued to be sharply drawn. Even those who had numerous siblings depict themselves as somehow living apart from the mainstream of family life, alone in mind, if not in body. The Quaker, Mary Howitt, whose sister Anna was her close companion in childhood, was surrounded by withdrawn and reclusive adults. 'It is impossible to give an adequate idea of the stillness and isolation of our lives as children,' she afterwards declared. When she and her sister went to school in Croydon, she again felt out of key with her new world, and began a longing for what was dignified and cultured. 'I feel a sort of tender pity for Anna and myself when I remember how we were always seeking and struggling after the beautiful, and after artistic production, though we know nothing of art,' she recalled.[46]

Others went further still, reviving experiences of extreme alienation from their families. Both Harriet Martineau and Beatrice Webb contemplated suicide, and armed themselves with suitable means; Fanny Kemble thought of poisoning her sister; and Eliza Lynn Linton, as Christopher Kirkland, dreamt that she was not her father's child at all, 'but a foundling, some day to be reclaimed and taken home by his own who would love and understand him'.[47] Maggie Tulliver's escape to her 'own people', the gypsies, in *The Mill on the Floss*, is a fictional analogue of the same experience, a need to be appreciated by, and included in a group of sensitive doubles of the self. Sara Coleridge subsequently came to see her own children as her 'secondary *selves* . . . because they *are* self in a second edition'.[48]

Extreme experiences of childhood isolation, as recalled by Victorian women autobiographers, helped foster a significant degree of independence and emotional self-sufficiency in those who later became actresses, philanthropists, scientists and novelists. If this chapter has stressed the similarities between autobiographers' childhood memories, rather than the differences between them, it is because the autobiographers themselves seem to have gained their unusual (or 'unfeminine') awareness of their personalities from this very experience of alienation and the 'hidden life'. By learning not to depend on other people, and to invent a private, more congenial level of existence where they were able to occupy centre-stage, many Victorian women created themselves as their own heroines in childhood and adolescence, thus preparing the way for their achievements in adult life. Transforming dislocation into distinction, they were able to resist familial or cultural pressures to shed what made them different, and discover an enduring identity of their own. In this, they had much in common with contemporary male autobiographers. Though less pressurised by social restrictions, autobiographers such as John Stuart Mill, Anthony Trollope and John Ruskin, passed much of their childhood away from other children, and in a state of emotional deprivation. The transition from childhood amusements to adult occupations was easy and scarcely noticed; the ambitions aroused by their respective upbringings quickly demanded satisfaction. 'Ambition and desire of distinction, I had in abundance,' John Stuart Mill remembered; while Trollope had wanted to write a novel ever since he left school.[49] Separation from other children, with their more commonplace ideals, inevitably threw both male and female autobiographers on their own inner resources, and established an early consciousness of their unique qualities.

For women, however, this consciousness was trammelled by the values of their society, which their writing shows they partially internalised. They knew it was wrong to crave distinction, so they craved martyrdom; they knew it was 'unhealthy' to dwell too much in imaginary states, so they tried to behave normally by day, but could not repress the outbreak of terrors by night, especially revenge dreams against their parents. Of course, children of both sexes experience night-terrors; the significant point is that few male autobiographers of the nineteenth century, after the Romantics, delineate in detail, as the women do, the psychological landscape of their childhood minds. Female autobiographers, on the whole, avoid interpretive types, especially in their reconstruction of childhood. Images of Eden or of Exodus, as used, for example, by Ruskin and Carlyle respectively, rarely appear in the non-fictional self-writing of Victorian women; and where the paradisal myth is used by George Eliot in *The Mill on the Floss*, its idealised assumptions are questioned by the uncomprehended suffering of Maggie's girlhood. Instead, Victorian women begin again with their own reality. The 'world of instincts, perceptions, experiences, pleasures, and pains', as Anna Jameson called the unexplored 'mystery of childhood', rather than the external world of national or family events, is the focus of their attention as autobiographers and their natural outlet for veiled protest against the ordained direction of their adult lives.

It was easier for them to protest through recollections of their childhood, than when they were writing about any other aspect of their lives. They risked relatively little in describing a remote period of their history, when their emotions were irrational or exaggerated, and would be seen as such by their audience, or else, in George Eliot's words, seen as 'pathetic and interesting'. Protests against needlework and other female occupations occur safely enough in the childhood sections of autobiography, and are usually atoned for at a later stage. So are allusions to youthful ambition and precociousness, devotion to brothers and occasional criticism of unfeeling parents. Everyone could sympathise with the story of an unhappy child, especially as the novelists, both male and female, had familiarised Victorian audiences with this kind of narrative. A child is only partially socialised, not yet fully absorbed into the cultural system, and therefore both freer to protest and more readily excused. With hindsight, many Victorian women seem to have recognised the beginnings of their absorption into a repressive code, and used their childhood reminiscences to highlight the split between their emotional and intellectual needs and the meagre provision made for them by society. This split remained with them for the rest of their lives, but as adult novelists and reformers they were often forced to compromise. As children, they had not yet learnt the meaning of the word, and the revival of childhood frustrations with a practice they could not understand was the directest form of autobiographical resistance against the values and priorities of their age, the sharpest attack on all that made them aliens.

Notes

1. Jameson, *A Commonplace Book*, pp. 117–21.
2. Jean-Jacques Rousseau, *Emile* (1762; trans. Barbara Foxley, London and New York: Everyman, 1974), p. 1.
3. See especially Richard N. Coe, *When the Grass was Taller: Autobiography and the Experience of Childhood* (New Haven and London: Yale University Press: and London, 1984); Peter Coveney, *Poor Monkey: The Child in Literature* (London: Rockcliff, 1957); and Lawrence Stone, *The Family, Sex and Marriage in England 1500–1800*.
4. Coe, p. 10; p. 40; Coveney, p. ix.
5. Thomas De Quincey, *Suspiria De Profundis*, *The Posthumous Works of Thomas De Quincey*, ed. Alexander H. Jupp (London: Heinemann, 1891), p. 7. See also Lamb's Essay 'Witches and other night-fears', in *Essays of Elia* (1823).
6. LuAnn Walther, 'The invention of childhood in Victorian autobiography', in Landow (ed.), *Approaches to Victorian Autobiography*, pp. 64–83.
7. See, for example, Susanna Egan, *op. cit.*, Linda H. Peterson, *op. cit.*, Avrom Fleishman, *op. cit.*
8. *George Eliot Letters*, VI, 353; V, 458.
9. Sigmund Freud, 'Fragment of an analysis of a case of hysteria', *The Standard Edition of the Complete Psychological Works of Sigmund Freud* (London: The Hogarth Press, 24 vols, 1953–74), VII, 16.
10. Coe, p. 51.
11. Mark Pattison, *Memoirs* (London: Macmillan, 1885), p. 1; Gavin de Beer, ed., *Charles Darwin, Thomas Henry Huxley, Autobiographies* (London and New York: Oxford University Press, 1974), p. 101.
12. *The Autobiography of Charles Darwin, 1809–1882*, ed. Nora Barlow (London: Collins, 1958), p. 22; p. 25; Martineau, *Autobiography*, I, 14.
13. Anthony Trollope, *An Autobiography* (1883, Worlds Classics edition, Oxford: Oxford University Press, 1980), p. 1.
14. See, for example, Dinah Mulock's reverence for 'the *house-mother*' in *A Woman's Thoughts About Women* (London: Hurst & Blackett, 1858), p. 122.
15. George Eliot, *Impressions of Theophrastus Such* (1879; Illustrated Copyright Edition, London: Virtue & Co., 1913), p. 6.
16. Christabel Coleridge, *Charlotte Mary Yonge: Her Life and Letters* (London: Macmillan, 1903), p. viii.
17. Barrett, 'Two autobiographical essays', pp. 119–21.
18. Elizabeth Barrett Browning, *Aurora Leigh* (1857; ed. Cora Kaplan, London: The Women's Press, 1978) Book I, lines 477–80, p. 52.

19. Josef Breuer and Sigmund Freud, *Studies on Hysteria, The Complete Works of Freud* (Standard Edition, London: The Hogarth Press, 1955), II, 41.

20. *The Mothers of England: Their Influence and Responsibility*, by the author of the 'Women of England' [Sarah Ellis] (London: Fisher, Son & Co., 1843), p. 323.

21. *A Commonplace Book*, p. 131; p. 135.

22. Deborah Epstein Nord, *The Apprenticeship of Beatrice Webb* (London: Macmillan, 1985), p. 65.

23. Herbert Spencer, *An Autobiography* (London: Williams & Norgate, 2 vols, 1904; repr. London: Watts & Co., 1926), I, 76.

24. Besant, p. 42; p. 57; Charlotte Elizabeth, *Personal Recollections*, p. 25.

25. T. J. Wise and J. A. Symington (ed)., *The Brontës: Their Lives, Friendships and Correspondence* (Oxford: Basil Blackwell, 1932) II, 49–50.

26. *Memoirs and Letters of Sara Coleridge edited by her Daughter* (London: Henry S. King & Co., 2 vols, 1873), I, 25.

27. Melanie Klein, 'Early analysis' (1923), in *Love, Guilt and Reparation and Other Works 1921–1945*, ed. R. E. Money-Kyrle (London: The Hogarth Press and the Institute of Psycho-Analysis, 1975), p. 79.

28. *Praeterita: The Autobiography of John Ruskin (1885–1889)*, ed. Kenneth Clark (Oxford and New York: Oxford University Press, 1978), p. 36; *The Autobiography of Leigh Hunt: A new edition, revised by the author* (London: Smith, Elder & Co., 1850, 1859), p. 50.

29. Virginia Woolf, 'Sara Coleridge', *Collected Essays* (London: The Hogarth Press, 1967), III, 226.

30. Quoted by Gordon R. Lowe in *The Growth of Personality: From Infancy to Old Age* (1972; Harmondsworth: Penguin, 1985), p. 100.

31. Freud, 'Inhibitions, symptoms and anxiety', XX, 143.

32. Yonge, *Life and Letters*, p. 120.

33. Simone de Beauvoir, *The Second Sex* (1949; trans. H. M. Parshley, Harmondsworth: Penguin, 1972, 1983), p. 642.

34. *Memoirs of Margaret Fuller Ossoli* (London: Richard Bentley and Son, 3 vols, 1852), I, 9–10.

35. *On Some of Shakespeare's Female Characters*, pp. 5–6.

36. *Record of a Girlhood*, I, 48, 69; Kemble also enjoyed *Paradise Lost*, which her father read to her.

37. *Harriet Martineau's Autobiography*, I, 45.

38. 'Old woman's gossip', *The Atlantic Monthly* XXXVI (Cambridge, Mass. August, 1875), p. 157.

39. *The Autobiography of Elizabeth M. Sewell, edited by her niece, Eleanor L. Sewell* (London: Longmans, Green and Co., 1907), p. 15. She says her 'vague dreams of distinction' were 'kept under from the sense of being a girl', p. 16.

40. *The Second Sex*, pp. 644–5.

41. *The George Eliot Letters* I, 173; contrast Martha Ronk Lifson, 'The myth of the fall: a description of autobiography', *Genre* XII (Spring 1979), 45–67. She argues that paradisal, Edenic scenes in autobiography parallel an effort by their authors to define themselves against 'a fragmented and shapeless world' (p. 57). For women, a private dream-world or some form of autobiographical protest usually replaces the traditional images of Eden.

42. George Eliot, *The Mill on the Floss* (1860; ed. A. S. Byatt, Harmondsworth: Penguin, 1979/1987), p. 123.

43. Sara Coleridge, II, 107.
44. *Life of Frances Power Cobbe*, I, 33, 35, 99.
45. Oliphant, *Autobiography*, p. 244; Martineau, *Autobiography*, II, 324.
46. Mary Howitt, *An Autobiography*, edited by her daughter Margaret Howitt (London: William Isbister Ltd, 2 vols, 1889), I, 45, 95.
47. Mrs Lynn Linton, *The Autobiography of Christopher Kirkland* (London: Richard Bentley and Son, 3 vols, 1885), I, 62.
48. Sara Coleridge, I, 124.
49. John Stuart Mill, *Autobiography* (1873; ed. Jack Stillinger, London and Oxford: Oxford University Press, 1971), p. 66; Trollope, *An Autobiography*, p. 52.

Chapter 4

Recollections of a Literary Life
novelists as autobiographers

'One thing is pretty clear,' Mrs Gaskell told Eliza Fox in 1850, '*Women*, must give up living an artist's life, if home duties are to be paramount.'[1] By the end of the century, when George Eliot, the Brontës, Elizabeth Barrett Browning and Mrs Gaskell herself had proved that women could combine the literary and the domestic, critical strictures were forced to relax; but there remained a deeply ingrained sense that no normal, happy woman would have either the time or the inclination to write a novel. 'It is different with men, whose home duties are so small a part of their life,' Mrs Gaskell's thoughts continued. Yet for women, the life of the imagination offered undoubted therapeutic relief:

> I am sure it is healthy for them to have the refuge of the hidden world of Art to shelter themselves in when too much pressed upon by daily small Lilliputian arrows of peddling cares; it keeps them from being morbid as you say; and takes them into the land where King Arthur lies hidden, and soothes them with its peace. I have felt this in writing, I see others feel it in music, you in painting, so assuredly a blending of the two is desirable. (Home duties and the development of the Individual I mean.)

Writing a novel was perhaps the most acceptable outlet for female literary ambition, though even this was fraught with risks of emotional exhibitionism and self-betrayal, and some of the minor women novelists preferred to distance themselves from those such as George Eliot, who gave the morality of their profession a bad name. When they came to write their autobiographies, they often took George Eliot as a negative example, stressing in their own lives their economic and family commitments, and their unimpeachable relationships.

Women novelists make especially interesting autobiographers, because their professional writing life has already given them the oportunity to experiment in ways of narrating women's experiences within the constraints imposed on them by society's notions as to what was suitable for publication. Many had already, to some extent, fictionalised their lives before writing their autobiographies, and knew just what it meant to shape, idealise, or distort the pattern of experience in order to make it aesthetically or emotionally more fulfilling. The prospect of telling the plain, unadorned truth about themselves must have been daunting. Moreover, the chief topic of most fiction by Victorian women was courtship and marriage: a theme on which they are emphatically silent in autobiographical accounts of their lives. Margaret Oliphant mentions refusing her husband's first proposal, then changing her mind six months later. 'It is not a matter into which I can enter here,' she insists, a little tartly.[2] In the hands of many women novelists, from Jane Austen to George Eliot, and beyond, this would have been the central concern of the whole work.

The experienced novelist was also used to the conditions of omniscience. She could see into the minds of her characters and manipulate them as she saw fit. When she came to write her own autobiography, she 'knew what was going to happen' in much the same way, but could read only her own mind: the motivation and thought-processes of the other people in her life remained largely unconfirmed and unguessable, limited as she was to the first-person narrator's vision. Nor had the autobiographer-novelist access to the same literary tech-niques as she would have used in a novel: the language of autobiography, at least in the nineteenth century, is by unspoken consensus of its practitioners as close as possible to the language of truth. Elaborate symbolism, or other kinds of metaphorical language were not generally used, and nor were concentric or enclosed narratives, like the Brontës'.

Faced with her professional knowledge of fiction-writing, the auto-biographer approached the construction of her own life-story with an acute awareness of its difficulties. The question of emphasis, of what to omit or include in the shaping of her tale, was perhaps the largest problem, closely followed by choice of style. Too much attention to her professional life (an area rarely covered by novels, in any case) would make the author look conceited, while too much attention to her private life would violate the sacred notions of decency. She therefore had to look for other subjects, such as charitable work, the founding of schools, family life, or harmless literary parties. This gives the appearance of the finished text a desultory air, and explains why so many autobiographies by Victorian women novelists lack the taut structure one might expect from an experienced professional. Because of their unease about auto-biography, writers such as Oliphant and Sewell often stopped and started, leaving their narrative untouched for months or years at a time, while their novels were usually written in concentrated stretches to meet deadlines and raise money. Their style suffers accordingly, and is inconsistently humorous or self-pitying as occasion demands. For all her attempts to conceal as much as she reveals, the novelist-autobiographer exposes many of her deep-seated perplexities, and generally fails to resolve them. She may even admit, as Sewell does, to revealing more about herself in one of her novels, sending the reader on a trail of comparison and contrast between a series of semi-autobiographical texts.

Alfred Kazin has suggested that the creative writer 'turns to autobiography out of some creative longing that fiction has not satisfied'.[3] This may be truer for Victorian women than appears on the surface. Writing about how imaginary women have supported their families through misfortune may have proved unfulfilling to Margaret Oliphant in the long run. Her *Autobiography* proved once and for all that she and she alone had been responsible for holding together her remarkably unlucky clan. Similarly, Elizabeth Sewell, so often overlooked as unimportant, reveals, in her *Autobiography*, if not always intentionally, the full extent of her contribution. But the finished texts of Victorian women novelist-autobiographers are densely ambiguous. Because of their known experience in writing, it is harder to dismiss their work as naive or careless, and it seems cruel to see it as disingenuous. If, as Philippe Lejeune has argued,[4] autobiography is as much a mode of reading as a mode of writing, the burden of interpretation for the reader of this group of autobiographies becomes correspondingly heavier.

The most direct way in which women novelists were able to anticipate and deflect hostile attacks against their self-portrayal, was by deprofessionalising the act of authorship. Sometimes the author's family did this for her, as in Sara Coleridge's case. 'The letters of Sara Coleridge were not acts of authorship, but of friendship,' wrote her daughter Edith in the preface to her mother's fragment of autobiography; 'we feel, in reading them, that she is not entertaining or instructing a crowd of listeners, but holding quiet converse with some congenial mind.'[5] Her mother had already decided to construct her autobiography, or 'little sketch' of her life, as she preferred to call it, round a series of letters to her daughter, thus reducing the public aspect of her private recollections. As it was, she died before she could relate the circumstances of her first publication, and the rest of her memoirs were put together from letters selected by Edith.

Mary Russell Mitford, author of *Our Village* (1824–32) gave the subtitle 'Books, Places, and People' to her *Recollections of A Literary Life* (1852), a title which she admitted gave a 'very imperfect idea of the contents':

Perhaps it would be difficult to find a short phrase that would accurately
describe a work so miscellaneous and wayward; a work where there is far
too much of personal gossip and of local scene-painting for the grave preten-
sion of critical essays, and far too much of criticism and extract for anything
approaching in the slightest degree to autobiography.

Declining her rights to the professional term, Mary Mitford offers
instead a survey of her favourite authors, and attaches to each one
fragments of personal reminiscence, mostly about her childhood. Her
intention, as expressed in the Preface, was 'to make others relish a few
favourite writers' as heartily as she had relished them herself.[6] In her
appreciation of the poet Catherine Fanshawe (1765–1834), she set out
the qualities of an ideal literary woman: 'a woman, who, with powers to
command the most brilliant literary success, contents herself with a
warm and unenvying sympathy in the success of others':

> It has always seemed to me that one of the happiest positions – let me say the
> very happiest position, that a woman of great talent can occupy in our high
> civilisation, is that of living a beloved and distinguished member of the best
> literary society; enjoying, listening, admiring; repaying all that she receives
> by a keen and willing sympathy; cultivating to perfection the social faculty;
> but abstaining from the wider field of authorship, even while she throws out
> here and there such choice and chosen bits as prove that nothing but
> disinclination to enter the arena debars her from winning the prize. How
> much better to belong to that portion of the audience which gives fame to the
> author – that class of readers to whom the writer looks for reputation – than
> to figure as actor or as author oneself. (pp. 249–50)

After this, it comes as no surprise to hear that one of Miss Mitford's
favourite authors was Dr Johnson; her ideal literary society sounding
distinctly Augustan, though with a hint of Mrs Ellis's and Ruskin's
Angel-Queen originator of *bons-mots*. Significantly, Mitford compares
the displaying author with an actor, and her references to the 'arena',
'prize', and 'audience' reinforce her dislike of garish publicity. 'Enjoying', 'listening', 'admiring' and 'abstaining' are all more acceptable
feminine roles, although Mitford seems to overlook the fact that both
Catherine Fanshawe and herself have published their writing, and would
otherwise have gone unrecognised as women 'of great talent'. The image
of a talented woman suppressing her brilliance purely for reasons of
womanly modesty proved too self-effacing even for its earliest reviewers. Mrs Oliphant, who was usually critical of egotistical autobiographers, suggested that while Miss Mitford was 'one of the most
womanly and unpretending' of 'feminine writers', she had written the
reminiscences of a reader, rather than a writer, and raised 'fruitless
expectations'. The personal details of her work 'are so tempting, that one
longs for more, and rather grudges at the long extracts, however fine they

may be in themselves, which might be got elsewhere, whereas nowhere else is it possible to find Miss Mitford, and her friends, and her home'.[7] Men, too, regretted her choice of emphasis. William Henry Smith, for *Blackwood's*, attributed her modesty to fear of her audience's response, 'the charge of being too personal, too egotistical'. While this was 'very natural', Smith insisted that 'if Miss Mitford had boldly recalled her own intellectual history . . . she would have produced a far superior work to that which lies before us.'[8]

The only female autobiographer of the nineteenth century to give anything like 'her own intellectual history' was Harriet Martineau, and she was accused by Margaret Oliphant of inflating her book throughout with 'self-applauses'.[9] Although most female autobiographers refer in some detail to their childhood reading, they are more interested in the imaginative impact of early impressions than in the long-term intellectual influence of their mature reading. Nor did many produce spiritual autobiographies, or even secular versions of the same form, as Linda Peterson has demonstrated in her discussion of Harriet Martineau.[10] Again, the warning against excessive self-absorption must have deterred many would-be spiritual autobiographers; while Evangelicals, who were commanded to study themselves minutely, tended to write diaries, which enabled them to keep a daily watch on their spiritual condition. Others simply lacked the education and authority to use Biblical typology. Most nineteenth-century women who wrote autobiography preferred to evolve their own form, rather than adopt the forms established by their male contemporaries.

Even the Evangelical novelist, 'Charlotte Elizabeth' (Mrs Tonna), who does use the spiritual autobiography, adapts it to her own purposes, and combines it with other forms. Her *Personal Recollections* (1841), one of the earliest full-length female autobiographies of the nineteenth century, is written as a series of letters, opening with an apology for her decision to 'go public'. An author is already the property of her audience, Charlotte Elizabeth argues, and if she does not tell her own story, some unscrupulous biographer will make her 'the heroine of some strange romance'. She sets out her apology in the form of a reply to an importuning friend: 'I have given my best consideration to the arguments by which you support the demand for a few notices of events connected with my personal recollections of the past,' she begins, so that the reader seems to be entering the autobiography in the middle of a debate that has gone on for some time. This absolves Charlotte Elizabeth from having any inappropriately egotistic feelings about her own importance: 'and if the charge of egotism be brought,' she continues, 'let the accusers lay their hands upon their hearts, and declare that they would not have sanctioned another in performing for me, as a defunct writer, the office which nobody can fulfil half so well, because nobody can do it half so correctly as myself.'[11]

Having defended the principle of autobiography, and asserted its superiority over biography, Charlotte Elizabeth interrupts her narrative from time to time to discuss some other aspect of the mode. While she was writing, new difficulties occurred; she noticed apparent inconsistencies or dangers and rushed to defend them, as, for instance, passages of self-condemnation in the private journal or autobiography. How could the reader believe they were true, that the author really felt like that, especially if he were not yet in a state of grace? 'This consideration might well cause the pen of auto-biography to drop from a Christian's hand,' she admits; except that all her writing goes to 'glorify God in his merciful dealings' (p. 22). Much of the book is concerned with precisely this glorification of God, but her first four chapters (or 'letters') reveal a number of significant tensions between her repressed ambition and her acceptance of the religious role to which she adapted all her writing and her life itself. As a child, she was romantic, dreamy and imaginative, rejecting specifically the female contribution to domestic life and allying herself with her father and brother. When her brother left home, she turned 'wholly' to her father,

> never desiring to pass an hour out of his society, and striving to be to him both daughter and son. My mother was a perfect devotee to household cares, every thought occupied in seeking to promote the domestic comforts of her family; while I, indulging a natural antipathy to all that did not engage the intellectual powers, gave her no help there. (p. 72)

Her confession of 'a natural antipathy' to all that was *not* of intellectual interest, seems a deliberate inversion of the usual claim that all women were 'naturally' fond of housework and caring for children. Her father, by contrast, was the only member of the family who shared her interest in politics and literature; and her constant companionship with her male relatives made her habitually submissive to male authority (p. 67). Not until her father's death was she able to consider a career; then, like many other Victorian women novelists, she was compelled to think about it, from economic necessity. 'A small annuity was all that my mother could depend on, and I resolved to become a novel-writer, for which I was just qualified, both by nature and habits of thinking, and in which I should probably have succeeded very well, but it pleased God to save me from this snare' (p. 73). Her use of conventional religious tags sorts oddly with her more worldly boast about her potential as a novelist; as it was, she went to London, and met her first husband, Captain Phelan, thereby delaying the beginning of her literary career.

In a significant number of Victorian women's autobiographies, the discovery of a career is preceded by a period of dullness and dissatisfaction, roughly corresponding to the mood of hopelessness associated, in spiritual autobiography, with a first conviction of sin. In secular autobiography, the writer is acutely conscious of her boredom or emotional turmoil; she feels isolated, or somehow different from those around her, but is unable to do anything to help herself. She waits, like Bunyan, in *Grace Abounding to the Chief of Sinners*, in a state of active passivity, to be 'called' by a force outside herself. When Rachel Curtis, heroine of Charlotte Yonge's novel *The Clever Woman of the Family* (1865) declares 'My mission has come to seek me,' she expresses succinctly that fusion of longing and inertia that characterises the mood of many Victorian women immediately before the discovery of a fulfilling occupation.[12] In Charlotte Elizabeth's case, her childhood daydreams gave way to a religious fanaticism, and 'a restless, unsatisfied, unhappy feeling, that seemed in quest of some unknown good' (p. 96). This period of her life, when she was in Ireland with Captain Phelan, is recalled through images of enclosure and seclusion. She decided to become 'a sort of Protestant nun', and fancied her garden 'with its high stone walls, and little thicket of apple-trees, a convent inclosure' (p. 111). This was followed by a bout of illness, during which she read a religious biography of a son by his father, her understanding was opened, and the 'veil' removed from her heart. 'I was like a person long enclosed in a dark dungeon, the walls of which had now fallen down, and I looked round on a sunny landscape of calm and glorious beauty' (p. 115). Harriet Martineau, inverting the usual pattern of spiritual autobiography, employs a similar image of release and escape to celebrate her loss of religious faith when she found herself 'a free rover on the broad, bright breezy common of the universe'.[13] For Charlotte Elizabeth, however, escape from her prison meant release from vainglorious fanaticism into true religion, and the beginning of her literary career.

If she had been only a novelist, after her father's death, she would have entered a 'snare'; by becoming a religious writer after her conversion, she was serving others; and her account of how she came to write her first book is mediated through the language of passivity and surprise. One day she was sent a parcel of tracts:

> Presently the thought flashed upon me, 'Since I cannot give them money, may I not write something to be useful in the same way?' I had just then no work before me; and a long winter evening at command. I ordered large candles, told the servants not to interrupt me, and sat down to my novel task. I began about seven o'clock, and wrote till three in the morning; when I found I had produced a complete little story, in the progress of which I had been enabled so to set forth the truth as it is in Jesus, that on reading it over I

was amazed at the statement I had made of scriptural truth, and sunk on my knees in thankfulness to God. (p. 127)

By suggesting throughout that she was no more than an instrument of divine teaching, Charlotte Elizabeth deflects the reader's attention away from her apparent presumption in thinking she could write for publication. She is only 'enabled' to set forth the truth, and afterwards she is as 'amazed' as if she had written in a trance, or at another's command. Her prayer at the end shifts still further the responsibility for what she has done, on to the mysterious workings of God's will. 'I was absolutely awe-struck by this very striking incident,' she comments. 'I saw in it a gracious acceptance of my freewill offering at His hands to whom it had been prayerfully dedicated' (pp. 127–8). Certainly there was 'freewill', as evidenced by the brisk commands to her servants, but this is subsumed into a larger force, which her narrative shows she could not resist.

The story of Charlotte Elizabeth's conversion into a religious novelist shows how one woman found a way of reconciling her literary ambition with her self-censorship as a woman and a Christian. The letter–form reminds her constantly that her autobiography is subject to the judgement of a critical audience, while her religious commitment colours retrospectively every stage of her earlier life, and builds in a self-regulating system of gratitude for the fortunate outcome of her experiences. Although few nineteenth-century women adopt the paradigm of spiritual autobiography, religion provides them with a habit of thankfulness that makes them both accept the external conditions of their lives, and disclaim the possession of any exceptional qualities.

Another way in which Victorian women novelist-autobiographers reassured their audiences that they had not been hardened or unsexed by a literary career was by devoting relatively little of the autobiography to an account of their artistic activities. Both Margaret Oliphant and Elizabeth Sewell found it difficult to keep up any sustained review of their writing beyond the momentous epoch of their first breakthrough, and appear to fall back more comfortably on descriptions of their home lives. At the same time, both autobiographies disclose an undercurrent of resentment, envy and repressed ambition, which frequently disrupts the tenor of the upper narrative. These two competing drives pull the autobiographies in opposing directions, producing unusually choppy texts, and inviting the reader to question the sincerity of their repeated self-denigration.

With uncanny foresight, Elizabeth Sewell declared as a girl that she would never be 'a useful aunt', for aunts, she felt, were 'put upon'. If her brothers married, they must take care of their own children (*Autobiography*, p. 155). What she failed to predict was that her brothers' wives would die young, and the care of nine children would fall to their maiden aunts, especially Elizabeth. Another of her 'girlish declarations', equally prophetic, if equally ineffective, was that 'women ought not to write books'. On her forty-fifth birthday in 1860, she noted her misgivings about translating a lived life into written language, and decided: 'How untrue any biography – even an autobiography – of any human being must be! How much there is which can never be told except to God, but on which all that is really life has depended' (p. 163).

Elizabeth Sewell's own autobiography is structured as a family history, supplemented by journal entries, which are generally bolder and more direct than her usual narrative style. Several times in the autobiography itself, she admits to pouring her innermost feelings into one of her heroines, such as Myra Cameron in *A Glimpse of the World* (1863), Mrs Anstruther in *Home Life and After Life* (1891) and Sarah in *The Experience of Life* (1853). Although she does draw on events from her own life, the novels mostly gave her an opportunity to vent emotions that were presumably inappropriate to a devoted aunt. For Susan, one of the heroines of *Ivors* (1856) she felt a special sympathy 'in her calm unselfishness, and her quiet acceptance of the life-long pain of a disappointed affection' (p. 146); while Myra Cameron 'knew perfectly well how alive she was to what she called her own rights, and how determined upon asserting them, whether they interfered with those of others or not'.[14]

Evidence from her journal and novels suggests that Elizabeth Sewell longed to voice her often ambitious or resentful feelings to a sympathetic audience, but was unable to do so, except under cover. At the age of twenty, she succumbed to a bout of ill-health, which she attributes to a form of self-absorption. 'I was longing for some one to take an interest in me, and had not yet learnt to make life happy by taking an interest in others' (*Autobiography* p. 51). Soon after this, she apparently masters her moodiness, and says no more about it; but her ambivalent attitude to praise suggests that she had not altogether stifled her ambitions. 'Praise given me to my face,' she explains, 'made me feel extremely awkward, and I have never conquered my dislike to it. Written praise was quite different, and is so still, but spoken words were and are trials' (*Autobiography* p. 76). This passage closely echoes another of Myra's opinions: that when praise was 'implied, she could enjoy it; when written, it was delightful to her; but spoken praise was suffering' (*A Glimpse*, p. 63). Since written praise can be read and re-read, and used as private therapy, these statements argue that Sewell even derived a covert satisfaction from praise. Indeed, the second half of the *Autobiography* leaves more than a tang of discontent at missed recognition, when she declares that *Home Life and After Life* 'deserved a more cordial welcome than it received' (p. 198), or that she was 'no longer a recognised popular authoress' (p. 202).

The beginnings of her literary career are recalled in circular, self-contradictory sentences, which re-enact the battle between ambition and passivity. Her attitude to other women novelists is strongly marked by a sense of competition, as when she told her mother:

> 'You know, mamma, Miss Edgeworth has written stories, and so perhaps I might be able to do the same'; a speech followed by a painful consciousness of having been terribly conceited, for I had all the time a great dislike to authoresses, and once startled a young lady who was dining with us by stating it as my opinion that women had no business to write. No one certainly could have had less perception in childhood or youth of possessing any power of imagination, or indeed of having any talent of any kind than I had. (p. 54)

The boast about Miss Edgeworth is soon erased by a torrent of self-denigration, several times as long as the original transgression. It shows that as a child, Elizabeth Sewell obviously tried her best to internalise the values of a male-dominated society, playing the role of disapproving elder to the flighty female dinner guest; but no amount of denial can conceal the fact that she also enjoyed writing, and thought she could compete with the best of her contemporaries.

The urge to deny all perhaps derives partly from the 'strange scrupulous fancies' she experienced as a child (p. 24). These were self-tormenting obsessions with keeping vows, and, more importantly for autobiography, telling lies. Unable to confide in anyone, she devised a system of psychological self-help based on stringent repression. 'I accustomed myself, whenever the troublesome thoughts came into my head, deliberately to count to six, and then say to myself, "No, I won't think of it," and thus the thoughts, being constantly kept down, after a time went away' (p. 25). The habit, once established, seems to have remained with her, in the form of perpetual self-censorship, for the rest of her life. On her last night at school, she felt 'proudly ambitious for the future. I was going into a new world, and in that world I was resolved to make my mark' (p. 30). Yet she soon declined into poor health and a secluded existence at home with her sisters. She tries to persuade her audience that the one interest of their lives was their set of motherless nieces and nephews, replacing within her 'any desire for literary society, or any craving for literary fame' (p. 84).

The bulk of Elizabeth Sewell's *Autobiography* concerns family relationships and financial difficulties. Her mother dominates the opening pages; her brothers William, Robert and Henry the remainder.

Her father, whom she remembers as 'irritable and cold-mannered, but most benevolent and really tender-hearted' (p. 9), is quickly dismissed with the usual Sewell formula of prohibited outspokenness, followed by dutiful apology. Although she is careful not to criticise her brothers, they emerge through the interstices of the text as incompetent and selfish, especially in their mismanagement of practical affairs. After their father's death, they rerouted their sisters from an independent existence to one that better suited their brothers:

> We calculated upon having £500 a year to live upon; and I had a vision of a little cottage in the country, and a life of extreme quietness. But my brothers had a different plan in view. They thought that it would be better for us at once to remove to Pidford.
> Pidford as a residence had always been in idea our great aversion. (p. 71)

A few years later, William found them a house at Bonchurch: 'a most odd-looking place' (p. 79). When, in 1852, she finally bought it and built on, her apologies seem unnecessary:

> Theoretically I dread and dislike having house property, and for many reasons it might have seemed better for persons situated as we were to have our money differently invested; but looking back I cannot see that we could have done otherwise than build. The landmarks of life seemed to point that way, and events have proved that the decision was wise. (p. 141)

Harriet Martineau had made no such apologies in her *Autobiography*, published thirty years earlier (and written twenty years before that) for building the Knoll at Ambleside: for her the ultimate symbol of freedom and self-sufficiency. Yet it becomes clear, reading between the lines of Sewell's writing, that she was the main prop of her entire family, displacing her brothers from the role that she realises should have been theirs. Her first novel, *Amy Herbert* (1844), gave her mother emotional support; her second, *Laneton Parsonage* (1846–8), paid the bills:

> My writings had now become a pecuniary necessity for the whole family. My mother fully recognised it, for she said to me one day that she would rather be dependent upon me than upon any one else. Not that my brothers failed in assisting us to the utmost of their power, but the business claims were still a perpetual anxiety, and the pressure upon us all was so great that any one who made or could make money was called upon, as a matter of course, to give it to the general fund. (pp. 101–2)

Again, the structure of this passage shows an assertive statement about her own contribution to the family, her independent wage-earning capacity, undercut by defence of her brothers, and an abstract argument in favour of doing one's duty. The fact remains that it was Elizabeth who made the largest contribution, bought a house, ran a school, supported all her nieces and nephews, and was for years a best-selling novelist. A journal entry included in the *Autobiography*, notes that in 1845 a clergyman told her that ten thousand copies of *Amy Herbert* had been circulated in America, 'and there might be ten thousand more, for it had been published by two houses' (p. 121).

How self-aware, then, was Elizabeth Sewell? The question is impossible to answer with any degree of certainty, since every positive thrust in her *Autobiography* is contradicted by a tantalising circularity of style, or overt denial of her achievement. Like many women of her time, she seemed to have the underlying instincts of a successful novelist and businesswoman, but had been well trained to mouth – and perhaps really believed – the theories of the age. Certainly, in her *Note-Book of an Elderly Lady* (1881), a series of debates on women's education, the proto-feminist Miss Brown, is repeatedly put down by the careful arguments of Sewell's spokeswoman Mrs Blair. The 'elderly lady' of the title believes that 'what women can do they will do, and what women can't do they will be obliged to leave alone, ultimately', the standard response of the moderate Victorian middle-class woman.[15] On the other hand, Miss Brown has the stronger side of the debate, urging more direct action. To her, men are innately selfish, their interests too firmly entrenched to give the women's cause much help. Although her readers were presumably meant to find Miss Brown too strident, Elizabeth Sewell at least demonstrates that she had a good grasp of the feminist arguments. Her novels, too, show single women in the forefront, resisting the downward path into marriage, and taking command – albeit in traditionally female roles. To practised modern eyes, her autobiographical apologies are unconvincing, and the gap between reiterated self-denigration and assertion of her achievements leaves her reader questioning the real extent of her lip-service.

Margaret Oliphant's *Autobiography* reveals a very similar uncertainty about her professional standing. As Linda Peterson has shown, 'the real issue of the *Autobiography* was not to separate the artist from the mother but to define the relationship between the two.'[16] Like Elizabeth Sewell, Margaret Oliphant was acutely aware of other women novelists, but whereas Sewell usually believed her own work was superior, Oliphant felt 'very small, very obscure, beside them, rather a failure all round' (p. 8). 'No one even will mention me in the same breath with George Eliot,' she admitted, having been tempted to start her *Autobiography* by Cross's *Life* of George Eliot, which she read critically in 1885 (p. 7). By then, she had reviewed the autobiographies of Harriet Martineau, Fanny Kemble, Mary Russell Mitford and the Duchess of Newcastle, besides writing a general series of articles on autobiography for *Blackwood's* and contributing other reviews on women's issues. 'I don't think any one will like George Eliot better from this book, or even come nearer to her,' she confessed to John Blackwood, adding later: 'It is quite astounding to see how little humour or vivacity she had in real life. Surely Mr Cross must have cut out all the human parts.'[17] Always bristly on the subject of 'women's rights', Margaret Oliphant perferred women novelists to be cheerful, pleasant and unaggressively feminine. Fanny Kemble's *Record of a Girlhood* won her approval because it was 'an entirely pleasant book, full of many bright pictures, and no bitterness', while Harriet Martineau's *Autobiography* was just the opposite. Mrs Oliphant enjoyed anecdotes of notable people, but only if they threw 'no dart of deadly scandal either at the living or the dead'.[18] The Duchess of Newcastle also charmed her with the 'rambling but delightful description' she gave of herself; and Mary Russell Mitford with her 'pure womanly' judgements and 'unaffected pages'.[19] Within the *Autobiography* itself, further comments on her contemporaries, male and female, help clarify her moral and literary values. Trollope's *Autobiography*, published two years before she began writing her own, astonished her 'beyond measure' with its solemn talk about the characters in his own books: 'I am totally incapable of talking about anything I have ever done in that way.'

> As he was a thoroughly sensible genuine man, I suppose he was quite sincere in what he says of them, – or was it that he was driven into a fashion of self-explanation which belongs to the time, and which I am following now though in another way? I feel that my carelessness of asserting my claim is very much against me with everybody. It is so natural to think that if the workman himself is indifferent about his work, there can't be much in it that is worth thinking about. I am not indifferent, yet I should rather like to forget it all, to wipe out all the books, to silence those compliments about my industry, &c., which I always turn off with a laugh. (pp. 4–5)

Sharing Elizabeth's Sewell's much-vaunted dread of praise, she regards herself as a reluctant follower of literary fashion, in this case for autobiography. Hers is essentially the story of a writer who keeps forgetting she's a writer, or wishes she had never been one. It also tries to entertain – she told John Blackwood it had sometimes given her 'a little amusement to write it' – but often crumples into acute sadness, as one by one, her family die away, and she is left the sole survivor. The book she wrote for her sons, especially Francis, or 'Cecco', the younger, is redirected half way through to the general public, and its tone adjusted accordingly: 'I am now going to try to remember more trivial things, the incidents that sometimes amuse me when I look back upon them, not merely the thread of my life' (p. 65). In fact, the change of tone is barely noticeable. Mrs Oliphant clings, as before, to every pleasant memory of her sons, to every occasion when they were still happy, well and successful. When she reaches the disappointing careers and premature deaths of both sons, her incentive to write and her autobiography end simultaneously: 'And now here I am all alone. I cannot write any more' (p. 150).

As an experienced critic of autobiography, Margaret Oliphant knew what the public would expect of literary memoirs, and produced a handful of suitable anecdotes; all, however, rather withered round the edges. When she visited Tennyson in London, he paid no attention to her, 'as was very natural' (p. 136); while at the start of her career, she was dismissed by the American novelist Grace Greenwood, as 'a little homely Scotchwoman' (p. 36). With Jane Carlyle, she succeeded better, perhaps because Jane reminded her of her own mother, and because both were fond of East Lothian (p. 78); but Margaret Oliphant was no casual name-dropper. 'It is rather a fictitious sort of thing recalling those semi-professional recollections,' she admits. 'It is by way of a kind of apology for knowing so few notable people' (p. 138).

She is clearly jealous of other women whose success has been more outstanding than her own. Having introduced Dinah Mulock to the publisher Henry Blackett, she was dismayed when *John Halifax, Gentleman* 'raised her at once to a high position':

> She made a spring thus quite over my head with the helping hand of my particular friend, leaving me a little rueful, – I did not at all understand the means nor think very highly of the work, which is a thing that has happened several times, I fear, in my experience. Success as measured by money never came to my share. Miss Mulock in this way attained more with a few books, and these of very thin quality, than I with my many. (p. 83)

She felt much the same about Mrs Humphry Ward, whose success seemed 'fabulous' and inexplicable to 'poorer writers' like herself (pp. 70–1). Again, her mood is 'rueful': a mixture of self-pity, regret and incomprehension, as she remembers the less sensational popularity of her own Carlingford series: 'a series pretty well forgotten now, which made a considerable stir at the time, and *almost* made me one of the popularities of literature. *Almost*, never quite, though "Salem Chapel" really went very near it, I believe' (p. 70). Like Elizabeth Sewell, she had outlived her own fame: 'and yet I have done very well for a woman, and a friendless woman with no one to make the best of me, and quite unable to do that for myself' (p. 70).

Of all the Victorian female autobiographers, Margaret Oliphant is the one most conscious of her difficulties as a woman, and the most alienated by male versions of the genre. Not only was she unable to discuss her novels, as Trollope had done; she also shied away from the introversion of John Addington Symonds, whose autobiography she read during the composition of her own. The difference between her 'prosaic little narrative' and his 'elaborate self-discussions' almost made her laugh (p. 80).

'I might well give myself up to introspection at this sad postscript of my life,' she admits; but any attempt at discussing herself 'like Mr Symonds' would 'end in outlines of trouble, in the deep, deep sorrow that covers me like a mantle.' A strong, indestructible woman among men weak in body and spirit, she hoped her maternal anxieties would be understood by other women in her invisible audience, especially a 'woman in the passion and agony of motherhood' (p. 147). In the struggle between the author and the mother, the mother wins, because her triumphs and agonies strike deeper. Only her first novel, *Passages in the life of Mrs. Margaret Maitland* (1849), is recalled with any real sense of elation, partly because it was her first, but also because it 'was the most extraordinary joke that ever was', written at her own pace, and not to support a needy family. She was still unmarried, and her mother, who was everything to her, 'laughed and cried with pride and happiness and amazement unbounded' (p. 19). Neither her father nor her husband, both shadowy figures in the narrative, played an important role in her development as a novelist; whereas her first attempts at writing began by her mother's bedside. Significantly, the chief character in this first exercise was 'an angelic elder sister, unmarried, who had the charge of a family of motherless brothers and sisters': an alarmingly prophetic picture of her own future altruism, towards her brother Frank's family, as well as her own (p. 16). 'At my most ambitious of times,' she confesses, 'I would rather my children had remembered me as their mother than in any other way, and my friends as their friend' (p. 130).

If women, specifically mothers, are the strong, supportive figures in her narrative (and also in many of her novels, particularly *The Doctor's Family*, 1863, and *Hester*, 1883), Mrs Oliphant was afraid that as a mother, she might, after all, have failed. As one by one her children were taken away from her, she wondered whether her priorities had been mistaken, her decisions tragically wrong. A winter in Rome had killed her only surviving daughter Maggie, making her ask whether God found her 'unworthy of bringing up a woman', as she confessed to a friend a year later (p. 200). Perhaps she remembered Mary Howitt's dour warnings a decade earlier: 'a mild, kind, delightful woman, who frightened me very much, I remember, by telling me of many babies whom she had lost through some defective valve in the heart, which she said was somehow connected with too much mental work on the part of the mother, – a foolish thing, I should think, yet the same thing occurred twice to myself' (p. 36). By 1895, when all her children were dead, she was pondering upon 'a sadder theory still', that her easygoing attitude to money had made them too dependent and inactive, 'so that I seem sometimes to feel as if it were all my doing, and that I had brought by my heedlessness both to an *impasse* from which there was no issue but one' (p. 106). When her elder son, Cyril 'missed somehow his footing', she often thought that she 'had to do with it, as well as what people call inherited tendencies' (p. 147). This bleak, Ibsenish conclusion emphasises the sad futility of all her efforts to keep the family afloat, though by this stage of the *Autobiography* she is too subdued by loss to express any more specific regrets.

Mrs Oliphant's guilt about her children is offset by an occasional gleam of pleasure in the act of writing. From the beginning, she admits that she enjoyed her work, which was her 'natural' way of occupying herself (p. 5) at a time when caring for children was considered a more 'natural' occupation for a woman. Frequently, in Mrs Oliphant's life, her roles as a woman and as a novelist completely coalesced, as when she wrote by her mother's bedside, or corrected proofs on her wedding morning, or talked to Jane Carlyle about Cecco's convulsions. Though she laughs at the way she is distracted from discussing her novels by 'a couple of baby stories', she admits to being 'ever more really satisfied by some little conscious felicity of words than by anything else' (p. 86). Her writing was something private and mysterious, responsive to her emotions, yet still independent of her outward sorrows:

> I have always had my sing-song, guided by no sort of law, but by my ear, which was in its way fastidious to the cadence and measure that pleased me; but it is bewildering to me in my perfectly artless art, if I may use the word at all, to hear of the elaborate ways of forming and enhancing style, and all the studies for that end. (p. 86).

Like Elizabeth Sewell, Margaret Oliphant first expresses pleasure in the hidden and lawless act of writing; then attempts to cleanse it of all professional associations. Throughout the *Autobiography*, she insists that writing came naturally to her, but a self-regarding preoccupation with technique she dismisses as fundamentally alien, with sometimes a suggestion that only male authors (such as Trollope and Symonds) take their own creations so seriously.

Her style in the *Autobiography* also strengthens the unprofessional, 'human' quality of her recollections. Although she passes over the most intimate relationship of her life, her marriage, on all other matters she seems to be thinking aloud; qualifying over-hasty assertions, questioning the truth of what she has just said, producing a more accurate reflection of her instinctive opinions, though always with a consciousness of what people will think. Her problem throughout the narrative is to say what she feels, while retaining the sympathy and trust of her always potentially critical audience. Hardest of all is the task of persuading them that she was really not proud of her books, or unduly occupied by them:

Other matters, events even of our uneventful life, took so much more importance in life than these books – nay, it must be a kind of affectation to say that, for the writing ran through everything. But then it was also subordinate to everything, to be pushed aside for any little necessity. (p. 23).

She often gives the impression of not being fully in control of her narrative. Its unplanned, conversational mode allows her to express, then repress, unsuitable opinions, to discuss with herself whether certain subjects should be introduced. After describing what she did for her brother Frank's children, for example, she stops herself from saying too much and boring her readers: 'But it is not likely that such family details would be of interest to the public.' Then second thoughts suggest otherwise. 'And yet, as a matter of fact, it is exactly those family details that are interesting, – the human story in all its chapters' (p. 122).

On the supremacy of the 'human story' over the 'artless art', Mrs Oliphant rests her case, but as with Elizabeth Sewell the reader is left wondering how much the author really believes in this particular portrayal of herself. Mrs Oliphant's *Autobiography* suggests that she does not know what to bring forward and what to hide; whether her audience will approve of her more as a mother or an author, for she can be seen as more successful in her 'unnatural' role than in her domestic efforts, though ultimately, perhaps, a failure in both. There is more honest bewilderment here than in Elizabeth Sewell's *Autobiography*, as is usually the case in self-writing by married women. They were meant to be more invisible than single women, more staunchly devoted to the cause of home and family. Having outlived her children and her celebrity, Margaret Oliphant had no heart to go on 'making pennyworths' of herself (p. 75): preparing for the public a face that could never be entirely her own.

When Eliza Lynn Linton was urged to give her 'unveiled Reminiscences' to the world, 'her eyes blazed at me through her spectacles as she raised her hands and beat her knees, with a characteristic gesture, and cried, "Oh, lor'h! oh, lor'h! George, my dear, I dare not! I know too much; I dare not".'[20] Her friend Beatrice Harradan pleaded that 'Mrs. Linton's pen was even harsher than her speech, and those who loved and knew her have the right to emphasise this fact'[21]; but whitewashing such an outspoken novelist as Eliza Lynn Linton was no easy matter, since besides her 'official' recollections, *My Literary Life* (1899), she had also written an 'unofficial' transvestite autobiography of a 'moral derelict', Christopher Kirkland.[22] 'I have put my very Soul, my Life into these pages and I feel as if I am being slowly killed through them,' she complained when publication was delayed. She considered it not only 'the book' of her whole career, but also 'the best I have ever done';[23] yet the critics were largely unimpressed. *The Saturday Review*, Lynn Linton's own customary outlet for scathing attacks on 'the girl of the period', dismantled the book into two parts of personal recollections and reflections by the author, and one of the 'fictitious autobiography of Christopher Kirkland'. The last it considered 'neither exciting nor edifying' and Kirkland himself a 'thoughtful oaf' who rings the changes on 'Unitarianism, Necessitarianism, Humanitarianism, Spiritualism, Altruism, Mind-Stuffery, and Comic Emotion in a sufficiently depressing manner'.[24] Julia Wedgwood, writing in *The Contemporary Review*, more perceptively observed that the fictitious male autobiography publicised one specifically female experience, 'the fact that Christopher is allowed to grow up without any education whatever being the only sign we can call to mind that we are in reality reading the story of female life.'[25]

The Autobiography of Christopher Kirkland (1885) is essentially an exaggerated version of Eliza Lynn Linton's unhappy childhood, marriage, literary life and outspoken opinions. Her biographer, Herbert Van Thal, suggests that she fictionalised her autobiography and changed the sexes because 'for so frank a credo she would be unable to identify the partners of her "love affairs" or of many of those close to her, though she freely gives the true identity of her many friends and acquaintances.'[26] There has been much debate as to whether women who use male first-person narrators are dodging the issue, or subverting, from within, patriarchal assumptions. For Sandra Gilbert and Susan Gubar such a choice of viewpoint 'may involve a female writer in uncomfortable contradictions and tensions', possibly leading to 'radical psychic confusion'.[27] What it chiefly allows Lynn Linton to do is express violent passions which would have been unpublishable in a work purporting to be by a woman. As a young man, for example, Christopher is fascinated by the subject of virgin births; he develops a tremendous crush on a neighbour Mrs Dalrymple; he tests his ability to withstand torture by gouging out a tooth with a knife; and yearns to 'be famous and do great things':

> I would cover my name with glory, and all those who had not believed in me with confusion; and my own should be proud of me. I used to dream of the senior wranglership at Cambridge and of the leadership of the House of Commons. I would go to the bar and be Lord Chancellor, or remain a free lance and be Prime Minister. I would make a name; I would be great. Whatever I did I would succeed. And I felt as if I could not fail.[28]

In real life, Eliza Lynn persuaded her father to let her try a year's intellectual activity in London; in the novel, Christopher Kirkland persuades himself that 'self-assertion was not selfishness', and that the sacrifice of 'a real vocation for no one's good and simply because of the arbitrary opposition of a parent' is neither absolute nor imperative (I, 224). As a man, he is able to pitch his ambitions at the highest offices in the country, providing Lynn Linton with a broad outlet for the expression of her own necessarily confined aspirations, and the mechanism for a female revenge drama.

By the end of the novel, however, Kirkland has paid heavily for his freedom. Unhappily married, as Lynn Linton was herself, old and alone, he preaches the 'annihilation of self' and the 'practice of altruistic Duty as the absolute law of moral life' (III, 320). All the sorrows and disappointments of his life have taught him the futility of egoism and the value of a Dorothea-like renunciation as the moral evolution of the human race builds towards a higher being. Sinking his individuality in the collective mass, he looks forward to the glorious future of humanity. The end of Harriet Martineau's *Autobiography* celebrates a similar triumph of human reason based on a recognition of impersonal and immutable laws governing the universe.

If Christopher Kirkland learns by his mistakes, the women he meets on his egotistical progress through life embody fixed positions of femininity that help define the ideal woman. The first of these is the hero's mother, instantly idealised as 'sweet and gentle and very beautiful' (I, 11). 'If our dear mother had lived, things would have been different. She would have understood each and would have done justly by all,' Christopher believes (I, 75). In the British Museum, he observes a girl who is perhaps a sketch of Lynn Linton herself: 'one of the vanguard of the independent women; but she did her life's work without blare or bluster, or help from the outside' (I, 253). By the time of his marriage to Esther Lambert, who is dedicated to women's emancipation, Christopher has developed a dislike of bloomers, women doctors and mixed nude drawing classes. Sexual difference, in his view, necessarily entails a separation of spheres: 'Nor can I deny the value of inherent modesty; nor despise domestic duties; nor look on maternity as a curse and degradation' (III, 4). Many of 'these extremely advanced women' he finds antagonistic to his concept of 'feminine charm', the cause undeniably suffering with him 'because so many of its advocates were ungainly and unlovely' (III, 5).

When he marries Esther, Christopher insists that she gives up her public life and keeps house like any other wife and mother; but her political activities have 'unsexed' her; clean tablecloths, she declares, in a speech of defiance, are not the centre of life, and she flounces off to America. Now separated from her, Christopher consoles himself with a series of surrogate sons and daughters, whose perfections emphasise the shortcomings of Esther. 'Obedient, gentle, steadfast, unselfish, Claudia was a typical woman of the best kind – thinking of others more than of

herself,' he says of an eighteen-year-old girl left in his care by her father
(III, 237). In turn, an older woman, Felicia Barry, looks after him during
an illness, the 'type of the Ideal Woman . . . strong, hopeful and unselfish'
(III, 300). Together with the quiet girl in the British Museum, they
compensate for Lynn Linton's own aggressive determination, despite
her anti-feminist standpoint, to lead an independent life as a journalist.
Comparison with one of the few personal passages in *My Literary Life*
shows that Lynn Linton was herself 'as much an insurgent as the rest, and
despised all that was old and proved in favour of all that was new and
untried' (p. 31). Several of her memories in the later autobiographical
work incorporate responses to female propriety. W. S. Landor, who
appears in both books as an idealised father-figure, is remembered in the
second as having old-fashioned ideas about women, and a dislike of
slang; George Henry Lewes shocked her with his open references to 'the
most delicate matters of physiology' (p. 18), and an unsuccessful attempt
to kiss a pretty young girl on her departure from the family; while she
herself was so quiet that a young man once complimented her on her
ability to keep silent: an attribute rarely associated with Eliza Lynn
Linton in her bolder middle age. At this stage of her life, she was still
suffering from a conventional upbringing along the lines of 'childish
effacement and womanly self-suppression', and taught that she ought to
have no opinion of her own, and certainly no desire to express it (p. 36).

Eliza Lynn Linton was in an awkard position. By the time she was
ready to write her autobiography, she was a notorious defender of old-
fashioned womanly ways, a tireless campaigner against the new bloomer-
clad, made-up, fast-living, slang-shouting 'Girl of the Period'; yet in her
own life, she had refused to stay at home with her father; she had gone to
London and established herself as an independent woman; she had married late, and unsuccessfully, having no children and separating from her
husband; and finally she had published her sufficiently embarrassing
history under a thin masculine disguise that the critics had penetrated
without difficulty. Sixteen years earlier, in *Ourselves*, a collection of
essays about women, Lynn Linton had discussed the problem of what
she called 'Feminine Extremes', or the difficulty of achieving moderation
of temper and behaviour. Self-restraint is their rarest characteristic, she
complained of women, though it is 'the very essence of masculine
strength':

> But women get so 'mixed up' by emotion, desperation, passion, and
> defiance, that no after-restraint is possible when once the curb is slackened;
> so that, unless they are held in subjection by the fear of God, the world, or
> the devil, they go headlong to destruction, and neither reason nor
> philosophy touches them.[29]

Identified with 'Passion', while his brother Edwin was 'Patience', Christopher Kirkland demands a mental arena of distinctly unfeminine proportions (I, 67). His *Autobiography* is Lynn Linton's opportunity to investigate a forbidden emotional landscape, which she explores as an altruistic wise elder, chastened by experience. While on the surface it reinforces the lesson of feminine self-restraint, Christopher's rampant ambition and longing for adventure, his outspoken support for easier divorce laws and 'the cause of freedom in general' (II, 261) produce a more subversive subtext of aspiration that would have been unthinkable in Lynn Linton's own voice.

Women novelists had long been using male pseudonyms, and even male narrative personae in their writing; but the range of pseudo-male autobiographies by women is relatively small. Where this form is chosen, the woman behind the masculine disguise usually expresses views that are particularly unacceptable by normal female standards. For instance, Beryl Gray, in the afterword to the 1985 Virago edition of George Eliot's *The Lifted Veil* (1859), sees the hero, Latimer's persistent quest for fulfilment as 'no more than a quest for self-gratification', the exact opposite of Maggie Tulliver's altruistic devotion to her brother Tom.[30] As such, *The Lifted Veil* may be seen as cathartic autobiography, leaving George Eliot free to resume her more positive study of inalienable ties in *The Mill on the Floss*, which she had interrupted to write the shorter tale. 'Cursed with an exceptional mental character', an exaggeration of George Eliot's sybilline wisdom, Latimer is able to foresee the moment of his own death, and before that time comes, longs for the sympathetic understanding of his fellow men.[31] He has no near relatives, and will leave no works for posterity to remember. 'It is only the story of my life that will perhaps win a little more sympathy from strangers when I am dead, than I ever believed it would obtain from my friends while I was living' (p. 4).

The pattern of his childhood is in some ways similar to Margaret Oliphant's and Eliza Lynn Linton's. The mother is idealised, the father strict and unbending. 'There is no need to dwell on this part of my life,' Latimer suggests. 'I have said enough to indicate that my nature was of the sensitive, unpractical order, and that it grew up in an uncongenial medium, which could never foster it into happy, healthy development' (p. 8). His father only begins to care for him when his brother Alfred is dead, and finds him too dreamy and wayward to be worth educating for a career. Latimer's physical and psychological characteristics are in fact a caricature of the female neurotic's. He is held to have 'a sort of half-womanish, half-ghostly beauty' (in contrast to George Eliot's heavy and horselike features), a face 'framed for passive suffering' (p. 20), and a transient capacity for 'rapt passivity' (p. 14). He tries to stimulate his imagination with poetic memories, his self-consciousness heightened 'to that pitch of intensity in which our own emotions take the form of a drama which urges itself imperatively on our contemplation, and we begin to weep' (p. 36):

> I felt a sort of pitying anguish over the pathos of my own lot: the lot of a being finely organised for pain, but with hardly any fibres that responded to pleasure – to whom the idea of future evil robbed the present of its joy, and for whom the idea of future good did not still the uneasiness of a present yearning or a present dread. (p. 36)

In effect, George Eliot uses the autobiographical figure of Latimer to explore from within the psychological contours of a life distorted by egoism and alienated from the rest of the human race. At the same time, he embodies many of the characteristics of George Eliot as ominiscient novelist, whose interpretative wisdom penetrates the hidden processes of human thought and emotion. For Latimer, 'this superadded conscious-ness' becomes 'an intense pain and grief' when it opens up the souls of his closest associates:

> when the rational talk, the graceful attentions, the wittily-turned phrases, and the kindly deeds, which used to make the web of their characters, were seen as if thrust asunder by a microscopic vision, that showed all the intermediate frivolities, all the suppressed egoism, all the struggling chaos of puerilities, meanness, vague capricious memories, and indolent make-shift thoughts, from which human words and deeds emerge like leaflets covering a fermenting heap. (pp. 19–20)

Latimer's clairvoyant powers reduce society to a darkling plain of vapid clashing egos: a distortion of the insight into petty lives that George Eliot was to demonstrate in *Middlemarch*, aided by similar images of the web and instruments of scientific precision. What Latimer later calls a 'dis-eased participation in other people's consciousness' (p. 26) is here seen stripped of all benevolence, the compassion George Eliot subsequently feels for Maggie Tulliver and Dorothea Brooke. Instead, the world is full of Rosamond Vincys, blond water-nixies, indolent and egoistic, whose shallow malevolence drains the ominiscient author of tolerance and sympathy and drags him down to the common level of watchful sus-picion. If the surface text is a study of egoism, the muted story is the sensitive woman novelist's consciousness of her separation and differ-ence; her dread of discovering that the substance of other lives is only meanness, and that knowledge of it will inevitably isolate her from pro-ductive involvement with them. Nothing that Latimer sees in his visions brings him the creative pleasure normally enjoyed by the artist. His dream of Prague is of a sterile waste land populated by statues, its live inhabitants reduced to 'a swarm of ephemeral visitants infesting it for a day' (p. 12). Latimer's Prague is the obverse (or dehydrated travesty) of George Eliot's St Oggs, a nightmare vision of a society reduced to spiritual starvation, like T. S. Eliot's European capitals between the two World Wars.

Latimer is the opposite of George Eliot's other male autobiographical persona, Theophrastus Such, who gave his name to her last published work, a series of essays or 'impressions'. Unlike George Eliot herself, Theophrastus has apparently achieved little; 'and as to intellectual contribution, my only published work was a failure, so that I am spoken of to inquiring beholders as "the author of a book you have probably not seen".'[32] In the guise of another isolated and unloved (perhaps unlovable) male autobiographer, George Eliot examines the relationship between the needs of the individual and his commitment to society, and the differences between spoken and written explanations of the self. When he speaks his experiences aloud to another person, Theophrastus observes the all-too-obvious signs of boredom in his listener; the act of writing, however, 'brings with it the vague, delightful illusion' of a 'far-off, hazy, multitudinous assemblage, as in a picture of Paradise, making an approving chorus to the sentences and paragraphs of which I myself particularly enjoy the writing' (p. 17). Although writing may be a private act, Theophrastus is acutely conscious of his putative audience. 'If any physiognomy becomes distinct in the foreground, it is fatal. The countenance is sure to be one bent on discountenancing my innocent intentions' (p. 17). Consumed with self-doubt, and 'a permanent longing for approbation, sympathy, and love' (p. 8), he has established a habit of mind that at last protects him from undue absorption in his own anxieties. The 'diseased participation in other people's consciousness' experienced by Latimer is transformed into an active and positive interest in the lives of his neighbours: 'and I am really at the point of finding that this world would be worth living in without any lot of one's own' (p. 16).

The second essay 'Looking Backward' is, like *The Lifted Veil*, largely a study of the uneasy relationship between a father and son deprived of the mother-figure who, it is implied, would have smoothed the son's path through life. Quelling a blasphemous wish that he had had other parents, Theophrastus recreates a visionary picture of a slow rural England, in which he was his father's constant companion, and his affections were fledged in a 'warm little nest', which he left as a voluntary exile (p. 42). From the first, he explains, there have been such exiles: 'some of those who sallied forth went for the sake of a loved companion-ship, when they would willingly have kept sight of the familiar plains, and of the hills to which they had first lifted up their eyes' – presumably a reference to her own choice of London and Lewes over Coventry and her father and brother (p. 42). Older and wiser than Latimer, and ponderously philosophical, Theophrastus admits that the England of his affections may be 'half visionary', but illusions that began early 'have not lost their value when we discern them to be illusions' (p. 42).

Both pseudo-male narratives are concerned with the problem of the writer's egoism and alienation from conventional, uncomprehending societies; the male persona permitting George Eliot a less challengeable reconstruction of the creative artist's hidden fears and self-absorbed isolation. Both works, too, take liberties with the genre itself: Latimer predicting what remains unknown and unwritten to all autobiographers, the date and circumstances of the author's death; while Theophrastus insists that he is 'not indeed writing an autobiography' (p. 7), nor does he, selecting only a few impressionistic memories of his distant childhood, and some studied observations on his present temperament and increasing altruism, similar to the aged Christopher Kirkland's.

George Eliot's only piece of unreserved, unfictionalised autobiography, other than her accounts of herself in letters and the various 'Recollections' of places visited (which are mostly impersonal description), is the short, isolated statement 'How I Came to Write Fiction,' reprinted in Gordon Haight's edition of her letters.[33] Coming to it from the bizarre world of *The Lifted Veil* or the claustrophobia of *Theophrastus Such*, the reader is shocked by its meek simplicity. It begins with the frank admission that 'September 1856 made a new era in my life, for it was then I began to write Fiction' (p. 406). The discovery of her abilities is inseparable in the narrative from her relationship with Lewes, whose encouragement and criticism slowly build up her confidence, and run like a thread through every stage of her development from hesitant story-writer to established novelist. As in Margaret Oliphant's account of her beginnings, the invention of the Rev. Amos Barton is seen as something casual and accidental. The introductory chapter 'happened' to be among the papers she had taken with her to Berlin, and one evening 'something' led her to read it to Lewes. From that moment, according to the narrative's emphases, Lewes takes over the direction of her literary career: all the active urging is his, all the passive daydreaming hers. At first, 'he began to think that I might as well try, some time, what I could do in fiction'; subsequently, 'He began to say very positively, "You must try and write a story"' (p. 407). As, one by one, she disproves all Lewes's doubts about her ability to create this or that constituent of a publishable novel, each cleared hurdle is described in terms of Lewes's approval; all self-praise, therefore, mediated through the encouragement of a professional male journalist: 'The scene at Cross farm, he said, satisfied him that I had the very element he had been doubtful about – it was clear I could write good dialogue' (p. 408). When Lewes tells her proudly that her pathos is better than her fun, the last doubts disappear, and the way is clear for Lewes to send her story to John Blackwood and begin managing the business part of her professional career as a novelist. 'There was clearly no suspicion that I was a woman,' George Eliot comments (p. 408), and all the discussion about her takes place among men. The narrative, which was written as a private Journal entry on 6 December 1857, breaks off at the point where Blackwood has expressed unease about 'Janet's Repentance', and she has decided to end the series. The closing comment – 'we are still wondering how the public will behave to my first book' – ends the piece on a note of indefinite, continuing uncertainty, befitting George Eliot's lifelong distrust of her own abilities as a novelist. The future hangs suspended and unknown, as it does in the Brontës' diary papers, which were left unopened for several years after they were written.

The Oxford anthropologists, Shirley and Edwin Ardener, who have conducted an analysis of female culture, argue that women constitute a 'muted' group, whose cultural boundaries overlap, but are not wholly contained by the 'dominant' (male) group. Edwin Ardener has suggested that women are actually made 'inarticulate' by the male structure of public discourse, and display a 'necessary indirectness rather than spontaneity of expression'. Consequently, they 'might sometimes lack the facility to raise to conscious level their unconscious thoughts'.[34] Elaine Showalter has extended the Ardeners' argument to suggest that 'women writing are not, then, *inside* and *outside* of the male tradition; they are inside two traditions simultaneously.'[35] Victorian women novelists writing autobiography were torn between the 'insider' knowledge that male autobiographers usually structured their self-writing round the publication history of their books, and the realisation that such a structure would be considered unnatural and self-laudatory in the autobiography of a woman. The question of their 'unconscious thoughts' being raised to conscious level is particularly acute in this set of auto-biographers, whose professional work as novelists had accustomed them to handling emotional expression obliquely deflected through fictitious characters, usually women. It was perhaps harder for them than for any other group to place themselves in the position of 'characters' and, with-out the benefits of concealment, retell the story of their sorrows. Both Oliphant and Sewell had used their novels to explore the plight of women called upon to manage large families of dependants: writing about a similar situation in their own lives raised the new problem of blame and the risk of self-righteousness. Hence their recourse to a 'necessary indirectness', which in the cases of Lynn Linton and Eliot produced what might be called, at the cost of clumsiness, the pseudo-male, pseudo-autobiography, and in the cases of the other autobiographers discussed in this chapter, a duplicitous, self-denigrating style.

Yet all the women in this group enjoyed the act of writing. It gave them an inviolable world of their own, a place of power and recreation away from domestic duties that were often fruitless and repetitive. Although it was easier for the next generation of women novelist-autobiographers, such as Mrs Humphry Ward who was born in 1851, there remained a feeling of unease about their presentation of themselves. 'If these are to be the recollections of a writer, in which perhaps other writers by profession, as well as the more general public, may take some interest', begins Mrs Ward's tentative apology for talking about her theological 'best-seller', 'I shall perhaps be forgiven if I give some account of the processes of thought and work which led to the writing of my first successful novel, "Robert Elsmere".' Even so, she remembers that work on the novel was interrupted by her mother's serious illness – 'I was torn incessantly between the claim of the book, and the desire to be with her whenever I could possibly be spared from my home and children' – and that for a time she led a 'double life – the one overshadowed by my mother's approaching death, the other amid the agitation of the book's appearance, and all the incidents of its rapid success'.[36]

The notion of a 'double life' lacks this special resonance for male Victorian autobiographers. They may have belonged to more than one circle of family and friends, but there was no conflict, induced by society's expectations, between their public work and their private lives. Apart from a general feeling that excessive egoism, in either sex, is unattractive, there is no sense that it was wrong to discuss one's own works or to describe the development of a literary career. Women faced with an inappropriate pattern of professional autobiography had to make new decisions about the form and direction of their memories. The few who attempted anything approaching a serious analysis of their lives, faced a web of conflicting impulses and rival claims that silenced any real revelation of professional or personal feeling. All the critic can conclude with any certainty is that in the voice of the subtext speaks the roar that lies on the other side of silence.

Notes

1. *The Letters of Mrs. Gaskell*, ed. J. A. V. Chapple and A. Pollard (Manchester: Manchester University Press, 1966), p. 106.
2. Oliphant, *Autobiography*, p. 28.

3. Quoted by Francis R. Hart, 'Notes for an anatomy of modern autobiography', *New Literary History* I (Spring 1970), p. 487.

4. Quoted by Nancy K. Miller, 'Women's autobiography in France', p. 271.

5. Coleridge, *Memoir*, I, viii.

6. Mary Russell Mitford, *Recollections of a Literary Life: or, Books, Places, and People* (London: Richard Bentley and Son, 3 vols, 1852), Preface.

7. 'Mary Russell Mitford', *Blackwood's* 75 (June 1854), p. 658; p. 664.

8. 'Miss Mitford's "Recollections"', *Blackwood's* 71 (March 1852), p. 260.

9. 'Harriet Martineau', *Blackwood's* 121 (April 1877), p. 495.

10. Peterson, *Victorian Autobiography*, pp. 124–35.

11. *Personal Recollections*, p. 1; p. 4.

12. Charlotte M. Yonge, *The Clever Woman of the Family* (1865; London: Virago, 1985), p. 4.

13. *Harriet Martineau's Autobiography*, I, 116.

14. Elizabeth M. Sewell, *A Glimpse of the World* (London: Longman, Roberts, & Green, 1863), p. 70.

15. Elizabeth M. Sewell, *Note-Book of An Elderly Lady* (London: Walter Smith, 1881), p. 149. Sarah C. Frerichs argues that Sewell is not aware that she 'writes out of certain deep-seated psychological needs', but is 'partially aware' of her infatuation for her brother William, without intending to reveal 'the romantic, even sexual, coloration' to her feelings'. 'Elizabeth Missing Sewell: Concealment and Revelation in a Victorian Everywoman', *Approaches to Victorian Autobiography*, ed. Landow, pp. 175–99.

16. Linda H. Peterson, 'Audience and the autobiographer's art: the *Autobiography* of Mrs. M. O. W. Oliphant', *Approaches to Victorian Autobiography*, ed. Landow, pp. 158–74.

17. Oliphant, *Autobiography*, pp. 323–4.

18. 'Two ladies', *Blackwood's* 125 (February 1879), p. 224.

19. 'Margaret, Duchess of Newcastle', *Blackwood's* 129 (May 1881), p. 638; 'Mary Russell Mitford', *Blackwood's* 75 (June 1854). p. 670.

20. George Somes Layard, *Mrs. Lynn Linton: Her Life, Letters and Opinions* (London: Methuen, 1901), p. 247.

21. Mrs Lynn Linton, *My Literary Life*, with a Prefatory Note by Miss Beatrice Harradan (London: Hodder and Stoughton, 1899), p. 6.

22. Mrs Lynn Linton, *The Autobiography of Christopher Kirkland* (London: Richard Bentley and Son, 3 vols, 1885), II, 210.

23. Herbert Van Thal, *Eliza Lynn Linton: The Girl of the Period: A Biography* (London: George Allen & Unwin, 1979), p. 142.

24. *The Saturday Review* LX (1 August 1885), p. 155.

25. *The Contemporary Review* XLIX (April 1886), p. 594.

26. Van Thal, p. 142.

27. Sandra M. Gilbert and Susan Gubar, *The Madwoman in the Attic: The Woman Writer and the Nineteenth-Century Literary Imagination* (New Haven, Conn.: Yale University Press, 1978), p. 70; p. 66.

28. *Christopher Kirkland*, p. 109.

29. Mrs Lynn Linton, *Ourselves: A Series of Essays on Women* (London: G. Routledge & Sons, 1869), p. 174.

30. George Eliot, *The Lifted Veil* (1859; ed. Beryl Gray, London: Virago, 1985), p. 76.

31. *Ibid.*, p. 1.

32. *Theophrastus Such*, pp. 8–9.
33. *George Eliot Letters*, II, 406–10.
34. *Perceiving Women*, ed. Shirley Ardener (London: Malaby Press, 1975), p. 22; pp. viii–ix.
35. Elaine Showalter, 'Feminist criticism in the wilderness', *The New Feminist Criticism*, p. 264.
36. Mrs Humphry Ward, *A Writer's Recollections (1856–1900)* (London and Glasgow: W. Collins Sons & Co. Ltd, 1918), p. 162.

Chapter 5

Controversial Women

'It is scarcely possible to allude to Mrs. Somerville's achievements in science without some reference to her sex,' wrote the autobiographer and journalist, Edith Simcox, in 1874.[1] Mary Somerville, born nearly a century before, in 1780, rapidly became a byword for all that was truly domestic and 'womanly', though her editor-daughter, Martha, remained anxious for her mother's reputation. 'No one was more thoroughly and gracefully feminine than she was, both in manner and appearance,' Martha interposes at a convenient point in her mother's narrative; adding that 'no amount of scientific labour ever induced her to neglect her home duties.'[2] Similarly, Harriet Martineau, preparing an obituary for Florence Nightingale, who in fact outlived her by more than thirty years, insisted 'she was no declaimer but a housewifely woman . . . She was the most quiet & natural of all ladylike women; presenting no points for special observation but good sense & cultivation as to mind, & correctness in demeanour & manners.'[3] Certainly, if most mid-Victorian women novelists were eager to promote in their autobiographies a self-image of domestic efficiency, there was no shortage of female eulogists and friends to do the same for women scientists and campaigners, and preserve around them an aura of the most traditionally 'feminine' normality.

Preoccupation with the feminine ideal was at its height in the group of female activists born between about 1800 and 1840. As Martha Vicinus has shown in *Independent Women* (1985), pioneering women in all fields were faced by a shared double-bind: 'Despite often erratic schooling, they had to be equal to if not better than men intellectually, while not losing one iota of their feminine respectability.'[4] This made University women, for example, exert themselves to create an idealised homelike atmosphere in the new women's colleges at Oxford, Cambridge and London. Just as agnostics, such as George Eliot, tended to rely on a Christian vocabulary of altruism and fidelity, all the more for having discarded the mythology that generated it, pioneering women who had unsexed themselves by leaving home and demanding independent intellectual and social lives, were among the loudest exponents of domestic virtue and female duty. Frances Power Cobbe, who had waited patiently at home until her father's death when she was in her mid-thirties, before beginning a career of her own urged women in 1881 to 'give deep and well ordered reflection to the subject of morals in general, and of their own duties in particular', besides avoiding '"Bohemian" manners', and 'neglect of social *bienséances*': appearances were just as critical as actions. 'I fail to find words to say how important it seems to me that at this crisis of woman's history,' she urged, 'every one of us should, each in our small way, begin to tread the new path carefully, giving no just cause of reproach, or scandal, or ridicule.'[5] Harriet Martineau, Josephine Butler and Frances Cobbe shared Sarah Ellis's conviction that women had higher domestic instincts than men, and however unusual their attainments in a competitive public field, created a home, or more often a 'Home', wherever they went. Josephine Butler even argued circuitously that far from endangering the institution of marriage, the emancipation of women from a purely domestic arena 'would utimately, though not very soon, tend to the increase of marriage, for the worth, and therefore the attractiveness of women would be increased, and undoubtedly it would tend to the preservation of all that we wish to preserve in existing homes.'[6]

Women confronted with unconventional achievers of their own sex often reacted negatively to them, and were quick to identify 'unfeminine' characteristics in their behaviour or appearance. Fanny Kemble remained uncertain about women doctors, observing that while all the 'lady physicians' she knew appeared clever and intelligent, they had 'something hard and dry in their manner', which made her wonder whether 'something especially and essentially womanly – tenderness, softness, refinement – must either be non-existent or sacrificed in the acquirement of a manly profession and the studies it demands'.[7] For many women, this was the crux of the problem. However unfeminine their own achievements (and Fanny Kemble was not only an actress, but a divorcee), most Victorian professional women of the earlier generation were suspicious of those who had abandoned their reticence or their ladylike manners. By far the most spiteful criticisms of George Eliot came not from men, but from other women, who were unable to reconcile the all-wise, humane spirit of her narrative voice with the known facts of her unconventional lifestyle. Those who were unorthodox themselves, such as Eliza Lynn Linton and Harriet Martineau, regarded their own choice of career as unrepresentative, and generally felt that the majority of women would prefer domestic affection and responsibility.

In her *Autobiography*, Harriet Martineau makes out a special case for herself as a single woman, without disparaging the value of home ties. 'The veneration in which I hold domestic life has always shown me that that life was not for those whose self-respect had been early broken down, or had never grown. Happily, the majority are free from this disability,' she argued, placing herself in the unfortunate minority.[8]

The ideological paradox faced by all achieving Victorian women was that whereas self-assertion and independence were indispensable weapons in their armoury, the first glint of steel was likely to draw upon them not only the distrust of male politicians and administrators, but also the enmity of many of their own sex. To write about achievements won through any form of self-display, and invite applause for them, was to repeat the transgression; or, as Nancy K. Miller has put it, 'to *reinscribe* the original violation'.[9] If this was a danger for women novelists turning to autobiography, the risks were twice as great for women scientists, actresses and campaigners. Many tried to project their work as an extension of the feminine role, for example through teaching, nursing or philanthropy; but whereas novel-writing or running a charitable institution could be seen as ladylike activities, it was difficult to defend acting or lecturing in a similar way. At the same time, many of these women were acutely conscious of their individuality, the enduring sense of self that had helped them to survive. Much of their lives had been spent scribbling letters to devoted friends, and watching the success of contemporaries in related fields. Few wished to see themselves as eccentric outsiders: most, towards the end of their lives, wanted to entertain the public, and make both their peace and a comfortable pension. Some degree of compromise was nearly always unavoidable.

'the manners of a gentlewoman': Mary Somerville

The woman who most successfully reconciled the seemingly incompatible roles of dedicated wife and mother with a professional career was Mary Somerville, the mathematician, who won male recognition for her work on Laplace's *Mécanique Céleste*, and female approval for her impeccable home life. Her *Personal Recollections* (1873) succeeded in recounting a struggle for intellectual fulfilment without incurring any serious bitterness of tone in the narrative: hence the warm reviews by other women. Her development as a scientist seems to have occurred through alternating periods of perseverance and passivity. There were times when she had to wait in abeyance; others when her studies took a dramatic leap forward. But the underlying theme of her autobiography is a sense of injustice to her sex in matters of education. 'From my earliest years my mind revolted against oppression and tyranny,' she reports, 'and I resented the injustice of the world in denying all those privileges of education to my sex which were so lavishly bestowed on men.'[10] She was encouraged, like so many other women, by the work of an earlier female professional; in this case, the conduct writer, Hester Chapone. The traditional girlish occupation of sewing was, as so often, rejected as a symbol of the chosen life. 'I was annoyed that my turn for reading was so much disapproved of, and thought it unjust that women should have been given a desire for knowledge if it were wrong to acquire it' (p. 28). The word 'unjust' occurs as often as it does in the opening pages of *Jane Eyre*; yet the narrative voice is less disturbed than Mrs Oliphant's, and more certain of itself. She knew from an early age that she was 'intensely ambitious to excel in something' (p. 60) and quietly found her way round every obstacle that her old-fashioned mother and aunt placed in front of her. Presently, her scientific interests become such an integral part of her life, that allusions to them are made with matter-of-fact ease. After her first marriage, to Samuel Greig, for example, she comments: 'I was alone the whole of the day, so I continued my mathematical and other pursuits . . . as I did not go into society, I rose early, and, having plenty of time, I resumed my mathematical studies' (p. 75, pp. 77–8).

In fact, her account of this marriage makes it clear enough that Mr Greig was seriously out of sympathy with her interests, and 'had a very low opinion of the capacity of my sex' (p. 75). Soon widowed and left with two sons, she acquired enough authority to resist any further pressures from her own family; though then, as always, she maintained an orderly household: 'A great part of the day I was occupied with my children; in the evening I worked, played piquet with my father, or played on the piano, sometimes with violin accompaniment' (p. 80). When she married a second time, her husband, William Somerville, encouraged her work, although his sister hoped Mary would give up her 'foolish manner of life' and 'make a respectable and useful wife' (p. 88). Useful the new Mrs Somerville certainly proved to be, interrupting her honeymoon to make her sick brother-in-law some currant jelly: 'I made some that was excellent, and I never can forget the astonishment expressed at my being able to be so useful' (p. 89).

Half way through the autobiography (which relies increasingly on extracted letters), Mrs Somerville contrasts her 'timidity of character' with the determination exercised in the pursuit of her studies. 'They were perpetually interrupted, but always resumed at the first opportunity. No analysis is so difficult as that of one's own mind, but I do not think I err much in saying that perseverance is a characteristic of mine' (p. 141). She puts it with evasionary modesty, but her impression is borne out by the shape of her narrative, which is a tale of quiet determination and the undramatic overturning of conventional notions as to a woman's duties. Like John Stuart Mill in *The Subjection of Women* (1869), she recognised that a woman's time for private study was liable to intrusion:

> I rose early and made such arrangements with regard to my children and family affairs that I had time to write afterwards; not, however, without many interruptions. A man can always command his time under the plea of business, a woman is not allowed any such excuse. At Chelsea I was always supposed to be at home, and as my friends and acquaintances came so far out of their way on purpose to see me, it would have been unkind and ungenerous not to receive them. Nevertheless, I was sometimes annoyed when in the midst of a difficult problem some one would enter and say, 'I have come to spend a few hours with you.' However, I learnt by habit to leave a subject and resume it again at once, like putting a mark into a book I might be reading; this was the more necessary as there was no fireplace in my little room, and I had to write in the drawing-room in winter. Frequently I hid my papers as soon as the bell announced a visitor, lest anyone should discover my secret. (pp. 163–4)

This passage is quoted at length to show the pendulum movement of obstacles intruded and overcome by steady perseverance. First, she attends to her household responsibilities; then well-meaning but unwelcome visitors barge in; and all the time she is training herself to adapt to the rhythms of interruption, as Jane Austen did. The general reference to differences between male and female working habits shows her theoretical awareness of a much larger problem than her own; yet she avoids any stridency, merely stating her opinion in the same calm, measured tones as in the rest of her narrative. Just as she does not question the absence of a fire in her room (or wonder why it could not be exchanged for one with a fireplace), she accepts the inconveniences of her life and navigates round them.

Mary Somerville remained conscious all her life of her inadequate education and poor training in argument. At the end of her *Personal Recollections* she attempts a summary of her own character, which emphasises all the deficiences she shared with other women of her generation.

> In my youth I had to contend with prejudice and illiberality; yet I was of a quiet temper, and easy to live with, and I never interfered with or pryed into other people's affairs... I was not good at argument; I was apt to lose my temper; but I never bore ill will to any one, or forgot the manners of a gentle-woman, however angry I may have been at the time. (pp. 347–8)

This last admission strikes a curiously archaic ring; yet to Mary Somerville, it was clearly important. Similarly, when Lord Brougham invited her to write an account of the *Mécanique Céleste* for the Society for the Diffusion of Useful Knowledge, she was sure that her 'self-acquired knowledge was so far inferior to that of the men who had been educated in our universities that it would be the height of presumption to attempt to write on such a subject, or indeed on any other' (p. 163). Accordingly, she declared her doubts, but accepted the advice of Brougham and her husband, and wrote the book. 'Thus suddenly and unexpectedly the whole character and course of my future life was changed' (p. 163). This turn of events is typical of the erratic pattern traced by many women's autobiographies in the nineteenth century. Unlike Trollope, who trained all his life as a professional novelist, or John Stuart Mill, who was trained by his father to the work of a political economist, or Ruskin, who worked steadily as an art critic, many Victorian women record a moment of triumphant breakthrough, when at last their interrupted, half-secretive efforts seemed justified. The key word here is 'unexpectedly', and the passive construction of the sentence underlines the ultimate powerlessness of even the most determined woman at a time when male validation of her work was essential. Her excitement is considerably more transparent and naive than anything to be found in a male autobiography of the time. 'I was surprised and pleased beyond measure to find that my book should be so much approved of by Dr. Whewell, one of the most eminent men of the age for science and literature.... I was astonished at the success of my book; all the reviews of it were highly favourable; I received letters of congratulation from many men of science' (pp. 172–3).

'I wrote because it was impossible for me to be idle,' Mary Somerville states soon after retelling this episode (p. 203): a sequence of cause and effect that is less obvious and matter-of-fact than it would appear. Throughout her *Personal Recollections*, she tries to minimise her own unconventionality; to explain in the most reasonable terms how she managed the conflicting interests of her life. Adding to the otherwise completed book in 1872, when she was ninety-two years old, she confessed to a continuing taste for the problems of higher algebra. 'Sometimes I find them difficult, but my old obstinacy remains, for if I do not succeed to-day, I attack them again on the morrow' (p. 364). This seems to have been her solution to the more intractable problems of being a woman of science in a patriarchal society.

'no organised surface': Fanny Kemble and Ellen Terry

If science was considered an unsuitable profession for a woman, the stage was rated hardly better than prostitution: at least in the 1820s, when

Fanny Kemble made her debut as Juliet at Covent Garden. Kemble herself regarded acting as 'public exhibition, unworthy of a woman',[11] although she never lost a sense of exhilaration at *becoming* the part she was playing, or pronouncing the greatest soliloquies in Shakespeare, when she subsequently made a career from giving public readings. In an article for the *Cornhill*, in 1863, long after she had left the stage, even for the second time, she described the 'dramatic art' as combining for her 'elements at once so congenial and so antagonistic' to her nature.[12] It had never been necessary for Mary Somerville, at any stage in her career, to apologise for the antagonistic effects of the higher algebra, which was, after all, a study that could be pursued quietly at home, as innocently as if it were music or drawing. The reputation of actresses had, to some extent, been redeemed by Kemble's aunt, Sarah Siddons, and the Kembles were viewed collectively as a respectable enough theatrical dynasty; but many critics, male and female, were uneasy about the long-term effects of a stage career on the volatile emotions of a woman. J. W. Croker in the *Quarterly*, reviewing Kemble's *Journal* (1835), felt the life of an actress, with her 'habits of individual thought, study and exertion', 'acquired confidence', and 'familiarity with bargains, business, and bustle', must all tend to 'weaken the sense of feminine dependency':

> An actress lives fast: her existence is a perpetual wrestling-match, and one *season* gives her more experience – and with experience, more of the nerve and hard features of the world – than a whole life of domestic duties could do. In short, a *young actress* may be in mind and character an *old woman*.[13]

Over twenty years later, reviewers were still conscious of a prejudice, among their readers, against the theatre as a career for respectable people. 'The objection to the theatre which most good people make,' said the *Saturday Review*, 'is, that actors and actresses are not virtuous characters, or rather, although modesty and prudery may forbid them saying so plainly, they do not much care about the men, but they think that the women are bad.'[14] Here, too, the all-pervasive double-standard, so rampant in Victorian society, made what was more or less acceptable for men (Dickens's friend, William Charles Macready, though an actor, was a decent family man), decidedly risky for women. To the *Saturday Review*, as to many other uncomfortable commentators, the stage was a place of vanity and temptation, where a woman was taught to acquire artificial manners, to weep and laugh and fall in love on demand. 'The life of an actress is to the world at large a curious *terra incognita* peopled by forbidding phantoms of evil or seductive visions of pleasure and success,' the *Englishwoman's Journal* concluded in 1859, thirty years after Fanny Kemble's debut; 'as a gifted woman's devotion to art, or the honest and laborious means by which she earns her bread, the vocation of the actress is understood by few.'[15] Responses to the great tragic actress Rachel, particularly from other women, revealed a deep-seated fear of artificially invoked female passion. Charlotte Brontë's famous recreation of Rachel's dramatic powers, as Vashti in *Villette* (1853) embodies everything that frightened her awe-struck audiences. 'I found her something neither of woman nor of man: in each of her eyes sat a devil,' remembers the cautious female narrator, Lucy Snowe. 'Hate and murder and madness incarnate she stood.'[16] Even Fanny Kemble felt slightly queasy watching Rachel in 1841, when she ran through the full gamut of turbulent passions for which she was noted: 'scorn, hatred, revenge, vitriolic irony, concentrated rage, seething jealousy, and a fierce love which seems in its excess allied to all the evil which sometimes springs from that bittersweet root.'[17]

Fanny Kemble never smouldered as ominously as Rachel, but she clearly understood the moral uncertainties of a theatrical career. Yet compounding one moral nightmare with another, she married an American planter and slave-holder, Pierce Butler, in 1834, published her journals, including a critical account of her residence on her husband's plantation in Georgia, slipped her traces as a married woman and spent long holidays back in London with her family, returned to the stage (not altogether successfully) in 1847, was divorced two years later, and occupied the rest of her life giving public readings, travelling to and fro across the Atlantic, and publishing volumes of her personal memoirs. The first of these, *Record of a Girlhood* (1878), was serialised in the *Atlantic Monthly* and is the best of her tripartite and leisurely ramble through the pleasanter aspects of her theatrical history. She purposely omitted anything that would be disturbing, either to herself, or to her conjectural reader. 'My motive in publishing is *purely sordid*,' she told William Dean Howells of the *Atlantic Monthly*;[18] and the act of composition was assisted by the vast collection of her own letters to her lifelong friend, Harriet St Leger, who obligingly kept and returned them, for Kemble to sift and burn. 'My letters constitute a ready written autobiography,' she realised in 1875, surprised at the wealth of material they contained.[19] 'In going over the immense mass of letters you returned to me,' she informed Harriet St Leger, 'I am astonished at the minute and abundant details of the events of my life which the all but daily history of it, in my correspondence, conveyed to you.' By then, she felt that quite so much detail was unfortunate; the letters themselves might well appear 'monotonous and dull to almost as great a degree as they are egotistical'. Already, in 1847, she had begun to have doubts about the worth of her letters. She thought they were more like 'imperfect essays than letters', because of her 'tendency to discussion', and she had neither room nor time in them to say anything as she wished to say it. 'Then, I have an indescribable impatience of the mere mechanical process.' She even wondered whether writing so many letters prevented her from producing something more genuinely 'literary', a novel or a play, perhaps.[20]

However unsatisfactory she found the letter as a medium of communication, Fanny Kemble continued to use it throughout her life. What she originally said to Harriet St Leger, or anyone else, about her husband, Pierce Butler, and the difficulties of their marriage, was carefully excised from the published version of her experiences, which were arranged primarily for the reader's entertainment:

> I have come to the garrulous time of life – to the remembering days, which only by a little precede the forgetting ones. I have much leisure, and feel sure that it will amuse me to write my own reminiscences; perhaps reading them may amuse others who have no more to do than I have. To the idle, then, I offer these lightest of leaves gathered in the idle end of autumn days, which have succeeded years of labour often severe and sad enough, though its ostensible purpose was only that of affording recreation to the public.[21]

The faint escape of discontent towards the end of her light-hearted introduction is soon blocked off, and not allowed then, or at any other point in her reminiscences to cloud the atmosphere. The most truly autobiographical portions come at the beginning of her *Record*, when she had no letters to quote. The two subsequent books, *Records of Later Life* (1882) and *Further Records. 1848–1883* (1890), are put together almost entirely from letters, with the minimum of explanatory commentary, and for that reason can hardly be treated as autobiography in the structural sense. They make no attempt to see her life as a coherent whole; only as a succession of adventures and collisions with other people. Henry James's observation that 'Mrs. Kemble has no organised surface at all,' could be applied equally well to the presentation of her life in its numerous volumes.[22]

As Mrs Oliphant noticed, in her review of the *Girlhood* titles, the most interesting part is the story of Fanny Kemble's entrance into the world as an actress.[23] As so often in Victorian women's autobiography, the chance beginning of her career is described in terms of resonant ambiguity. A rebellious child, she plunged into a restlessly romantic adolescence. 'I had become moody and fantastical for want of solid wholesome mental occupation, and the excess of imaginative stimulus in my life, and was possessed with a wild desire for an existence of lonely independence,' she recalls of the months immediately before her family decided to try her on the stage.[24] Extracted letters to Harriet prove that acting was the very reverse of her inclinations, and she had adopted it only to help her father, who was in severe financial straits. From the beginning, however, she enjoyed the intoxicating effects of what she called 'dramatic persona-tion', as her account of a voice-trial for Juliet shows:

> Set down in the midst of twilight space, as it were, with only my father's voice coming to me from where he stood hardly distinguishable in the gloom, in those poetical utterances of pathetic passion I was seized with the spirit of the thing; my voice resounded through the great vault above and below me, and completely carried away by the inspiration of the wonderful play, I acted Juliet as I do not believe I ever acted it again, for I had no visible Romeo, and no audience to thwart my imagination. (*Record*, II, 7–8)

The structure of every sentence accentuates her lack of responsibility for what she was doing: she was 'set down', 'seized with the spirit of the thing', and 'completely carried away' by the beauty of her speeches, and perhaps by the God-like quality of her father's disembodied voice booming out of the darkness. Mesmerised into obedience, with no Romeo to inhibit her 'unfeminine' display of sexual feeling, she acquired a new kind of boldness, expressed by 'my voice resounded' and 'I acted Juliet as I do not believe I ever acted it again'.

At least she was conscious of the dangers gaping for an exhilarated Juliet, and forced herself into a round of 'systematic pursuits and monotonous habits':

> Amid infinite anguish and errors, existence may preserve a species of outward symmetry and harmony from this strong band of minute obser-vance, keeping down and assisting the mind to master elements of moral and mental discord and disorder, for the due control of which the daily and hourly subjection to recurring rules is an invaluable auxiliary to higher influences. The external practice does not supply, but powerfully supple-ments, the internal principles of self-control. (II, 58)

This last sentence – if not the whole paragraph – might have been taken from Mrs Ellis, or some other tight-lipped conduct-writer of the time. As it was, other professionally successful women who had led erratic lives claimed to prefer the monotonous routines of home and family responsibilities to the public attentions of their professional lives. Mrs Oliphant was happiest bathing her children and putting them to bed; Harriet Martineau bored Robert Browning with accounts of her custard and gingerbread making; Ellen Terry claimed to have enjoyed pottering about in the country with ducks and children.[25]

Fanny Kemble, meanwhile, emphasised that her going on the stage was an act of filial obedience: 'of duty and conformity to the will of my parents, strengthened by my own conviction that I was bound to help them by every means in my power' (*Record*, II, 13). As frenzied lover, she was risking herself in an anarchic role; as dutiful daughter, helping to save her family from economic ruin, she was behaving with exemplary unselfishness and fortitude. 'And so my life was determined, and I devoted myself to an avocation which I never liked or honoured, and about the very nature of which I have never been able to come to any decided opinion' (II, 60–1). She says this so often and in so many different contexts throughout her life, that one must take her at her word, though it gives her autobiographical writing an uneasy instability. On the one hand, she is clearly stimulated and excited by her success, particularly at the beginning of her theatrical career; on the other, her innate modesty seems to have shrunk from the gaze of audiences, and her genuine piety, instilled by her education, distrusted the exhibitionism of young female roles.

In the second volume of her *Record*, Fanny Kemble tries, spasmodically, to understand her own dislike of the stage. After all, her parents both acted, and never discussed the moral dangers of their profession; 'but the vapid vacuity of my aunt Siddons's life had made a profound impression upon me' (II, 64). As so often in women's autobiography, the example of another woman's professional experience made a deeper impact than the less comparable one of a man. 'Were it possible to act with one's *mind* alone, the case might be different,' she conceded a year after her debut; 'but the body is so indispensable, unluckily, to the execution of one's most poetical conceptions on the stage, that the imaginative powers are under very severe through imperceptible restraint. Acting seems to me rather like dancing hornpipes in fetters' (II, 171). The more she worried about it, the more self-absorbed she seemed, and the guiltier she felt. 'You see', she told her friend, Harriet St Leger, 'I write as I talk, still about myself; and I am sometimes afraid that my very desire to improve keeps me occupied too much about myself, and will make a little moral egotist of me' (II, 174).

Distrusting introspection, though at various times in her life she obtained relief from keeping a journal, Fanny Kemble began to question the nature of her own identity and the kind of communication open to isolated individuals. 'Then, upon reflection, few things have ever puzzled me more than the fact of people liking *me* because I pretended to be a pack of Juliets and Belivideras, and creatures who were *not* me,' she confided to Lady Dacre in 1840, by which time she had retired from the stage, and was unhappily married. 'Perhaps *I was jealous of my parts.*'[26] Professionally trained to be anyone but her real self, she had to rediscover her identity, which was, in any case, lost in her new name of Mrs Pierce Butler and her amphibious life as an American planter's wife during some months of the year and the pet of London hostesses on her prolonged visits to England. As it was, she noticed 'the abyss of individualism which separates one human being from another'. 'Do you not know that to misunderstand and be misunderstood is one of the inevitable conditions, and, I think, one of the especial purposes of our existence?' she asked Harriet St Leger.[27]

It was especially the case for a divorced actress in the middle of the nineteenth century. The diarist, Charles Greville, who met her in 1842, when her marriage was not yet over but was visibly strained, thought she would have done better to study her husband's character, and acquire a sense of domestic duty, instead of writing journals, tragedies and poems. He added that 'she now casts many longing, lingering looks back towards the stage, the scene of her triumphs, the source of independence, and compares the condition from which she once so desired to escape with her present lot.'[28] Clearly, Fanny Kemble's uncertainty about her selfhood, at once so separate, yet merged into all the parts she had acted, was compounded by a continued attraction to the stage. On the question of women's rights, she also remained uncertain. She believed that women should be better educated, but that their ultimate destiny of motherhood was perhaps inevitable, and should not be neglected for anything else. That she chose to preserve letters in which she makes these declarations implies that as she was compiling her autobiographies, these were the views she wanted to endorse. 'I do not think nature intended mothers to be authors of anything but their babies,' she told the unmarried Harriet St Leger rather primly in 1836. 'I cannot read a book through quietly for mine; judge, therefore, how little likely I am to write one.'[29] Four years later, she was telling Anna Jameson, also childless:

> My serious interest in life is the care of my children, and my principal recreation is my garden; and though I formerly sometimes imagined I had faculties whose exercise might demand a wider sphere, the consciousness that I discharge very imperfectly the obligations of that which I occupy, ought to satisfy me that its homely duties and modest tasks are more than sufficient for my abilities; and though I am not satisfied with myself, I should be with my existence, since, such as it is, it furnishes me with more work than I do as it should be done.[30]

In fact, she was profoundly dissatisfied. Even after rigorous pruning, her letters from America chafe with boredom and frustration at the lack of any intellectual stimulus or interesting social life, while her frenetic interludes in London, dining out and visiting, were like oases in her marital desert. In the 1870s, when she began work on the autobiographies, she was friendly with Frances Power Cobbe, whose views on women she found somewhat extreme. Despite her own unsatisfactory marriage, Fanny Kemble continued to declare the bearing and care of children 'woman's natural calling'; whereas 'Fanny Cobbe ... believes she may find or make a better business for herself, with which opinion I do not at all agree.'[31] Like Harriet Martineau, Fanny Kemble thought that women should be allowed to do whatever they could, even be soldiers if they wanted to; but she still felt there was a 'natural law, by which women are constituted and constitute themselves the *subjects* of men'.[32] This remained her utter conviction throughout her life, although she allowed her *Records* to express occasional dissatisfaction with this so-called 'natural' law. 'Oh, how I wish I was a man! How I wish I owned these slaves!' she declared, appalled by conditions on her husband's plantations; while from Philadelphia, she followed the news at home and wished she could participate. 'If I were a man in England, I should like to devote my life to the cause of national progress, carried on through party politics and public legislation.'[33]

Being a woman, she was unable to do anything of the kind, and like many of her contemporaries, atoned for her unconventional way of life by issuing soundly traditional advice. The woman who had always resisted her husband's will, and believed that marriage was a partnership of equals, decided in 1847 that the whole value and meaning of life 'lies in the single sense of conscience – duty'. Her passionate impersonation of Juliet subsided into reverent readings of Shakespeare at a table; an attempt to use her 'small gift *dutifully*', inspired by the '*virtue* of Shakespeare's works'.[34] Seeing the course of her life as 'determined' by circumstances beyond her control, all she could do was adapt, and make the best of things.

From time to time, the elderly Fanny reproves the naive effusions of the young married self discovering America, but clearly all the more painful passages of her life have been removed. Even her success as Juliet is transformed into a Cinderella story, in which the heroine exchanges the 'faded, threadbare, turned, and dyed frocks' that she normally wore, for 'fashionably made dresses of fresh colours and fine texture'. As she herself recognises, every condition of her life had been altered, 'as by the wand of a fairy'. The fairy tale analogy both reduces the extent of her active participation in the metamorphosis and provides an emotional outlet for her retrospective exhilaration. But to placate the disapproving, she mingles delight with dark warnings. 'God knows,' she ends balefully, 'how pitiful a preparation all this tinsel sudden success and popularity formed for the duties and trials of my after-life.'[35] Mrs Oliphant admired the 'total absence of all self-assertion and independence' in the narrative.[36]

Fanny Kemble evades a full investigation of her developing self by deliberately setting out to entertain, and keeping to the safe, well-trodden path of anecdotal memoirs. Ellen Terry, writing thirty years later, evades the same unwelcome subject by claiming literary amateurism and narrating instead a tribute to her theatrical partner, Henry Irving, who dominates the second half of the book. Virginia Woolf saw the self-written Ellen Terry as essentially splintered; a contradictory bundle of scattered sketches: 'mother, wife, cook, critic, actress', and possibly painter.[37] Ellen Terry's Introduction to *The Story of My Life* (1908) reinforces this notion of a disconnected narrative. She has put off telling her story for so long that her recollections are 'hazy and fragmentary', and her old diaries destroyed. Even the diaries, composed of newspaper cuttings, telegrams, photographs, letters and dried flowers, had become 'a bursting, groaning dustbin of information, for the most part useless'.[38] From this welter of chaos, a rejection of conventional literary form, eventually emerged a more sober narrative, but still a fragmented one, omitting the details of her unsuccessful marriage to the painter G. F. Watts when she was sixteen, and glossing over the years she lived, unmarried, with Edward Godwin. Tacked to the end is an 'Apologia', in which she says, somewhat disingenuously, one suspects, that a good deal has been left out 'through want of skill in selection', and 'some things have been included which perhaps it would have been wiser to omit' (p. 212).

In fact, Ellen Terry was keenly aware of the generic problems facing the intending autobiographer, and the most interesting parts of her book are those where she tries to address them. Like many other Victorian women, she makes it clear that the impulse to write her own life came from outside. It was 'suggested' to her, and as she had had an eventful life, 'something would be expected' of her (p. vii). She wished that she could write about her childhood as Tolstoy had done, or her girlhood, like Marie Bashkirtseff: 'But it is not given to all of us to see our lives in relief as we look back. Most of us, I think, see them in perspective, of which our birth is the vanishing point. Seeing, too, is only half the battle. How few people can describe what they see!' (pp. vii–viii). When urged by a male friend to write down the first thing she could remember, she realised that she was 'not leaving a human document for the benefit of future psychologists and historians, but telling as much of my story as I could remember to the good, living public which has been considerate and faithful to me for so many years' (p. viii). Once her task was deprofessionalised and given a human, personal face, the train of memories was released, and she was able to begin.

Nevertheless, her doubts returned; and in the 'Apologia', she confronts the impossibility of writing a life. 'During my struggles with my refractory, fragmentary, and unsatisfactory memories, I have realised that life itself is a point of view: is, to put it more clearly, imagination' (p. 213). At this juncture, she constructs a defensive dialogue with an implied 'disappointed interlocutor', who says the autobiography has said a great deal about life in the theatre,

> but after all, your whole life has not been lived in the theatre. Have you nothing to tell us about your different homes, your family life, your social diversions, your friends and acquaintances? During your life there have been great changes in manners and customs; political parties have altered; a great Queen has died; your country has been engaged in two or three serious wars. Did all these things make no impression on you? Can you tell us nothing of your life in the world? (p. 213)

These, presumably, are the contents of the 'human document' Ellen Terry declined to write for the benefit of psychologists and historians. Instead, she confesses to having lived very little 'in the world', as the life of an actress belongs to the theatre. 'When I am not acting, the best part of my time is taken up by the most humdrum occupations' (p. 213). In place of the observations on political parties and changing customs, she concludes with a piece on the death of Henry Irving, extracts from letters to her, and 'Bits from my Diary', 'almost worthless' for her present purposes: 'Yet because things written at the time are considered by some people to be more reliable than those written years afterwards when memory calls in imagination to her help, I have hunted up a few passages from my diaries between 1887 and 1901' (p. 236). In a final curtain call, she concludes: 'If I have not revealed myself to you, or succeeded in giving a faithful picture of an actor's life, perhaps I have shown what years of practice and labour are needed for the attainment of a permanent position on the stage' (p. 240). The actress, who by virtue of her profession, concealed her essential self within the parts she played, and gives only a discontinuous picture of her personal life, thus remains hidden to the very end of the autobiography.

Like Fanny Kemble, Ellen Terry is torn between loyalty to her own love of acting, and apparent desire to conciliate an audience aware of grave irregularities in her lifestyle: in this case, three marriages, one liaison, and two illegitimate children. Contemporaries seemed to make generous allowances for her chequered history. Lady Salisbury considered her *'never* immoral, only rather illegal'; while Christopher St John, a woman friend, who edited Terry's correspondence with George Bernard Shaw, called her 'a woman of very exceptional virtue without having the smallest respect for the law'.[39] Ambiguity is decidedly the hallmark of her autobiography, as she shuttles cheerfully between her years of temporary retirement and her triumphant returns to the stage. Describing herself as 'more woman than artist', she contrasts her tastes with Henry Irving's; he entirely lacking her *'bourgeois* qualities – the love of being in love, the love of a home, the dislike of solitude. I have always thought it hard to find my inferiors. He was sure of his high place' (p. 95). Like the Kembles, the Terrys were a respectable theatrical family, and in any case, acting was becoming a more acceptable, and certainly a more popular, profession for women during the second half of the century. Nevertheless, perhaps because of her own problematic history, Ellen Terry depicts herself essentially as a 'womanly woman' (p. 211), the character by which she was known on stage. 'Never at any time in my life have I been ambitious,' she insists (having, like Fanny Kemble, gravitated naturally towards a theatrical career): 'I was just dreaming and aspiring after another world, a world full of pictures and music and gentle, artistic people with quiet voices and elegant manners' (p. 30) – in other words, the very opposite of the theatrical world, where voices were loud and manners crude. It was also a deceptive daydream, leading to the disastrous marriage to G. F. Watts. About this episode, she is particularly evasive, her narrative dissolving into impressionistic flashes whenever her subject becomes potentially awkward. As so often in autobiography by Victorian women, she says little about how she met her husband, or the process of courtship. With a retentive memory for clothes (though not, apparently, for lines), she says far more about what she was wearing on her wedding day than what she felt about it. 'It all seems now like a dream – not a clear dream, but a fitful one which in the morning one tries in vain to tell. And even if I could tell it, I would not' (p. 33). At the end of the same chapter, she says that the past is now 'like a story in a book' that she once read (p. 37): in each case, she transmutes her experience into other narrative forms, an incoherent, half-forgotten dream, and a distant, completed story, both forms that evade interpretation. She clings instead to shapes and colours, non-verbal, primal memories: her brown silk gown, her white bonnet, her sealskin jacket with coral buttons, her swollen nose (from crying, which Mr Watts considered inartistic), and the fair hair of her brothers and sisters whom she bathed for the last time on her wedding morning.

The marriage itself is mostly described in terms of the famous people she met through her husband's literary and artistic contacts. Throughout this section of her narrative, Ellen Terry preserves an air of innocence and trance-like passivity, which minimises her sexual commitment to the marriage. 'I wondered at the new life, and worshipped it because of its beauty. When it suddenly came to an end, I was thunderstruck; and refused at first to consent to the separation, which was arranged for me in much the same way as my marriage had been' (p. 37). Afterwards, she was at pains to explain that the marriage had been less unhappy than people thought, whatever the rumours; 'and I forestall them by saying that it in many ways was very happy indeed. What bitterness there was effaced itself in a very remarkable way' (p. 37).

Her elopement with Godwin was less easy to whitewash, though his name is never mentioned, and her children enter the narrative (and evidently the world) without a father:

> Soon afterwards I left the stage for six years, without the slightest idea of ever going back. I left it without regret. And I was very happy, leading a quiet, domestic life in the heart of the country. When my two children were born, I thought of the stage less than ever. They absorbed all my time, all my interest, all my love. (p. 47)

Her announcement of this change is authoritative, calm and simple, as if to silence questions or criticisms. On the next page, she compares her departure from the stage with her sister Kate's, though Kate left to get married, and surrounds her new life with the altruistic aura of an act of self-sacrifice. 'I have been happiest in my work when I was working for some one else. I admire those impersonal people who care for nothing outside their own ambition, yet I detest them at the same time, and I have the simplest faith that absolute devotion to another human being means the greatest *happiness*' (p. 49). Such protestations reduce the element of conflict that inevitably affected her commitment both to career and children; and she implies, again through the use of timeless, unstructured impressions, that her six years of family life in the country could have gone on indefinitely, had she not been called back to the stage. Her baby-stories recall Mrs Oliphant's preference for these over descriptions of her books, and the self-mockery of her half-apologies for them. 'I feel that if I go maundering on much longer about my children,' says Ellen Terry, 'some one will exclaim, with a witty and delightful author when he saw "Peter Pan" for the seventh time: "Oh, for an hour of Herod!"' (p. 51). Memories of her children and their naive sayings make her want to cry, but she questions whether anyone else would be interested. The gap between the private and the public aspects of her life fissures the connectedness of her story, as she appears to recognise herself. On her return to the stage, 'Teddy' and 'Edy', in their little Japanese costumes, 'disappear from these pages for quite a long time. But all this time, you must understand, they are educating their mother!' (p. 54).

Much as she enjoyed her rural idyll, Ellen Terry admits that Henry Irving would hardly have left the stage for six months, let alone six years (p. 49), and when she was back herself, her exhilaration was all too obvious. Playing Portia in *The Merchant of Venice* she described as 'a wonderful time' (p. 68), during which it was difficult to maintain the correct air of womanly propriety. 'Everyone seemed to be in love with me! I had sweethearts by the dozen, known and unknown.' While Shylock completely failed, she enjoyed 'the feeling of the conqueror' which comes to an actress perhaps once in a lifetime. 'Elation, triumph, being lifted on high by a single stroke of the mighty wing of glory – call it by any name, think of it as you like – it was as Portia that I had my first and last sense of it' (p. 67). Her greatest anxiety, when she acted the same part later at the Lyceum was lest she had shown 'too much of a "coming-on" disposition in the Casket Scene'. Any suggestion of *'indelicacy'* in her treatment of a part, she added, always 'blighted' her (p. 118). She adds maternally that it was for her children's sake that she was most glad of her increasing prosperity as an actress (p. 86).

More unconventional than Fanny Kemble, Ellen Terry also finds a way of repeating praise for her more successful parts. Whereas Kemble quoted mostly harmless descriptive extracts from her own letters, Terry interpolates letters from other people, complimenting her on her performances; in *Much Ado About Nothing* for instance ('The Terry was glorious', A. J. Duffield wrote to Henry Irving, who passed the letter on to Terry 'because it had some ridiculously nice things about me in it', p. 146); and *Macbeth*, which was praised by Edward Burne-Jones via a letter from Lady Pollock (p. 197). Occasionally, she even applauds herself directly, noting that as Lucy Ashton, in an adaptation of *The Bride of Lammermoor*, she was able to make an effect with hardly a word to say. 'The love scene at the well I did nicely too' (p. 200). The sense of propriety that made Fanny Kemble recoil from self-praise was no longer so potent by 1908 when Ellen Terry was reviewing her life; and her marriages and partnership with Henry Irving having ended, she sought acknowledgement of the real successes she had achieved.

In 1907, she had, however, married for the third time, and the closing sections of the autobiography become a scrapbook of letters, diary entries and hasty recollections, designed primarily to amuse. She concluded on the last page that actors and actresses *see* many people, but *know* very few; and in any case, she thinks as little of the future as she does of the past. 'The present is for me!' (p. 240). Her final comment connects neatly with her first memory: of being locked in an attic while her parents were at the theatre, and having the sunset, some 'flaming forges' and the oak bureau to contemplate. The powerful sensory impressions of the present, not a disturbing interpretation of a constant core of self, compose the essence, both of Ellen Terry's autobiography, and of Fanny Kemble's.

'the Duties of Women': Frances Power Cobbe and Annie Besant

When she was wondering what to do with her memoirs, Fanny Kemble showed them to her feminist friend, Frances Power Cobbe, who induced her to take them back and publish them herself as autobiography. Otherwise, decided Frances Power Cobbe twenty years later, she would have written Fanny Kemble's biography. Instead, she enjoyed reading the published 'delightful *Records*' of her friend, and even borrowed Kemble's intended title of 'Old Woman's Gossip' for use in the preface to her own autobiography, the *Life of Frances Power Cobbe* (1894). She also reviewed Mrs Somerville's *Personal Recollections* for the *Quarterly*, and took great interest in the work of her female contemporaries. She concluded that she had met most of them, except George Eliot and Harriet Martineau, and so when she spoke of her work for women's rights, she did so 'with practical personal knowledge of what women are and can be, both as to character and ability'.[40]

Although she campaigned for the admission of women to university degrees, the medical profession and other forms of employment, besides improvements in the married women's property law, and extension of the suffrage to women, Frances Power Cobbe maintains in her *Life* that women are 'the equivalents, though not the equals, of men'.[41] The ambiguity is characteristic of her stance throughout the *Life*. On the one hand, she was a completely fulfilled single woman, who enjoyed her professional life; on the other, she knew she had experienced special difficulties because of her social role as a woman. Yet 'duty' was the lesson she preached above all others, as the natural concomitant of 'rights'. Her object in giving six lectures in 1881 on the *Duties of Women*, she explains, 'was to impress women as strongly as might be in my power, with the unspeakable importance of adding to our claims for just *Rights* of all kinds, the adoption of the higher standard of *Duty*' (II, 233). Hence her retreat in the *Life* from overt rebellion against the limitations of her lot. Her method, like Mary Somerville's, was to work patiently, and circumvent immovable obstacles.

Frances Cobbe tried to make her *Life* 'the true and complete history of a woman's existence *as seen from within*; a real LIFE, which he who reads may take as representing fairly the joys, sorrows and interests, the powers and limitations of one of my sex and class in the era which is now drawing to a close' (I, iv–v). She therefore intended her autobiography to have a fully representative quality, in accordance with a contemporary interest in character, rather than action, as outlined earlier in her preface. Her method was to build up a picture by 'small touches' and 'trifling memories', a retrospect which was 'a pleasure' to compile. Of all the autobiographers in this section, Cobbe seems the happiest, and she had the least to hide; yet if her personal life was irreproachable, her opinions were not. Quite apart from her feminism, which Fanny Kemble, for one, found overpowering, there was her 'deconversion' from Evangelicalism, through agnosticism, to Theism, and her outspoken campaign against vivisection. Her allusion to the 'powers and limitations' of her sex in fact defines the divided impulses of her *Life*, which alternately affirms her enjoyment of an independent career, and upholds the importance of female altruism and usefulness.

Beginning with a reference to her strong physical health, Frances Power Cobbe declares:

> Had I been a man, and had possessed my brother's faculties for entering Parliament or any profession, I have sometimes dreamed I could have made my mark and done some masculine service to my fellow-creatures. But the woman's destiny which God allotted to me has been, I do not question, the best and happiest for me; nor have I ever seriously wished it had been otherwise, albeit I have gone through life without that interest which has been styled 'woman's whole existence'. Perhaps if this book be found to have any value it will partly consist in the evidence it must now afford of how pleasant and interesting, and withal, I hope, not altogether useless a life is open to a woman, though no man has ever desired to share it, nor has she seen the man she would have wished to ask her to do so. (I, 4–5)

Even Fanny Kemble had wished to be a man, so that she could devote herself to the cause of national progress: Cobbe, a more earnest activist, clearly knew her social and legal disabilities as a woman had obstructed her work as a reformer. Nevertheless, she uses the rest of the passage to demonstrate that she is satisfied with her lot, and to justify the feminine usefulness of a life without marriage. Yet her terms are hesitant, and leave room for doubt. An undercurrent of wishing and dreaming disturbs the confidence of her avowals. She has never 'seriously' wished her life had been otherwise, she does not 'question' it (though the opening sentence does, by implication); she hopes a 'not altogether useless' life is open to an unmarried woman, and she is conscious throughout the passage that her position is anomalous and lacking. How, therefore, can it be the 'real LIFE' or representative female experience she outlined in her preface?

Cobbe worked hard as a journalist to redeem the single woman from a history of mockery and pity. Her *Essays on the Pursuits of Women* (1863) were aimed specifically at unmarried women, and in a signed article for *Fraser's Magazine*, 'Celibacy v. Marriage' (1862), she insisted that 'the "old maid" of 1861 is an exceedingly cheery personage, running about untrammelled by husband or children . . . "My life, and what I shall do with it?" is a problem to which she finds the happiest solution ready to hand in schools and hospitals without number.' If 'untrammelled' was a negative account of the single woman, Cobbe concluded that she has 'not fewer duties than other women, only more diffused ones'.[41] The image of the 'cheery personage, running about' and assuming wider duties than those available to most married women, is precisely the impression given by Cobbe's self-portrait in her *Life*.

'If I have become in mature years a "Woman's Rights' Woman" it has not been because in my own person I have been made to feel a Woman's Wrongs,' Cobbe explains carefully at an early stage of her autobiography (I, 31). Beginning with her solitary childhood as the only daughter and youngest child of ageing parents, she depicts herself as 'a very merry little chick' (p. 35), devoted to her mother, and growing up free from distracting romances. After a purely ornamental education at a boarding school in Brighton, she embarked, like so many of her female contemporaries, both in fiction and in real life, on a more substantial course of private study; for many women, the most rewarding way of transcending the limitations of their role. Aware that her passion for History and Greek was uncharacteristic of most young women's interests, Cobbe boasted that her geometry tutor said he was able to teach her 'in one lesson as many propositions as he habitually taught the undergraduates of Dublin College in two' (I, 70). Then she hastily assures her readers that she was properly attentive to her household duties, which she accepted 'with pleasure':

> I love a well-ordered house and table, rooms pleasantly arranged and lighted, and decorated with flowers, hospitable attentions to guests, and all the other pleasant cares of the mistress of a family. In the midst of my studies I always went every morning regularly to my housekeeper's room and wrote out a careful *menu* for the upstairs and downstairs meals. (I, 75)

Even when she lost her religious faith and was sent away, because of her 'heresies', to cool off for a while on her brother's farm in the wilds of Donegal, she remained fully conscious of, and committed to her 'duties.' Her first book, arising from guilty feelings during an attack of bronchitis at the age of thirty, was motivated by apparent altruism, the desire to help other people discover, as she had done, a system of ethics which supplied grounds other than religious ones for a life of duty.

Even so, her writing time was limited to evenings and early mornings. 'I had a great deal else to do – to amuse and help my father (then growing old); to direct our household, entertain our guests, carry on the feminine correspondence of the family, teach in my village school twice a week or so, and to attend every case of illness or other tribulation in Donabate and Balisk' (I, 111). When the proofs were corrected, and she had only the preface to write, how was she to find a quiet hour? Reconstructing this moment of crisis in her *Life* betrays Cobbe into a rare burst of resentment on behalf of herself and her sex:

> Like most women I was bound hand and foot by a fine web of little duties and attentions, which men never feel or brush aside remorselessly (it was

only Hooker, who rocked a cradle with his foot while he wrote the Ecclesiastical Polity!); and it was a serious question for me when I could find leisure and solitude. Luckily, just on the critical day, my father was seized with a fancy to go to the play, and, equally luckily, I had so bad a cold that it was out of question that I should, as usual, accompany him. Accordingly I had an evening all alone, and wrote fast and hard the pages which I shall presently quote, finishing the last sentence of my *Preface* as I heard my father's knock at the hall-door. (I, 113)

Cobbe's conflict of duties was therefore resolved purely by chance, and the preface got written without any fundamental alteration of the *status quo*. Her father's knock at the door symbolically terminates her independence as a writer, like the stroke of midnight restoring Cinderella to her rags. In fact, Cobbe accepted these conditions until her father's death released her from all her household duties, and from the sense that girls should learn 'accomplishments' and refrain from working for money. When she finally became a journalist, and found it 'a delightful profession', she was still conscious of her father's old prejudices, although she was now free to ignore them. 'What my poor father would have felt had he known that his daughter eked out her subsistence by going down in all weathers to write articles for a half-penny newspaper in the Strand,' she confessed, 'I cannot guess. My brothers happily had no objection to my industry' (II, 76). Her last sentence shows that she still respected the force of male permission. One wonders what she would have done if her brothers had disapproved.

As it was, Cobbe found it hard not to boast of her success. For seven years, on the *Echo*, she never once failed to keep an engagement, 'and thus proved, I hope, once and for all, that a woman may be relied on as a journalist no less than a man. I do not think indeed, that very many masculine journalists could make the same boast of regularity as I have done' (II, 69). About the quality of her achievements as an essayist and campaigner, she remains ambivalent. As Patricia Meyer Spacks has argued in a survey of late nineteenth-century political women, whose work was carried out in the first half of the twentieth century, the theme of accomplishment rarely dominates the narrative of women's autobiography. 'Indeed, to a striking degree they fail directly to emphasise their *own* importance, though writing in a genre which implies self-assertion and display.'[42] Where Cobbe does advertise her strength and reliability, it is as a representative of her sex, rather than as an individual who deserves admiration for some personal distinction. Cobbe saw herself as an essayist who had

> done very little in any other way than to try to put forward – either at large or in a book or in a magazine article, or, lastly, in a newspaper-leader – which was always a miniature essay, – an appeal for some object, an argument for

some truth, a vindication of some principle, an exposure of what I conceived
to be an absurdity, a wrong, a falsehood, or a cruelty. (II, 76)

She therefore subordinates her own achievements to the larger impact of
a cause, and becomes no more than a voice employed on behalf of the
oppressed. The part of her work for women which gave her most
satisfaction was her efforts on behalf of battered wives, though even
there she had to work through MPs, who were inevitably men. Her
literary career she considered 'moderately successful'; her *Life* only
'scrappy souvenirs' with no pretensions to a place in the history of
autobiography. 'At best, a woman's knowledge of the eminent men
whom she only meets at dinner-parties, and perhaps in occasional quiet
afternoon visits, is not to be compared to that of their associates in their
clubs, in Parliament and in all the work of the world' (II, 81). This
modest account of her opportunities to mingle with the great implies that
she was the wife of a politician, rather than an achiever in her own right:
'Fanny Cobbe', for all her extreme notions which disconcerted Fanny
Kemble, ensures to the last that her self-portrayal is acceptably low-key.
She may have led an unrepresentative life, but she never unsexed herself
in her writing.

Among the readers of her theological books was Annie Besant,
twenty-three years her junior, and author of an autobiography published
just a year before Cobbe's. Whereas the older woman's book was praised
for its 'optimism' and 'healthy and buoyant tone', Annie Besant's was
attacked as egotistical and complacent. 'She fails to realise how extremely
selfish some of her sacrifices were,' complained the *Spectator*, detecting
an exaggerated longing for martyrdom.[43] Besant herself believed she had
travelled 'through storm to peace', and identified the keynote of her life
as a 'longing for sacrifice to something felt as greater than the self'.[44] Like
Cobbe's response to the duties and campaigns of her life, this implies a
complete subordination of the self to a larger cause, though both autobiographies recount the discovery of a voice in a woman who had been
silent for the first twenty-five or thirty years of her existence. A cross
between Dorothea Brooke and Jane Eyre in her desire first for a wider
life of service through self-sacrifice, and then for rebellion and defiance,
Annie Besant develops in her autobiography from a romantic fanatic to a
vocal and self-confident campaigner. Even here, however, one finds
substantial concessions to the Victorian feminine ideal: the longing for
self-devotion to another, the emphasis on duty and usefulness, the
taboos against anything savouring of egotism.

Annie Besant is unusual in that she herself draws attention to the
contradictory impulses in her character, displaying a greater degree of
self-awareness than is common among her contemporaries. 'I have ever

been the queerest mixture of weakness and strength, and have paid heavily for the weakness,' she confesses in her *Autobiography* (1893, p. 82). She saw herself as combative on the platform in defence of a cause, but a coward at heart in private, with a dread of confrontations. 'An unkind look or word has availed to make me shrink into myself as a snail into its shell, while on the platform opposition makes me speak my best' (p. 83). Besant wrote with the overt aim of 'trying to state things as they were', rather than giving 'mere conventionalisms' (p. 68): her earlier *Autobiographical Sketches* (1885) had been written 'to satisfy friendly questioners, and to serve, in some measure, as defence against unfair attack'.[45] Both works (which are substantially the same, the later *Autobiography* being an extension of the earlier *Sketches*) emphasise Besant's dedicated religious fanaticism. She studied, fasted, even flagellated herself to see if she could bear physical pain: she seemed to be training for the 'pathway trodden by the saints', taking Christ and her mother as the two ideals of her childhood and youth. She even thought of becoming a Sister of Mercy, despite her mother's known objections, 'for ever that idea of escaping from the humdrum of ordinary life by some complete sacrifice lured me onwards with its over-mastering fascination' (*Autobiography*, p. 68).

Annie Besant's spiritual 'deconversion' is distinctly feminine, mediated through a series of marital and maternal crises. Like Dorothea Brooke, she married a clergyman because she thought her new life would bring her increased opportunities for doing good. The vocation of priest's wife seemed to her 'second best only to that of the nun' (p. 68), but she 'drifted' into an engagement with the Rev. Frank Besant without pretending to love him. She was as passive as Ellen Terry had been just a few years earlier in her marriage to G. F. Watts, and for both women, the loss of a supportive and happy family in favour of the bewildering conditions of married life came as a shock. Ellen Terry passes over it discreetly, but Annie Besant speaks out against the innocent ignorance in which unmarried girls were preserved, even by mothers as loving as hers.

> Looking back on it all, I deliberately say that no more fatal blunder can be made than to train a girl to womanhood in ignorance of all life's duties and burdens, and then to let her face them for the first time away from all the old associations, the old helps, the old refuge on the mother's breast. (p. 71)

While accepting that she must have been 'inexpressibly tiring to the Rev. Frank Besant' (p. 82), she blames her husband more than herself for the failure of their marriage, and says almost nothing in his favour. He held 'very high ideas of a husband's authority and a wife's submission' (p. 81), he was methodical and easily angered by his impulsive, proud wife, who had never been spoken to harshly or ordered to do anything when she lived at home with her widowed mother:

> And, in truth, I ought never to have married, for under the soft, loving, pliable girl there lay hidden, as much unknown to herself as to her surroundings, a woman of strong dominant will, strength that panted for expression and rebelled against restraint, fiery and passionate emotions that were seething under compression – a most undesirable partner to sit in the lady's armchair on the domestic rug before the fire. (p. 82)

In depicting herself as a Jane Eyre/Bertha Rochester figure concealed within the embodiment of the Victorian feminine ideal, Besant creates a subversive image of a demon by the hearth supplanting the Angel in the House. Certainly, the panting, seething rebellion of the clergyman's wife seems drastically out of place in the domestic context Besant supplies for it, but it led directly to her discovery of an individual voice. She attempted to transcend her unhappiness as a wife by writing stories, and was paid thirty shillings for them by the *Family Herald*. 'It was the first money I had ever earned, and the pride of earning was added to the pride of authorship' (pp. 84–5). She saw herself 'earning heaps of golden guineas', and supporting the household: but her excitement was short-lived, like her 'delightful sense of independence' at having earnings of her own, apart from her husband's. 'I had not then realised the beauty of the English law, and the dignified position in which it placed the married woman,' she comments ironically, recalling the shock of discovering the married woman's property laws (p. 85).

If her marital relations set in train a process of social and sexual disillusionment, her experiences as a mother triggered her passage from Christianity to atheism. Her baby daughter nearly died of congestion of the lungs, but whereas recovery from a serious illness could often bring about a spiritual awakening, watching her daughter's exhausting struggle struck the first blow at her belief in God as a merciful Father. Besant personalises the episode into a three-cornered battle between herself, Christ and the child Mabel. She had always regarded Christ as 'no abstract idea, but a living reality, and all my heart rose up against this Person in whom I believed, and whose individual finger I saw in my baby's agony, my own misery, the breaking of my mother's proud heart under a load of debt, and all the bitter suffering of the poor' (p. 91). Thus the contest widens to include her own mother, and the poor in general. Only 'mental diversion' – books on anatomy and science – were able to rouse her from the weeks of prostration which followed Mabel's recovery. Besant's husband considered her behaviour quite incomprehensible.

> Surely it was a woman's business to attend to her husband's comforts and to see after her children, and not to break her heart over misery here and hell

hereafter, and distract her brain with questions that had puzzled the greatest thinkers and still remained unsolved! (p. 98)

Besant insists that it was not a desire for moral licence that prompted her towards atheism: she was a blameless wife and mother, suffering from a sense of 'outraged justice and insulted right' (p. 100). Her doubts actually struck when she was 'in the guarded circle of the home, with no dream of outside work or outside liberty': a point she wishes to place on record against the diatribes of uncomprehending critics. The victim of social and sexual ignorance, an unsympathetic husband, and now her child's and her own illnesses, Besant discovered first an independent intellectual standpoint (even Dr Pusey in Oxford failed to resolve her doubts) and then a voice in which to declare it. The episode in which she recounts the delivery of her first speech has a symbolic quality that makes it a fit paradigm for many women's entry into male discourse. While she was practising the organ in her husband's church, the 'queer whim' came over her, that she would like to know 'how "it felt" to preach', though this was not, she emphasises, any kind of premeditated plan. 'I saw no platform in the distance, nor had any idea of possible speaking in the future dawned up on me. But the longing to find outlet in words came upon me, and I felt as though I had something to say and was able to say it' (p. 116). Alone in the silent church, she climbed into the pulpit, and delivered a lecture on 'the Inspiration of the Bible':

> I shall never forget the feeling of power and of delight – but especially of power – that came upon me as I sent my voice ringing down the aisles, and the passion in me broke into balanced sentences and never paused for musical cadence or for rhythmical expression. All I wanted then was to see the church full of upturned faces, alive with throbbing sympathy, instead of the dreary emptiness of silent pews. And as though in a dream the solitude was peopled, and I saw the listening faces and the eager eyes, and as the sentences flowed unbidden from my lips and my own tones echoed back to me from the pillars of the ancient church, I knew of a verity that the gift of speech was mine, and that if ever – and then it seemed so impossible! – if ever the chance came to me of public work, this power of melodious utterance should at least win hearing for any message I had to bring. (p. 116)

This passage can be compared with Fanny Kemble's account of her voice trial as Juliet at Covent Garden. In both cases, the speaker presents herself as a passive instrument in the power of an unsought force much greater than herself. Where Kemble was 'seized with the spirit of the thing', and 'completely carried away', Besant receives the 'gift of speech'. The feeling of 'power and of delight' 'came upon her', and the sentences flowed 'unbidden' from her lips. Each speaker is surprised by the strength of her own voice. Kemble's 'resounded through the great vault', and Besant's rang down the aisles and echoed back to her from the pillars of the church. But whereas Kemble feels uninhibited by the lack of a Romeo or an audience, Besant needs an audience, if only an imaginary one, to complete the impact of the experience. After a life of powerless submission to other people, she longs to sway the emotions of her listeners, the sense of power surpassing even the unfamiliar delight at her new-found skills.

Yet Besant quickly retreats from her euphoria. Her oratorical abilities remained a secret to all but herself 'for many a long month, for I quickly felt ashamed of that foolish speechifying in an empty church; but, foolish as it was, I note it here, as it was the first effort of that expression in spoken words which later became to me one of the deepest delights of life' (pp. 116-17). Having found a voice, however, Besant was reluctant to be silenced by male authority. When a separation from her husband was arranged, she was offered a home with her brother, on condition that she give up her heretical friends and 'keep quiet' (p. 119), but Besant was determined to be independent and support herself. The terms 'power' and 'delight' recur with striking frequency in the next few chapters, as she rejoices in her atheism, her freedom, and her efficacy as a public speaker: a role which also improved her health, and made her strong and vigorous. Although she always felt nervous before giving a lecture, 'all this miserable feeling vanished the moment I was on my feet and was looking at the faces before me.' As she heard her own voice 'ring out over the attentive listeners', she was 'conscious of power and of pleasure, not of fear' (p. 182). Her joyous acceptance of atheism is also described in terms of finding a voice. 'It was the cry of the freed soul that had found articulate expression, and the many inarticulate and prisoned souls answered to it tumultuously, with fluttering of caged wings' (p. 158).

Nevertheless, Annie Besant never loses her consciousness of propriety. She tries to expound her new philosophic stance in terms that would be familiar and acceptable to a more conventionally minded female reader. She also portrays herself as a devoted mother and daughter. If her husband is scarcely mentioned, the separation from her daughter and the death of her mother are given their full traumatic impact in the narrative, and Mabel's part in Besant's recovery from her failed marriage, inspires a peculiarly Victorian sentimentality otherwise absent from this normally vigorous text. 'The torn, bruised tendrils of my heart gradually twined round this little life,' reports Besant; 'she gave something to love and to tend, and thus gratified one of the strongest impulses of my nature' (p. 129). Similarly, when she and Charles Bradlaugh were involved in a controversy over a pamphlet on birth-control, she knew it meant the loss of the 'pure reputation' she prized, 'scandal the most terrible a woman could face'. 'The long suffering that followed,' she concluded, 'was a splendid school for the teaching of endurance' (p. 208). At the end of her autobiography, when she takes a ceremonial farewell of her readers, she assures them that 'quiet confidence has taken the place of doubt; a strong security the place of anxious dread' (p. 364). In this respect, Besant's autobiography is more like Harriet Martineau's than the garrulous memoirs of Fanny Kemble. Besant, like Martineau, has shaped the story of her life into a passage from girlish innocence to the tried and tested wisdom of a woman who has learnt to speak.

'the need of utterance': Harriet Martineau

Harriet Martineau's Autobiography provides a fitting conclusion to this survey of controversial Victorian women. Although it bears some of the hallmarks of other autobiographies of this class, it remains the most confident, forthright and deliberate work of the group, and perhaps the most interesting. I have considered it in detail elsewhere;[46] in this context, I propose to discuss it specifically as a *woman's* autobiography, in the light of issues raised by other works in this section.

In her recent study of Victorian spiritual autobiography, Linda Peterson suggests that Martineau revised the genre to comply with her Necessarian standpoint, and that her originality as a woman writer displays itself in a confrontation 'of a dominant male tradition, and its insistence upon gender-free patterns of human development'. In the debate over the modes of self-interpretation women should adopt, Martineau's position seems clear: 'women should engage the main tradition of autobiographical writing, and they should adopt universal patterns of interpretation, systems that apply to all humankind.'[47] Mitzi Myers, however, argues that Martineau's *Autobiography* is 'an archetypal female success story', and 'the emancipation proclamation of a female philosopher'.[48] Perhaps the two interpretations are not as incompatible as they sound, and Martineau may have written more self-consciously as a woman in some parts of the book than in others.

From an early point in her development as a reviewer and critic, she had been aware of the difficulties of expressing the essential meaning and characteristics of a human life in a written document. In 1830, reviewing *The Correspondence and Diary of Philip Doddridge* (1829), she bemoaned the imperfection and 'deception' of biography in its partial depiction of its subject. 'The histories of pious men and moralists are worth almost nothing at all, if the structure of their minds is hidden from the reader,' she complained, excepting only the *Life of Newton* published by the Society for the Diffusion of Useful Knowledge, and admitting that the subject contributed largely to this success. Newton's life was remarkably abstract, and free from the intricacies of social relations, whereas 'every other man's life, external and internal, is a system of checks and counter-checks; and in proportion to the balance of these checks is the happiness of his lot and the perfection of his soul.' As for autobiography, as a more revelatory form, Martineau argues that most people lack the will, the nerve or the power to write an auto-biography worth reading:

> If we consider for a moment how we should set about writing a history of ourselves, we shall find that so much of our character has been derived from the virtues of those with whom we live, and so much from their failings, that this consideration alone puts a seal on our lips, though we may be aware of the possession of some valuable facts which need not else be secret, and long to assist others with the experience which we have obtained from some peculiarity of circumstances whose results must be confined to ourselves through this restraint on the liberty of speech.[49]

Martineau broke through this veil of secrecy when she recounted all the miseries of her childhood, and her mother's failure to understand her need for demonstrative love. Like most other female autobiographers of her generation, she sees her writing as a means of helping others, a sharing of experiences at once peculiar, and yet representative. Unlike most of her contemporaries, however, she consciously shapes her written life for her readers' edification, and makes its internal structure evident from the opening. This was helped by her intense interest in a younger female life: that of her sister Ellen who was born when Martineau was nine. 'She was a pursuit to me, no less than an attachment,' Martineau recalls, and she remembered telling a friend that she would now 'see the growth of a human mind from the very beginning.'[50] Significantly, she saw this growth in terms of struggle, particularly in the acquisition of language, as she assumed the baby would have as much difficulty learning to speak as her sister had experienced in learning French.

Harriet Martineau had long seen it as one of the duties of her life to write her autobiography; and when she finally did, after many false starts, she rewrote her early attempts, so 'that the whole might be offered from one point of view, and in a consistent spirit' (I, 2–3). The expectation of sudden death – her reason for writing after so much delay – concentrated both her efforts and her sense of structure. She divided her life into distinct 'periods' marked by an advance in her views, her worldly position, or a major achievement; and it is essentially in the first volume that she alludes most often to her position specifically as a woman. After that, as she becomes less concerned with her own successes and perplexities, and more interested in the future of the entire race, in accordance with her positivist philosophy, she presents herself as a self-confident but controversial free-thinker, attacked for her agnosticism rather than her unwomanly behaviour. Besides, Martineau took care all her life not to appear unwomanly, but to insist on women's 'natural' enjoyment of housework and her own abilities in the kitchen. She also avoided direct association with other feminists, much as George Eliot did; largely because she found their stridency embarrassing and unhelpful.

In the *Autobiography*, Martineau is surrounded by negative female role models, from her mother to Mary Wollstonecraft; her encouragement comes from men, from her elder brother Thomas and younger brother James, to Isaac Perry, her schoolmaster, and the philosophers Joseph Priestley and David Hartley. Her final mentor was Henry Atkinson – 'that Mr. Atkinson', as Fanny Kemble called him[51] – who conducted her through an exploration of the powers of Man, and his position and destiny in the universe as a 'creature of necessity'.[52] The place where she is most passive in her behaviour is her account of how she first began writing for publication: a train of events started by her brother James, who advised her to write something while he was away at college, to console herself for his absence. 'What James desired, I always did, of course,' Martineau comments; and when the article was written, it was her elder brother Thomas who, ignorant of its authorship, read it to the family, and afterwards gave her permission to concentrate on her writing, with the oracular words: 'Now, dear, leave it to other women to make shirts and darn stockings; and do you devote yourself to this' (I, 120). As she recognised, in words no less oracular, 'that evening made me an authoress'. Until his premature death a short time later, Thomas Martineau watched over his sister's work and criticised it: 'from an anxious desire that I should work my way up to the high reputation which he felt I was destined to attain' (I, 120). The family's economic ruin in 1829 released the Martineau daughters from what George Eliot in *Middlemarch* calls the 'gentlewoman's oppressive liberty' into the real liberty of independent careers. 'It was truly *life* that I lived during those days of strong intellectual and moral effort' (I, 145); and from then onwards, her own ideas for essays or tales were thrust forward by the most determined efforts of her own, against the scepticism of critics. Her writing in the *Autobiography* becomes exceptionally forthright to reflect this new strength of will; for example over the plan for her *Illustrations of Political Economy*, which she describes as the 'strongest act of will' she ever committed herself to: 'and my will was always a pretty strong one' (I, 160).

This period of her life is recalled in confident language, but still with some remnants of respect for male authority. She is conscious of her difficulties specifically as a woman, in living at home in provincial Norwich, while all the literary business of the kingdom is done in London. 'I said to my mother, "You know what a man of business would do in my case." – "What?" – "Go up to town by the next mail, and see what is to be done."' Called in as final arbiter, her brother Henry commanded her to 'Go!' and go she did (I, 164). Summing up the events of this crucial 'third period' (after which she wrote her preface to the whole *Autobiography*), she maintains that it had, of all the stages in her life, the most 'intimate connexion with the formation of character' (I, 180). Her way of dealing with opposition was not, like Mary Somerville's, a patient by-passing of obstacles, but a head-on collision with them, in which she wears down the barrier between her career and her private life. As she gains confidence, she drops the passive constructions of her earlier sentences, and unlike Fanny Kemble, she openly declares her enjoyment of her work, and total contentment with her lot as a single woman. As she puts it at the end of this third section: 'I had now, by thirty years of age, ascertained my career, found occupation, and achieved independence,' and she felt no need to apologise for any of it (I, 181).

Martineau's commitment to her career is given added weight by the emphasis on business deals with publishers, and her methods of work. She even quotes a friend who remarked that Martineau's authorship was 'the fulfilment of a natural function, – conducive to health of body and mind, instead of injurious to either' (I, 188). It certainly gave her a strong sense of her own identity, and the ability to stand her ground against fierce opposition. At the age of thirty-two, she was telling Lord Althorp's private secretary how she would improve the Excise laws, and that his proposal to remove the tax on saddle-horses in the case of the clergy and dissenting ministers was ridiculous. Martineau recounts the episode in vivid dialogue, highlighting her own firmness in the matter:

> 'What shall I tell Lord Althorp that you think of this?' inquired the Secretary. 'Tell him I think the dissenting Ministers would like it very much if they had any saddle-horses,' I replied. – 'What! do you mean that they will not take it as a boon?' – 'If you offer it as a boon, they will be apt to take it as an insult. How should dissenting Ministers have saddle-horses, unless they happen to have private fortunes?' He questioned me closely about the dissenting Ministers I knew; and we found that I could actually point out only two among the Unitarians who kept saddle-horses, and they were men of property. (I, 264)

In all her public actions, Martineau portrays herself as self-disciplined, determined and courageous, impelled by an unshakeable belief in the value of what she was doing. Only in private did she sometimes waver, as on the occasion when she was offered the editorship of a new 'Economical Magazine'. 'If I do this,' she told herself, 'I must brace myself up to do and suffer like a man.' She recognised that her acceptance would open up the possibility of 'setting women forward at once into the rank of men of business' (II, 110); but when her brother James came down against the scheme, she immediately refused it. A stream of references to bodily illness also demonstrates at what cost she was combining an exhausting professional life with care of her mother and elderly aunt, but this declines, paradoxically as she believes herself to be fatally ill, though fully in charge of her own life.

By the end of her autobiography, Martineau writes less as a woman than as an optimistic seer, predicting the onward march of mind. Men and women have become subsumed into a mystical conception of 'Man', and her interests now concentrate on 'the nature and mode of development of the human being' (II, 458). Nevertheless, in the course of her narrative, she has revealed more of her feelings and asserted her own professional standing more than any other female autobiographer of her generation: a fact all the more remarkable in view of her early birth-date (1802). The *Autobiography* also relies far less than contemporary works on quoted letters. Comparison with Fanny Kemble's volumes of memoirs, published only a few years later, shows how much more rigorous was Harriet Martineau's shaping of her life into a coherent whole. Her respect for Atkinson's brand of physiological philosophy and her translator's familiarity with Comte gave her an unusually distinct awareness of human development theory: so much so, that long before she was dead, she was able to sum up her life in a self-written obituary, surely the oddest act of autobiographical writing in the history of women's introspection. Detached, trenchant, and analytical, the obituary, written in the third person, realistically assesses Martineau's contribution to literary history giving her credit, above all, for clarity of expression. 'In short, she could popularise, while she could neither discover nor invent.' 'Her stimulus in all she wrote, from first to last,' Martineau argued, 'was simply the need of utterance.'[53] She makes the strongest case since the Duchess of Newcastle's for the woman's natural instinct to express herself by the pen and not the needle.

Notes

1. Edith Simcox, 'New books', *Fortnightly Review*, 21 (January 1874), 114.
2. Somerville, *Personal Recollections*, pp. 346–7.

3. MSS Obituary of Florence Nightingale, Fawcett Library, City of London Polytechnic.

4. Martha Vicinus, *Independent Women: Work and Community for Single Women. 1850–1920* (London: Virago, 1985), p. 134.

5. Frances Power Cobbe, *The Duties of Women: A Course of Lectures* (London: Williams & Norgate, 1881), p. iv; p. 12.

6. *Woman's Work and Woman's Culture: A Series of Essays*, ed. Josephine Butler (London: Macmillan and Co., 1869), p. xxxiv.

7. *Further Records. 1848–1883. A Series of Letters by Frances Anne Kemble*, forming a Sequel to *Record of a Girlhood* and *Records of Later Life* (London: Richard Bentley and Son, 2 vols, 1890), II, 56.

8. *Harriet Martineau's Autobiography*, I, 132.

9. Miller, 'Women's autobiography in France', p. 263.

10. Somerville, *Personal Recollections*, pp. 45–6.

11. Kemble, *Record of a Girlhood*, II, 61.

12. 'On the stage', *Cornhill Magazine* VIII (December 1863), 736.

13. 'Journal of Frances Anne Butler', *Quarterly Review* 54 (July 1835), 40.

14. *Saturday Review*, 13 (22 March 1862), p. 321.

15. Quoted by Christopher Kent, 'Image and reality: the actress and society', in *A Widening Sphere: Changing Roles of Victorian Women*, ed. Martha Vicinus (Bloomington: Indiana University Press, 1977; London: Methuen, 1980), p. 94.

16. Charlotte Brontë, *Villette* (1853; ed. Tony Tanner, Harmondsworth: Penguin, 1979), p. 339.

17. Frances Anne Kemble, *Records of Later Life* (London: Richard Bentley and Son, 3 vols, 1882), II, 100.

18. J. C. Furnas, *Fanny Kemble: Leading Lady of the Nineteenth-Century Stage* (New York: Dial Press, 1982), p. 424.

19. 'Old woman's gossip', *Atlantic Monthly*, p. 152.

20. *Further Records*, I, 145; *Records of Later Life*, III, 156–7.

21. *Record of a Girlhood*, I, 1–2.

22. *Henry James Letters*, ed. Leon Edel, (London: Macmillan, 1978), II, 212.

23. 'Two ladies', *Blackwood's* 125 (February 1879), 219.

24. *Record of a Girlhood*, I, 202.

25. Oliphant, *Autobiography*, p. 85; *The Letters of Robert Browning and Elizabeth Barrett Barrett 1845–1846*, ed. Elvan Kintner (Cambridge, Mass.: The Belknap Press of Harvard University Press, 2 vols, 1969), I, 464–5; Ellen Terry, *The Story of My Life* (1908; Woodbridge, Suffolk:The Boydell Press, 1982), p. 50.

26. *Records of Later Life*, II, 34

27. *Ibid.*, II, 67.

28. *The Greville Memoirs, 1814–1860*, ed. Lytton Strachey and Roger Fulford (London: Macmillan, 1938), V, 61.

29. *Records of Later Life*, I, 54.

30. *Ibid.*, II, 22.

31. *Further Records*, I, 108.

32. *Ibid.*, I, 107.

33. *Records of Later Life*, I, 68; 4.

34. *Ibid.*, III, 247; 373.

35. *Record of a Girlhood*, II, 71.

36. 'Two ladies', p. 222.
37. Virginia Woolf, 'Ellen Terry', *Collected Essays*, IV (London: The Hogarth Press, 1967), p. 71.
38. Ellen Terry, *The Story of My Life*, p. vii.
39. Marguerite Steen, *A Pride of Terrys: Family Saga* (London: Longmans, Green & Co., 1962), p. 204; *Ellen Terry and Bernard Shaw: A Correspondence*, ed. Christopher St John (London: Reinhardt & Evans Ltd, 1931, 1949), p. xiv.
40. *Life of Frances Power Cobbe*, I, 197; II, 204.
41. 'Celibacy v. marriage', *Fraser's Magazine*, 65 (February 1862), p. 233; reprinted in Frances Power Cobbe, *Essays on the Pursuits of Women* (London: Emily Faithfull, 1863).
42. Patricia Meyer Spacks, 'Selves in hiding', in *Women's Autobiography*, ed. Jelinek, pp. 113–14.
43. 'Mrs. Besant's autobiography', *Spectator* (3 March, 1894), p. 309.
44. Annie Besant, *An Autobiography*, p. 363; p. 57.
45. Annie Besant, *Autobiographical Sketches* (London: Freethought Publishing Co., 1885), p. 3.
46. Valerie Sanders, *Reason Over Passion: Harriet Martineau and the Victorian Novel* (Hemel Hempstead: Harvester Wheatsheaf; New York: St Martin's Press, 1986), Ch. 6.
47. Peterson, p. 153.
48. Mitzi Myers, 'Harriet Martineau's autobiography: the making of a female philosopher', in *Women's Autobiography*, ed. Jelinek, p. 59, p. 53.
49. 'Doddridge's correspondence and diary', *Monthly Repository* 4 (January 1830), pp. 16–18.
50. *Harriet Martineau's Autobiography*, ed. Gaby Weiner, I, 52.
51. *Further Records*, I, 313.
52. Henry George Atkinson, F.G.S. and Harriet Martineau, *Letters on the Laws of Man's Nature and Development* (1851), p. 30.
53. *Harriet Martineau's Autobiography, with Memorials by Maria Weston Chapman* (London: Smith, Elder & Co., 3 vols, 1877), III, 470; 461.

Chapter 6

'I must write what I think'
into the twentieth century

'I was thinking the other night that there's never been a woman's autobiography,' Virginia Woolf told Ethel Smyth on Christmas Eve, 1940. 'Nothing to compare with Rousseau. Chastity and modesty I suppose have been the reason.'[1] Had nothing really changed since 1843, when Jane Carlyle assumed that *'decency forbids'* a woman from writing the story of her own life?

There had certainly been significant outward changes. The years between these two strikingly similar pronouncements had seen the transformation of women from tight-laced, superficially educated, unenfranchised, propertyless wives, widows and spinsters with a limited range of employment options, to suffragettes, war-workers, nurses, doctors, university teachers, campaigners and social investigators. Yet, as Elaine Showalter has argued, this did not necessarily entail a linear development towards feminist outspokenness. The lyrical and utopian protest literature of the 1880s and 1890s, by, for example, Olive Schreiner and Sarah Grand, was followed by a post-war 'retreat from the ego, retreat from the physical experience of women, retreat from the material world, retreat into separate rooms and separate cities'.[2] Showalter sees the post-war period as 'one of renewed conservatism about sex roles and gender issues', marked by the decline of late Victorian settlement houses and sisterhoods, and 'the shift of feminine interests away from questions of women's independence to questions of women's relationship to men'.[3] Virginia Woolf, in *A Room of One's Own*, noted a drift away from the autobiographical impulse in women's fiction, influenced perhaps by women's increased access to reading and criticism, and the attempt 'to use writing as an art, not as a method of self-expression'.[4] On the other hand, the 1914–18 War, which jolted women into unaccustomed professional roles outside the home, also released a new torrent of formal autobiography, particularly that concerned with the suffrage campaign, war work, or personal achievement.[5] Women autobiographers more readily assumed that the public wanted to know how they had won a court action or survived a prison sentence: a narrative many preferred to recount as a memoir, rather than as official history. Josephine Butler entitled her account of the campaign against the Contagious Diseases Acts *Personal Reminiscences of a Great Crusade*: so that she would not 'incur the blame which a professed historian would deserve for leaving *lacunae*, sometimes extensive ones, here and there, seeing that memory and the imperfect records I possess do not, and cannot, cover all the ground.'[6] Annie Besant's *Autobiography* similarly becomes a narrative of the battles she fought alongside Charles Bradlaugh for the distribution of birth control information, and the admission of non-believers to the House of Commons.

Inevitably, women writing autobiography around the time of the First World War, pitched their individual story against a backcloth of international devastation, which tended to dwarf their sense of significant individuality. An apocalyptic streak, which began with the ending of *Harriet Martineau's Autobiography*, written during the Crimean war, and reappears in the writing of Mrs Humphry Ward and Mrs Pankhurst, introduces a note of prophetic excitement about the future of mankind in general, rather than women in particular. Mrs Ward was temporarily distracted from world affairs by work on her *Writer's Recollections*, but in her Epilogue she recognises that 'the dream and the illusion are done'. The evening paper arrives, with more news of the Kaiser's speeches, and her *Recollections* end with a vision of the American forces coming to aid the Allies: 'The air thickens, as it were, with the sense of an ever-gathering host. On this side and on that, it is the Army of Freedom, and of Judgement.'[7]

Mrs Ward finished her autobiography on Christmas Eve, 1917; Mrs Pankhurst had finished hers three years earlier, in the late summer of 1914, when the armies of Europe were being mobilised for 'savage, unsparing, barbarous warfare':

> How mild, by comparison with the despatches in the daily newspapers, will seem this chronicle of women's militant struggle against political and social injustice in one small corner of Europe. Yet let it stand as it was written, with peace – so called, and civilisation, and orderly government as the background for heroism such as the world has seldom witnessed.

Contrasting the militancy of men, which though it has 'drenched the world with blood' has nevertheless been amply rewarded, with the harmless and righteous militancy of women, so far without results, Mrs Pankhurst writes with a sense of having been upstaged by the War. Her battles seem outdated and unimportant, compared with the approaching carnage of male global conflict, but she warns her readers that the suffrage campaign is only in abeyance. 'When the clash of arms ceases, when normal, peaceful, rational society resumes its functions, the demand will again be made.'[8]

Nevertheless, Mrs Pankhurst acknowledges the advantages of growing up in a militant age. In her opening chapter ('The Making of a Militant'), she draws a direct link between her activism and the atmosphere of anti-slavery opposition in which she was raised. From the beginning, however, she undermines the impression of aggressive enterprise by her insistence on a compensatory, 'womanly' instinct for reconstruction. *Uncle Tom's Cabin* and fund-raising events for the anti-slavery cause awakened in her the 'two sets of sensations' to which for the rest of her life she 'most readily responded':

> first, admiration for that spirit of fighting and heroic sacrifice by which alone the soul of civilisation is saved; and next after that, appreciation of the gentler spirit which is moved to mend and repair the ravages of war. (*My Own Story*, p. 3)

After describing her sight of prison gallows on which the Fenian rioters in Manchester were hanged, she explains that her 'development into an advocate of militancy was largely a sympathetic process' (p. 5). She had not suffered personally from any of the deprivations which bring so many people to a realisation of social injustice. Again, however, Mrs Pankhurst undercuts the effect of her own confident assertions. She admits that there was something lacking, even in her own home, 'some false conception of family relations', and her father's regret that she was not a boy (pp. 5–6). Her own and her sisters' education were considered less important than their brothers'; 'but I think I never decided that I regretted my sex' (p. 6). The awkward hesitancy of her conclusion would suggest exactly the opposite: and is conspicuously less confident than Frances Power Cobbe's acceptance, quoted earlier, of the 'woman's destiny' as 'the best and happiest' for her.

Emmeline Pankhurst studiously avoids all appearance of sexual antagonism or unreasonableness. Although she says very little about her marriage, she indicates that it was happy and normal, and that she had her husband's approval for her work. She makes a point of rebutting the usual taunt that 'suffragists are women who have failed to find any normal outlet for their emotions, and are therefore soured and disappointed beings. This is probably not true of any suffragist, and it is most certainly not true of me. My home life and relations have been nearly as ideal as possible in this imperfect world' (p. 12). Even when she had small children, her husband encouraged her interest in community affairs. 'Dr. Pankhurst did not desire that I should turn myself into a household machine' (p. 13). By page 31, however, Dr Pankhurst is dead, and the rest of the book, dictated to an American, Rheta Childe Dorr, on board a ship to New York in 1913, for serialisation in the magazine *Good Housekeeping*, is devoted to a largely impersonal account of the suffrage campaign, mainly for propaganda purposes.

Reviewers at this time had cause to complain that women's memoirs were too impersonal, as they had done about Mary Mitford's *Recollections of a Literary Life* (1852). When her friends urged Millicent Garrett Fawcett to write her reminiscences, she at first refused. '"The book would have to be I, I, I," she said. "I don't like that kind of book."' As Ray Strachey, her biographer, comments, 'she managed somehow to prevent the book from being full of "I, I, I,"; and indeed, the only criticism which was heard of it was that she had remembered too little about herself.'[9] Like Emmeline Pankhurst, Millicent Garrett Fawcett places her story in a dramatic political landscape. 'The year of my birth was the year of the Irish famine and the repeal of the Corn Laws, and the following year saw the downfall of half the old autocratic Governments in Europe.'[10] Family circumstances, in this case her father's support for her sister Elizabeth's career as a doctor, and her mother's opposition, heightened her awareness of sexual inequality; though her marriage, like Pankhurst's, was happy and supportive. Fawcett, too, emphasises her husband's concurrence in her campaign work. 'Without his perpetual encouragement I certainly should not have embarked on authorship at the age of twenty-one' (pp. 85–6). Like most women autobiographers born in the nineteenth century, however, Fawcett writes more readily of her parents than of her husband. Even her daughter Philippa is hardly mentioned until the episode of her resounding success in the Mathematics Tripos at Cambridge. 'Up to the present I have told little of Philippa,' Fawcett admits, 'but, of course, this is not because I remember little. At first, when she was a baby girl, I delighted in her rapidly developing mind, in her curiosity, and in her quaint expressions' (p. 137). Characteristically, Fawcett emphasises her daughter's intellectual brilliance, even as a baby: she says nothing about her own response to motherhood, and any conflict she might have experienced between caring for Philippa, assisting her blind husband, and pursuing her own career. Her work as a suffragist she describes as having been inspired by 'two accidentally heard conversations between women' (p. 116), giving her choice of career a random or fortuitous twist, despite the stimulating atmosphere in which she grew up. Whenever she does allude to anything personal or emotional, she apologises; as in her reference to the outbreak of the First World War. 'If I may be forgiven for referring to my own personal feelings, I may mention that the day on which we knew we were actually at war with the greatest military nation in the world was the most miserable of my life' (p. 221). Even so, this was strictly for personal reasons: 'so ill did I read the future that I thought the hope of women's freedom was indefinitely postponed, and that this was the supreme sacrifice asked of us at this stupendous moment.'

Neither Mrs Fawcett's nor Mrs Pankhurst's autobiography attempts to delineate the growth of a personality or the evolution of self-realisation. If anything, these autobiographies mark a retreat from the more genuinely introspective stance taken by Margaret Oliphant, one of the few Victorian women autobiographers to write about distinctively female experiences, especially motherhood, and the loss of her children.

To one male reviewer, writing in 1920, the paucity of genuine autobiography by women was perhaps inevitable, if regrettable. 'Orlo' (Orlando Cyprian) Williams (1883–1967) used his article in the *Edinburgh Review* on three 'Feminine Autobiographies' – by Liza Lehmann, Ella Wheeler Wilcox and Ethel Smyth – to investigate the apparent inability of women to write conventionally acceptable autobiography. His definition of the form rejects 'all the journals, sketches, and autobiographical reminiscences, all jottings about contemporary personages, and all those records of mere events which are shown as happening to a body that we have not seen, and touching the personality into which we are not allowed to penetrate.'[11] In other words, true autobiography is essentially concerned with internal, rather than external experiences. 'The true autobiography has one interest only, that of the author's personality as it appeared to himself' (p. 304), and it should recreate a 'unity of personality', through the triumph of an artistic imagination. He argues that 'anxiety' and 'agony' are 'inseparable from a great autobiographical creation' (p. 305) as the author attempts to communicate his own vision to others. Throughout the article Williams impresses the need both to objectify the recreation of the self, and to produce a sense of unified personality: demands which clearly sort ill with the random, discontinuous form of much women's autobiography.

Williams then attributes to women certain psychological characteristics which he assumes would normally make them skilled autobiographers. They are egotistical, morbidly introspective, and more self-conscious than men. On the other hand, they are more secretive about themselves. 'The physical and emotional frankness of men has for women something rather repulsive; they cling passionately to their last draperies even among themselves,' eschewing the voluntary appearance of nudity in public as 'an act of self-violation' (p. 306). The overtly sexual nature of Williams's criticism is complemented by his references to 'abstractions': women 'shy at propositions stated in general terms if they cannot immediately make some particular application of them'. The resulting self-image is 'more of a series of attitudes than of an elusive unity,' caused partly by the failure of most women to concentrate what egotism they have on the attainment of their ambitions. To make up for these deficiences, a woman calls on 'the cosmetic art of fiction'; busy with her 'make-up box' (while the man, 'more astute, attends to the lighting of the stage'), the female autobiographer prefers to 'touch herself up into the appearance of a heroine' (p. 307). With its picture of woman as a Pope's Belinda or second-rate actress, Williams's article indicates how in some branches of social life, at least since the war, the sharp division of gender roles and characteristics had returned to the position of perhaps fifty years earlier, and women were as far as ever from establishing a distinctive, yet acceptable, format for their non-fictional self-writing.

Two contemporary autobiographies by women which embodied some of these generic difficulties and won entirely opposite responses from (largely male) reviewers, were Ethel Smyth's *Impressions That Remained* (1919) and Margot Asquith's *Autobiography* (2 vols, 1920 and 1922). Although Ethel Smyth once said 'I am by far the most interesting person I know' (one sees why she nearly married Oscar Wilde's brother William), her first volume of autobiography was widely praised by the critics for its apparent lack of egotism, and its revelation of an inner life. 'The extraordinary intimacy and absence of egoism or self-consciousness begins very quickly to make a strong impression on the reader,' wrote W. I. Turner in the *New Statesman*; while the *Times Literary Supplement*, declaring it 'the most remarkable book of memoirs that has appeared in recent times', placed Smyth's *Impressions* well ahead of contemporary autobiographies by famous men such as Ludendorff and Lord French.[12]

Part of Smyth's success came from her attention to childhood memories which were, by her own admission, impersonal and representative. The daily life of the Smyth family of Sidcup might, she suggests, 'be that of any English family in analogous circumstances, and my own confessions the autobiography of any child'.[13] In her depiction of herself as a girl, Smyth is detached, witty, and self-mocking, setting her undoubted ambitiousness in a deflationary context. The 'main determination' of her life, which never wavered, was to go abroad and study music; subsequently, bitten by a passion for the opera, she decided that her 'greatest desire' was to have an opera of hers played in Germany before she was forty – 'an ambition fated to be realised'. Not only does Smyth openly confess her ambitions; unlike those of Pankhurst and Fawcett, they are unashamedly personal, or egotistical ambitions, not bound up with the good of mankind. Nevertheless, Smyth's awareness of her bumptious, even bullying self-confidence, anticipates and disarms the criticism of hostile readers, and seems to have charmed them into acquiescence. Moreover, in a later volume of autobiography, *As Time Went On ...* (1936), she candidly confesses that although she had become celebrated, or even notorious, for her eccentricities, she has not 'succeeded in becoming even a tiny wheel in the English music machine'.[14]

Although Ethel Smyth writes at length about the difficulties she encountered in her musical career, she pays at least as much attention to the development of her emotional life, the impact of friendships, and her experiences (mostly comic) at the hands of imperious royalty, namely Queen Victoria and the Empress Eugenie. In her second book of recollections, *Streaks of Life* (1921), she admits that her memories are a 'collection of papers' and 'no attempt at a connected story': the inevitable format, in her view, of contemporary autobiography. 'Dealing with modern times, continuity is impossible unless you are prepared either to hurt feelings, or to dip your pen in purest solution of rose-coloured amiability.'[15] The greatest challenge to Ethel Smyth's 'amiability' as an autobiographer, was to give an adequate explanation of her severed friendship with Elizabeth ('Lisl') von Herzogenberg, and her liaison with Harry Brewster while his wife Julia was still alive. 'Now why shouldn't you be not only the first woman to write an opera, but equally the first to tell the truths about herself?' Virginia Woolf urged her in 1940. 'Isn't the great artist the only person to tell the truth? I should like an analysis of your sex life. As Rousseau did his. More introspection. More intimacy.'[16]

In fact, Ethel Smyth had already been surprisingly outspoken in her first volumes of autobiography, twenty years earlier. Her preference for her own sex, Brewster's importance notwithstanding, is openly confessed at an early point in her *Impressions*: she was still a child when she drew up a list of over a hundred girls and women to whom, had she been a man, she would have proposed.[17] She recalls a certain rivalry over boyfriends with her sister Mary, whose 'more feminine helplessness' usually won over boys who had been at first attracted to Ethel's independence and proficiency at games. 'Now and again a very real feeling of mortification may have swept over me as I saw my admirers succumbing to the charms of Mary,' she remembers, 'but from the first my most ardent sentiments were bestowed on members of my own sex, and the love-affairs with boys were but imitative and trashy, I fear.'[18] Virginia Woolf had thought Smyth's *Impressions* badly written when she first read them in the year of publication, but admired the way she had 'ridden straight at her recollections, never swerving & getting through them honestly, capably, but without the power to still & shape the past so that one will wish to read it again'. In fact, she did read it again, attracted perhaps by the open portrayal of female relationships: 'friendships with women interest me,' she noted, even on her first critical reading.[19]

Margot Asquith wrote with a similar brisk directness, but the reviewers found it more offensive, largely because she had been outspoken about people who were still alive. 'It has its roots in vanity and self-love,' complained *The Times* leader, resuming the oldest cry of all against autobiography;[20] but although this was perhaps the most hostile review, it was by no means the only one. Desmond MacCarthy, in *The New Statesman*, noted that the *Autobiography* was 'crammed with quoted praise of herself', and suffered from 'lack of continuity and perspective'.[21] There is certainly no sense of all the events in Margot's thirty years of unmarried life leading up to her marriage with Mr Asquith: instead, every sketch of great men, every romp and escapade is retold for its own sake, as a piece of fun, or a remarkable experience that the reader might find amusing. Whole, extensive dialogues are recreated, with a romanticised Margot playing the part of heroine or chief inter-locutor; for example in her railway carriage confrontation with General Booth of the Salvation Army, or her chat with Lord Salisbury about Chamberlain.[22] Contemporary reviewers felt that she had no idea how to structure an autobiography. 'She lacks the seeing eye and the vivifying phrase,' argued *The Times Literary Supplement*, while *The Nation* suggested 'there is neither a diary of the heart, nor a true picture of the politics of nineteenth-century England to be made out of the story of an existence so external, so devoted to bodily pleasure.'[23]

Margot Asquith was asked to write her autobiography by Thornton Butterworth, the publisher, and encouraged by Arthur Balfour; but she was reluctant to use her diaries, which she had meant to leave to her two children to sell if they needed the money. On the other hand, she believed it was important to commemorate lives in writing. In 1906, she had tried to write her sister Laura Lyttleton's life, but left it incomplete; she had also asked her friend, Mary Drew, Gladstone's daughter, to 'write a sketch for me for posterity'. Meanwhile, her husband was writ-ing his own reminiscences, which Margot found flat and dull.[24] She was careful not to show her work to him, strictly maintaining that 'in this book I must write what I think':

> Had it been any other kind of book, the judgment of those nearest me would have been invaluable; but being what it is, it had to be entirely my own, since whoever writes as he speaks must take the whole responsibility; and to ask 'Do you think I may say this?' or 'write that?' is to shift a little of that responsibility on to someone else. This I could not bear to do, above all in the case of my husband, who sees this book now for the first time.[25]

Women's autobiography is repeatedly seen, throughout its history, as a private space, occupied without the knowledge or intervention of husbands; something a woman writes after her husband's death, or while he 'recreates himself with his pen' in another room and on another (more serious) work, as in the cases of the Duchess of Newcastle and Beatrice Webb. Frequently, it is the result of accumulated self-study, in diaries, letters, and experimental, self-conscious character-sketches produced on special occasions. In the first volume of her *Autobiography* Margot Asquith reprints studies of her parents' characters, written in her diary when they died; while Chapter VIII opens with a description of herself as she was in 1888, written, like Harriet Martineau's self-obituary, in the third person and noting her ability to survive antagonistic circumstances, in which she was assisted 'by having no personal vanity, the highest vitality and great self-confidence' (I, 90). The volume closes with another character sketch, written in 1906, nine weeks before the birth of her last baby. She begins, as in the previous sketch, with her appearance, perhaps because appearance counted first in the kind of society she knew. She preferred her earlier character-sketch, which was 'more external': 'after all, what can one say of one's inner self that corresponds with what one really is or what one's friends think one is?' (II, p. 250). This distrust of self-summary is increasingly the burden of women's autobiography written in the early twentieth century: hence Margot's frequent recourse to other authorities to support her impression of herself. Her first volume even includes responses to the *Autobiography* itself, from John Addington Symonds, who insists 'the absence of egotism is a great point', and from Henry James on her 'wonderful diary', which he praises as an 'admirable portrait of a lady' (I, 179). As with Beatrice Webb, the diary is more self-revealing, and a more accurate measure of emotional response to specific events than any reconstruction in the *Autobiography*.

In her second volume, Margot Asquith makes attempts to organise her memories more conventionally. Whereas her first volume was mainly about her family and friends before her marriage, her second, according to her Preface, is to concentrate on political events up to 1918. Yet the so-called 'political' volume soon digresses into 'My Last Riding Adventure' and 'My Theories upon Children and My Baby', which becomes an account of her neurasthenia. To further her readers' understanding of the condition, she cites another diary entry on her resistance to loss of health. For the first time in her life, she knew not only illness, but serious and regular duties, adding, however, outside the diary entry:

> Not the least sorrowful part of having neurasthenia is that your will-power, your character and your body are almost equally affected by it. Time, oxygen, and diet, added to regularity of hours and an untainted atmosphere,

are essential for complete recovery; and, what is even more vital, a patient
and perfect understanding in your daily surroundings. (II, 30)

She then quotes from her own paper on the upbringing of children,
having earlier, in Volume I, cited a diary account of her first experience of
childbearing. For a long time, she seems to avoid any direct account of
her children's characters and behaviour, finally admitting, in her tenth
chapter of Volume II, 'It is easier to talk than to write about one's
children; but in finishing this autobiography I can hardly leave them out'
(p. 178) – a reluctance well within the autobiographical tradition, both
for women as well as men. Husbands, sons and daughters, unless dead,
are apparently too close for cool and dispassionate analyses, or the autobiographer knows them too well to offer a simple summary. At any rate,
Margot Asquith again resorts to her diary for descriptions of her elder
child, Elizabeth, as she does for the death of Henry Asquith's son by his
first marriage, Raymond, who was killed during the First World War (II,
189–90). It is not only that the diary provides an emotional immediacy
that might be lacking in retrospective narrative: Margot Asquith, like
many autobiographers, especially other women, depends on the sincerity
and spontaneity of quoted diary entries to communicate her feelings on
the more personal and emotional occasions of her life. A dedicated role-
player, who seizes every opportunity to dramatise her relationships into
spirited, often comic exchanges, she relies on the diary to express the
devoted daughter, wife and mother. The vivid account of her sister
Laura's death – which 'had more effect on me than any event in my life,
except my own marriage and the birth of my children' – is again copied
from 'a short account of it', which she wrote at the time (I, 41).

The diary entries are also written in a consciously dramatic and visual
style, which would be less easy to project in a more formal narrative;
though all of Margot Asquith's *Autobiography* is peppered with dialogue
which heightens the dramatic effect. Despite her neurasthenia, she
portrays herself as a woman with a great zest for life. 'I am a simple
forthright person,' she declares in her collection of childhood autobiographies, *Myself When Young* (1938), culled from 'Famous Women of
To-day'. Here too, she suddenly announces: 'I always wished that I had
been born a man, as for what reason I do not know, I never understood my
sex, and although I have many women friends – [lists them] – I have many
more men, and I can truly say that I have never lost a man friend. . . .'[26]
The keynote of her autobiographical essay is ambition, and its opposite,
missed opportunity, which she feels is still a feature of women's lives.
Surprisingly, she blames their lack of imagination. 'A few female writers
have had imagination,' she concedes, 'as shown by their novels, but little
in other ways, or there would have been more women poets, painters,

playwrights, and composers' (p. 9). Although most professions were by then open to women, she did not think they had made 'anything very audible of their lives' (p. 10). Hence the importance of childhood and youth, as the years in which a woman either decides on her career, or accepts a life of ease and little achievement.

Even within the small compass of this autobiographical essay, Margot Asquith frequently digresses: for instance, into a lament for the building of flats and closing of stately homes:

> But my readers will forgive me, as though I am a very authentic person I am a very amateur author, and my first book was so virulently attacked at the time of publication that I made up my mind that I would never write another – indeed had it not been repeated to me that Virginia Woolf – the greatest woman writer of to-day – admired my literary style I would never have published another volume. Before accepting to edit this book I re-read some of the pages of my Autobiography for the first time since I wrote it, and found nothing objectionable in them. The enterprising Penguin Press tell me that they have sold one hundred and eighty thousand copies of it in the last year; the greatest compliment ever paid me. (p. 36)

The opening lines of this apology have a curiously eighteenth-century cadence, underlining the continuity of generic history. Although she preferred men to women, and claimed to have been most influenced by three men, Gladstone, Jowett and her husband (p. 32), it is the encouragement of a woman, Virginia Woolf, that means most to her when her book has been attacked. At the same time, she cannot conceal a smirk of satisfaction at the end, when she mentions, quite casually, just how many copies of her *Autobiography* have been sold.

The most interesting essay in her collection is a piece by Amy Johnson, whose discovery of her vocation traces the same pattern of fantasy and self-repression that was a hallmark of most autobiography by successful Victorian women. Like Annie Besant, Anna Jameson, Elizabeth Barrett and Elizabeth Sewell, Amy Johnson was a great dreamer – Beatrice Webb called it 'my cursed habit of sentimental castle-building'[27] – and used to recreate fairy stories while her mother played the piano. 'Mother played like an angel and I would lie on the sofa with my eyes shut living a wonderful secret life of my own, full of exciting adventures in which I was always the heroine and the end was always happy and satisfying.'[28] Beginning life with what she calls a 'superiority complex' (because she was good at school, and dominated her younger sister), she was hit in the teeth with a cricket ball, and 'quickly adopted a most unfortunate inferiority complex which followed me through the rest of my life and probably had a most important bearing on my future action and character' (p. 140). Feeling like an outcast, she became introspective, and dreamed of escape. Her years at Sheffield University 'were relatively unimportant and had little bearing on my future life and career, or on my character and temperament' (p. 146). As she explains: 'I could not take any serious interest in a career because I imagined at that time that my career was to be a home and children' (p. 150).

The course of events that made Amy Johnson into a pilot are shown, as so often in women's autobiography, to be fortuitous and unplanned. She happened to be living in Maida Vale, and by chance, there was an aerodrome nearby. 'Then one day happened that trivial little incident which was to alter the whole course of my life.' She was on a bus going to the Stag Lane aerodrome, and the planes above came lower and lower; until she was tempted to run up Stag Lane, and see whether she could afford to have flying lessons. 'To flying as a subsequent career I never gave a thought. I merely wanted to fly a plane all by myself' (p. 155). Looking back on her history, she was not surprised at the outcome. She had been born into an adventurous family; but she is conscious of the difference between her lot as a woman, and what she might have done had she been a man. '. . . I might have explored the Poles, or climbed Mount Everest, but as it was, my spirit found its outlet in the air. Everything in my life has since spelt adventure and I hope it always will' (p. 156). From the second half of the nineteenth century to the middle of the twentieth, there seems to have been a special consciousness in women's minds of what they had lost by not being born men. Chief among these non-opportunities was entering Parliament, but having the freedom to achieve in a public and exceptional way is frequently mentioned with envy and regret.

At this point, it is instructive to pause, and consider some autobiographies written by men at roughly the same period. Although male autobiographers were often more introspective than their friends, and conscious of being different in some way, their desire to achieve usually took a more concrete form and they were able to train themselves, through the normal channels of school, and literary society, towards eventual success. In one of his *Autobiographies*, *The Trembling of the Veil* (1922), for example, W. B. Yeats declares: 'I thought it was my business in life to be an artist and a poet, and that there could be no business in life comparable to that.'[29] He therefore helped found the Rhymers' Club, but had already met 'most of the poets of my generation' (p. 164). From his childhood, Yeats had legitimate access to a rich cultural life that was denied most female autobiographers before Virginia Woolf. Ethel Smyth undoubtedly trained herself from an early age to be a professional musician, but before she could go to Leipzig she had to overcome massive prejudices in her father's mind. 'It is no exaggeration to say that the life I proposed to lead seemed to him equivalent to going on the streets.'[30]

H. G. Wells, writing his *Experiment in Autobiography* (1934), noted the consistency of his *persona* (in the Jungian sense, 'a complicated system of relations between individual consciousness and society . . . a kind of mask').[31] 'From quite an early age I have been predisposed towards one particular sort of work and one particular system of interests,' he observes in a prefatory essay. He talks of finding 'the pattern of the key to master our world and release its imprisoned promise,' besides seeing his life in terms of a clear evolutionary development. 'An autobiography is the story of the contacts of a mind and a world,' Wells suggests. 'The story will begin in perplexity and go on to a troubled and systematic awakening. It will culminate in the attainment of a clear sense of purpose, conviction that the great world of order is real and sure; but, so far as my individual life goes, with time running out and a thousand entanglements delaying realization.'[32] The autobiographies of Harriet Martineau and Beatrice Webb conform to this pattern, but for many women there was no such steady growth towards certainty, and consequently a more random structure to their writing. Women autobiographers are also a good deal less confident in prescribing genre expectations. There is rarely much suggestion in their autobiographical writing that the genre must include specific stages or relationships. Perhaps they recognised that the structure of their lives was often too variable and uncertain for it to accommodate the linear growth from 'perplexity' to 'attainment'; perhaps they simply felt the genre was not, by rights, theirs to formulate.

With the final pairing of autobiographers in this study, however, Isadora Duncan and Beatrice Webb, the sense of purpose is stronger than in any previous writer since Harriet Martineau. 'I believe that whatever one is to do in one's after life is clearly expressed as a baby,' Isadora Duncan announces at an early point in her autobiography, *My Life* (1928). 'I was already a dancer and a revolutionist.'[33] Nevertheless, she is constantly aware of the multiplicity of her selves and the conflicts between them, unlike H. G. Wells, who believed that his *persona* was consistent. 'How can we write the truth about ourselves?' asks Duncan, when even newspaper reports of one's character and appearance entirely contradict one another:

> So if at each point of view others see in us a different person, how are we to find in ourselves yet another personality of whom to write in this book? Is it to be the Chaste Madonna, or the Messalina, or the Magdalen, or the Blue Stocking? Where can I find the woman of all these adventures? It seems to me there was not one, but hundreds – and my soul soaring aloft, not really affected by any of them. (p. 10)

Duncan sees herself here in terms of stereotyped 'images of women', mostly of a derogatory kind established by men. She knew her life had been controversial, and that the public were aware of her numerous love-affairs, notorious opposition to marriage, and belief in a woman's right to have a child, without feeling obliged to marry the father. She herself had had three illegitimate children, one of whom had died shortly after birth, while the elder two had died in a horrifying motor accident. Yet she implies that there are other Isadora Duncans unrecognised by the hostile public; and here her perception of the individual identity closely parallels Virginia Woolf's in *To the Lighthouse*, published the previous year. Thinking of Mrs Ramsay, Lily Briscoe feels that she needs fifty pairs of eyes to see with: 'Fifty pairs of eyes were not enough to get round that one woman with, she thought.'[34]

Isadora Duncan finds language itself an inadequate reflector of real life. 'To write of what one has actually experienced in words, is to find that they become most evasive' (p. 10). Writing and lived experience operate on separate time-scales, and are at odds in emotional duration:

> As I advance in these memoirs, I realise more and more the impossibility of writing one's life – or, rather, the lives of all the different people I have been. Incidents which seemed to me to last a lifetime have taken only a few pages; intervals that seemed thousands of years of suffering and pain, and through which, in sheer self-defence, in order to go on living, I emerged an entirely different person, do not appear at all long here. I often ask myself desperately: 'What reader is going to be able to clothe with flesh the skeleton that I have presented?' I am trying to write down the truth, but the truth runs away and hides from me. (p. 339)

If she were a novelist, she concludes, she would have got nearer the truth by making novels of her life; as it is, her life as an artist would have required a separate story: 'for my artist life and thoughts of Art have grown quite aloof, and grow still, like a separate organism, seemingly quite independent of what I call my Will' (p. 339). Not for her, therefore, the 'Portrait of the Artist' kind of novel chosen as fictional autobiography by James Joyce or D. H. Lawrence; nor the female *bildungsroman* preferred by Charlotte Brontë and George Eliot.

As it is, Isadora Duncan mythologises her life, or at any rate, her lovers, by drawing on romantic legend to express the incommunicable passions of her various tragic liaisons. Her first sexual encounter was with a Hungarian actor she calls 'Romeo'; afterwards came Edward Gordon Craig, whom she compares with Endymion, Hyacinthus, Narcissus, Perseus, Shelley, and one of Blake's angels; her son Patrick was fathered by another man she calls 'Lohengrin'; Walter Rummel, the pianist she calls her 'Archangel'; while she herself was like Niobe when her children were killed, and otherwise like the heroines of Ovid's

Metamorphoses, constantly changing form and character 'according to the decree of the immortal gods' (p. 340). In fact, she confesses, she sometimes sees her life as 'a Golden Legend studded with precious jewels', and sometimes as 'but a series of catastrophes' (p. 361). With all her passion for Greece, and Greek forms of dance, she clearly identified with classical myth as a paradigm for her autobiography; a pattern quite unlike the commoner recurrent form based on Biblical typology.

Towards the end of her book, Duncan declares her alternative version of the 'Seven Ages of Man': a decidedly hellenic 'Four Ages of Woman':

> How mysterious it is to feel the life of the body, all through this weird journey on earth. First the timid, shrinking, slight body of the young girl that I was and the change to the hardy Amazon; then the vine-wreathed bacchante drenched with wine, falling soft and resistless under the leap of the satyr. I live in my body like a spirit in a cloud – and a cloud of rose fire and voluptuous response. (p. 373–4)

Soon after this vision of a Blakean 'fiend hid in a cloud', Isadora Duncan closes her autobiography, as so many other women had done before her, with an apocalyptic vision of a new world that will, she hopes, give her life more meaning than the old. She chooses to end her writing on the eve of her arrival in Russia, a world created by Buddha, Christ, Lenin, and all great artists: 'I was entering now into this dream that my work and life might become a part of its glorious promise' (p. 376).

Although she often seems to inhabit her own private visionary world, Isadora Duncan, like her predecessors in the genre, was still acutely conscious of the carping reader. Determined to go on with it to the end, she nevertheless heard 'the voices of all the so-called good women of the world saying: "A most disgraceful history." "All her misfortunes are only a just requital of her sins"' (p. 340). Little seems to have changed since Charlotte Brontë's autobiographical heroines defended themselves against the unsympathetic responses of narrow-minded readers convinced that they would have avoided the miserable experiences of Jane Eyre and Lucy Snowe.[35] Like Brontë's heroines, Duncan refuses to be cowed. 'But I am not conscious of having sinned. Nietzsche says, "Woman is a mirror," and I have only reflected and reacted to the people and forces that have seized me . . .' (p. 340). It is ironic that at this point in her self-defence, she cites such a misogynist as Nietzsche.

Of all her contemporary women autobiographers, Isadora Duncan is the most outspoken on specifically female life-events. Whereas Margot Asquith resorted to her diary for accounts of her sister Laura's death after childbirth and her own difficult deliveries, Isadora Duncan writes openly of her conflicting emotions and physical suffering on the births of her children. She was dismayed by the distortion of her body, and the threat to her success as a dancer (p. 207). 'And then, you may say, when I saw the baby I was repaid. Yes, certainly I had a consummate joy, but nevertheless I tremble with indignation even to-day when I think of what I endured, and of what many women victims endure through the un- speakable egotism and blindness of men of science who permit such atrocities when they can be remedied' (p. 209–10). At every stage, she anticipates the conventional response of her readers, and argues its banality; though she frequently contradicts herself, and seems untroubled by the inconsistencies of her emotional development. Inconsistency, alternate moods of euphoria and depression, belonged to her experience of pregnancy and motherhood: to the extent that having worried about the disappearance of her ambitions, she then saw the baby as a creation superior to any art. 'What did I care for Art! I felt I was a God, superior to any artist' (p. 210).

Nevertheless, to live with Gordon Craig was to renounce not only her art, but also her personality and individuality (p. 222). Although she believed he appreciated her art more than anyone, his pride, according to Duncan, 'would not allow him to admit that any woman could really be an artist' (p. 199). Viewing the dance as an art of liberation, Duncan came to realise that there would always be a conflict between her aspirations as an artist, and her private life as a woman; unless she could find a man prepared to accept her on terms very different from Gordon Craig's. Hence her taste for images of battle, and the structuring of her life-story round a series of violent myths. 'My soul was like a battlefield where Apollo, Dionysus, Christ, Nietzsche, and Richard Wagner disputed the ground' (p. 162). Finally, she sees it as her 'fate' that she attempted the impossible in trying to reconcile her love for Gordon Craig with the continuation of her career (p. 199). She stresses her own faithfulness, and reverses the usual misogynist sayings about the changeability of women, insisting she would probably not have left any of her lovers if they had been faithful to her. 'For just as I once loved them, I love them still and for ever. If I have parted from so many, I can only blame the fickleness of men and the cruelty of Fate' (p. 344).

If Isadora Duncan's autobiography emphasises the physical aspects of her life as a woman, it gives equal prominence to the visionary or spiritual side of her life as a dancer. Inspired by movements of despair and revolt, she recovered from each of her crises by returning to the stage. It comes as no surprise to learn that one of her heroines was Ellen Terry, the 'ideal' of her life (p. 72). When she was pregnant with her daughter, Deirdre, she dreamt three times of Ellen Terry, and the child herself turned out 'a perfect miniature of Ellen Terry' (p. 242). Gordon Graig was of course Terry's son, by an affair similar to Duncan's own with Craig, and both women experienced life as a conflict between the claims of love and art. 'I believe that in each life there is a spiritual line,' Duncan argues:

> an upward curve, and all that adhered to and strengthens this line is our life – the rest is but as chaff falling from us as our souls progress. Such a spiritual line is my Art. My life has known but two motives – Love and Art – and often Love destroyed Art, and often the imperious call of Art put a tragic end to Love. For these two have no accord, but only constant battle. (p. 252)

This Lawrentian vision of conflict could be transcended only by the transformation of her disillusionment and suffering into her art (p. 117). Even so, the form of her autobiography is random, in keeping with the unstructured, uncertain nature of her life as an itinerant performer. Her favourite image is of the sea. She believed that all the great events of her life had taken place by the sea, and her first idea of movement came from the rhythm of the waves (p. 18). 'My life and my Art were born of the sea.' As a 'free-spirited woman' (p. 26), Duncan expresses her affinity with all natural, untrammelled things. She remains aware of her audience, but openly defies convention. Having lost her children, she no longer seems to care about what people will think, and depicts her life as a series of resounding triumphs alternating with disasters. Appropriately, her first memory is of a fire, of screams and flames, and the security of being held by the policeman who rescued her (p. 17).

The critics were predictably hostile. *The Times Literary Supplement* saw Duncan as 'incapable of outer control or interior discipline'. Her sensations of 'sex and maternity' had nothing individual about them: 'they might be the experiences of any one of a thousand other women; they tell us nothing of the soul of Isadora Duncan'.[36] By contrast, the same journal particularly admired Beatrice Webb's *My Apprenticeship* (1926), concluding that 'by far the most remarkable and delightful aspect of the book is revealed in the diarist's entries concerning herself.'[37] Here at last was vindication of a form that was especially attractive to women autobiographers, the incorporation of diary entries into a larger exercise in self-writing. Nor was the *TLS* alone in its praise. Like Ethel Smyth's *Impressions*, *My Apprenticeship* was warmly welcomed for the attractive picture it gave of its author. Even its inevitable egotism was excused. 'Nobody will charge her with having written to gratify the vanity that plagued her in her youth,' the *New Statesman* assured her.[38] Virginia Woolf, who knew both the Webbs, found the book 'enthralling.' It set her thinking about how she would write her own life: 'But then there were causes in her life: prayer, principle. None in mine.' Unlike Virginia Woolf, Beatrice Webb seemed to belong to the process of history:

Mrs Webb's Life makes me compare it with mine. The difference is that she is trying to relate all her experiences to history. She is very rational & coherent. She has always thought about her life & the meaning of the world: indeed, she begins this at the age of 4. She has studied herself as a phenomenon. Thus her autobiography is part of the history of the 19th Century. She is the product of science, & the lack of faith in God; she was secreted by the Time Spirit. Anyhow she believes this to be so.[39]

Yet Beatrice Webb came to autobiography with as much reluctance as any of her Victorian predecessors, combined with a certain guilty pleasure in the process of sifting through her old diaries. Since the diaries have only recently been published in an extended form, edited by Norman and Jeanne MacKenzie, today's readers have an additional insight into the process of composition, beyond anything revealed by the diary entries included in *My Apprenticeship*. She started writing her autobiography in the winter of 1916–17, when she was tired of her investigations into economic theory. 'I want to summarise my life and see what it all amounts to,' she told her diary in 1918. She came to see it in terms of development, both emotional and intellectual; and from an early stage in her writing, she was looking for patterns as she tried to piece her life into 'a connected whole'.[40] Like John Stuart Mill in his *Autobiography*, she also wanted to express her personal philosophy of life: in her case, the meaninglessness of the scientific method without the presence of a religious impulse directing the purpose of her existence. But the work was not altogether healthy. 'There is a certain morbid tendency in writing this book,' she confessed in 1923. '– it is practically an autobiography with the love affairs left out – the constantly recurring decision of what degree of self-revelation is permissible and desirable. The ideal conduct would be to treat the diaries exactly as I should treat them if they were someone else's.'[41] Having begun by calling the work 'a book of my life' (3 January, 1917), she uses the term 'autobiography' with noticeable reluctance, as she does in the final draft of *My Apprenticeship*: 'Though for the purpose of describing my craft I quote pages from my M.S. diary, I have neither the desire nor the intention of writing an autobiography.' Yet the subject-matter of her science is society: 'thus I can hardly leave out of the picture the experience I have gathered, not deliberately as a scientific worker, but casually as a child, unmarried woman, wife and citizen.'[42]

When the writing was finished, and the realities of publication drew nearer, Beatrice Webb's anxiety expressed itself in familiar images. Publishing an autobiography was as unpleasant as 'selling your personality as well as your professional skill. You are displaying yourself like an actress or an opera singer – you lose your privacy.'[43] She was worried by the fact that her closest friends seemed less than enthusiastic about it. The

Bernard Shaws were discouraging; her husband Sidney Webb did his best to approve, but she sensed his doubts. 'In his heart he fears I am over-valuing it, especially the extracts from the diaries; the whole thing is far too subjective, and all that part which deals with "my creed" as distinguished from "my craft" seems to him the sentimental scribblings of a woman, only interesting because they are feminine.'[44] Like her Victorian predecessors, she tried to justify it on grounds of 'helpfulness' or simply as an account of 'Victorianism' (19 March, 1925). Nevertheless, Sidney's criticism lodged so firmly in her mind that she was remembering his exact phrase, the dismissive 'scribblings of a woman', six years later, in 1931, when she started the sequel to *My Apprenticeship*, *Our Partnership* which, from its inception was meant to be a more low-key, less demanding venture than the account of her life as a single woman discovering her craft and her creed.[45]

By the time she came to write *My Apprenticeship*, Beatrice Webb had read a good selection of autobiographies, both by other women, and by her male friends and contemporaries. One of the earliest to impress her was Harriet Martineau's, which she read in 1877, when she was only nineteen. In the rather prim style of her diary entries at that age, she noted that despite Martineau's indisputable egotism the book was candid and open, and conformed to a pattern. 'Her life, like most lives, begins with piteous whining at the unhappiness and wickedness of the world and intense egotism, and ends in a song of praise and an ignoring of self in the wider interests of humanity.'[46] This was to be very much the direction of Webb's own autobiography, when she had discovered her life's work many years later. About John Cross's *Life* (1885) of George Eliot, she felt less positive, while acknowledging the curious link, through Herbert Spencer (Webb's friend until his death), between their lives. Eliot's character, as revealed in her letters, seemed selfish, but she was interested in what the novelist had to say about 'inherited fate', the cause, Webb believed, of much misery in those who rebelled against it, longing for advantages which did not belong to them. '*Renunciation*, that is the great fact we all, individuals and classes, have to learn. In trying to avoid it we bring misery to ourselves and others.'[47]

In 1877, she read and made notes on George Sand's *Histoire de ma Vie* (1854), and in 1886 Herbert Spencer let her read in manuscript that part of his *Autobiography* (1904) which dealt with the growth of his ideas. She felt he had sacrificed the whole of his nature to the one aim of pursuing and proving his philosophy of society. 'I feel in reading his life what I have often felt about him in the flesh, that though there has been a grand struggle with outside circumstances, grandly borne, yet there has been and is no sign of a struggle with his own nature.' Four days later, she made a diary note of a conversation with Spencer, who told her that he had never been in love, and so there had been no feeling of sacrifice in pursuing his work and giving up everything to it.[48] This was exactly the opposite of Beatrice Webb's experience, following her physical attraction to Joseph Chamberlain and awareness of his despotic nature. She realised that if she married him, she would have to subordinate her own ideas to his political principles, whether or not she agreed with them. The whole affair left her with a profound sense of shame and embarrassment. 'I have *chattered* about feelings which should be kept within the holy of holies,' she told her diary (I, 117). Nevertheless, she urged Spencer to continue his *Autobiography*, whatever doubts she had about his chilly, self-absorbed habits of analysis.

Long after the publication of *My Apprenticeship*, Beatrice Webb continued to take a critical interest in other autobiographies. Havelock Ellis's *My Life* (1939) struck her as 'a sickly book, mostly self-exhibition in his love-affairs, which I failed to read through'; Wells's *Experiment in Autobiography* she found less antagonistic: 'this frank self-exposure interests me.'[49] Until the end of her life, however, Webb judged the self-writing of her friends by standards akin to those of her Victorian predecessors in the genre. The impulse to take stock of her life at frequent intervals, alternating between the day or week-long retrospect, and the summary of much longer phases of experience, was accompanied by a strong sense of shame at self-exposure. Occasionally, Webb conflates the concepts of diary and autobiography. A diary entry of 1887, for example, refers to the book in which she records the history of her own life – specifically of 'a woman's life' – as 'the autobiography,' from which she is anxious to exclude statistics of wages, hours of work, and her research. The important thing was 'to keep a record of individual growth', as in the tradition of Evangelical spiritual autobiography. 'So often have I found strength in turning over the back pages of my life, in watching the inevitable work its way, in spite of my desperate clutches after happiness, which were seemingly foredoomed to failure' (I, 220). The coalescence here of 'life' and 'autobiography', the lived existence and the written record of it, is unusual in the context of critical debate about the exact identity of the autobiographical self.

By 1888, Beatrice Webb was imagining an audience for her diary, by splitting herself into reader and writer: the reader detached and ironic, addressing the anxious writer as 'my dear' and 'Friend', and offering supportive advice on her career and relationships. She had already begun to wonder 'who it is to whom one writes in a diary,' deciding on 'some mysterious personification of one's own identity' (p. 280). She also called this ghostly reader her 'impersonal confidant' (I, 120). Certainly, its identity helped to establish the sense of a split personality, which permeates Beatric Webb's thinking about herself. In *My Apprenticeship*, she describes her mother, too, as being 'cursed with a divided personality', torn between her intellectual ambitions and her role as mother to nine daughters (p. 13).

It comes as no surprise to find that Beatrice Webb often discusses specifically female identity as a split consciousness. In 1886, she had read an article by Frederick Myers (1843–1901), an amateur psychologist and spiritualist, and founder of the Society for Psychical Research, 'on multiple personality, giving pathological cases in which absolutely different personalities appeared in the same person according as different parts of their brain were physically acted upon'. This, she felt, must also happen in response to mental agents, such as a change of ideas: 'And certainly in my own case I have noticed a duplex personality, and have been happy or unhappy as one or the other got uppermost in me.' The 'nethermost' being she linked with her mother, Lawrencina Heyworth: 'the gloomily religious – affecting asceticism and dominated by superstition' (I, 188). But her other side was 'light-hearted (because unegotistical)', essentially a realist and sceptic. It was this side that she saw as presenting special difficulties for women, because it springs from the 'sensual nature', and 'unless fulfilled in marriage, which would mean destruction of the intellectual being, must remain controlled and unsatisfied', venting its feelings in the one acceptable outlet, 'religious exaltation' (I, 189). The struggle between these two beings, similar to Charlotte Brontë's personified battles between Reason and Passion in the lives of Jane Eyre and Lucy Snowe, was intensified by her feelings for Joseph Chamberlain. She concludes, however, in Brontë's terminology, that 'womanly dignity and reserve side with Fate and forbid the inroads of Passion' (I, 189).

Reading through what she had written of *My Apprenticeship* fifty years later, Beatrice Webb, quarrying her old diaries, gathered that she saw herself 'as one suffering from a divided personality; the normal woman seeking personal happiness in love given and taken within the framework of a successful marriage; whilst the other self claimed, in season and out of season, the right to the free activity of "a clear and analytic mind"' (p. 279). Both the diary and the autobiography reiterate doubts about her own intellectual abilities, for which she was apparently sacrificing so much, but she was quite certain that 'the life of love and the life of reason' could not have been united. The fact that they were, in her marriage to Sidney Webb, is not allowed to obscure the very real sense of absolute choice between two incompatible alternatives, which is the dominant theme of *My Apprenticeship*.

At the same time, her choice is presented largely as a piece of good fortune, guided by the deaths of her parents at critical moments in her development. 'I have not despised the simple happiness of a woman's life,' she wrote in her diary in 1886, when her father was recovering from a stroke; 'it has despised *me* and I have been humbled as far down as a woman *can* be humbled. My way in life has been chosen for me' (I, 160). Whereas her mother's death in 1882 had 'revolutionised' her life by making her 'a principal, a person in authority' in her father's household (*My Apprenticeship*, p. 113), Richard Potter's illness seemed to destroy all the ground she had gained between 1883 and 1887 as a social investigator. Beatrice Webb saw these as the most important years of her life, during which she 'was transformed into, I will not say a professional, but a professed brain-worker, overtly out for a career of my own' (p. 257). Her reluctance to use the term 'professional' matches her general unwillingness, throughout *My Apprenticeship*, to protest against the special difficulties of her role as a woman and unmarried daughter.

In a preliminary retrospect of her life, written in 1901, Beatrice Webb noted the divergent paths of her experiences as a woman and as a professional. One half of her personality seemed able to thrive only at the expense of the other, exacerbated by physical irritations, from childhood illnesses to a dislike of overeating which is frequently mentioned in her diary. During the crucial years 1883–7, she believed her intellect had been leading a separate life from her emotions, until she acquired 'an almost religious resignation of the woman's life'. From that point, her intellectual interests steadily overtook her emotional development:

> The very month of my deepest humiliation as a woman, August 1887, was the very month that my first article was accepted by Knowles of the *Nineteenth Century*; the time of my greatest pain, November 1888, when Chamberlain was getting married to the charming American, I was 'starring' it at Oxford, acclaimed as a new light in a new science. (*Diary*, II, 192)

In *My Apprenticeship*, however, Beatrice Webb avoids writing about her crush on Chamberlain, and underplays her reluctance to marry Sidney. A painful courtship, constantly threatened by unwanted declarations of devotion on Sidney's part, and strict regulations on Beatrice's, is glossed over affectionately in the autobiography. Although she writes openly of her despair, she ascribes it to the general conditions of ill-health and purposelessness, rather than to the specific problem of her unrequited feelings for Chamberlain. From her position as omniscient narrator, she could afford an indulgent smile of pity over the sorrows of her earlier self. 'How little we mortals know what is good for us,' she comments after a diary entry on her 'slough of despond' in the 1880s. Looking back, she seemed to see a 'guardian angel' hardening her own purpose 'and perhaps another person's [Chamberlain's] heart' (p. 284). But in relying heavily on her diary entries, Beatrice Webb generally creates a dialogue with her former self, rather than 'being wise after the event': she lets the two Egos battle for supremacy, and tries to show her audience the *process* of struggle and recovery. 'Memory is a risky guide in tracing the ups and downs of belief; gaps in the argument are apt to be filled in, and the undulating line of feeling becomes artificially straightened' (pp. 92–3). Sometimes the diary entries are presented specifically as a dialogue between the two Egos (p. 96); but usually, they supply either a detailed account of her work, or a reliable transcript of her unhappiness: preserved as she experienced it, but written by a much earlier self, still gripped by unresolved anxieties about her future.

As the autobiography progresses, it becomes more impersonal: no surprise, perhaps, in one who 'delighted' in John Stuart Mill's *Autobiography* (p. 144). She relies increasingly on headings related to her work with Charles Booth on the condition of the London poor; reproduces tables and statistics; asks questions about social issues and answers them; and even allows Sidney to look over her shoulder and draw his own conclusions. Her name for him, 'The Other One', implies that he is a kind of *alter-ego* but inescapably different. '"What you needed," observes The Other One, "was not a tutor but a partner."' Beatrice, still struggling for an independent intellectual life at this point in her autobiography, rejects his premature diagnosis. '"But how could I select the partner until I had chosen the craft?" I ask' (p. 108). While she is perplexed about her relationship with Chamberlain (although he is not named), Sidney again intervenes with his complacent solution: '"Saved for me," interjects The Other One' (p. 284). Occasionally, Sidney's interventions are admonitory, as when he advises her against including an 'irrelevant' diary entry (p. 187), but she accepts them in good part, recognising, in any case, that when Sidney is with her she cannot talk to the 'Other Self' with whom she communed when she was alone (*Diary*, II, 330). Between the 'Other Self' and the 'Other One' lies an uncrossable gulf, though both are in a sense projections of Beatrice Webb's own identity.

In her discussion of women's autobiography in France, Nancy K. Miller suggests that a '*double* reading of George Sand's autobiography with her fiction 'would provide a more sensitive apparatus for deciphering a female self'.[50] In the case of Beatrice Webb, the double reading juxtaposes formal autobiography and informal diary, the public and the private, which Webb has sewn together in the proportions she selects. Although many contemporary critics not only accepted her method, but also admired it, it still screens the hidden interior world of the autobiographer/diarist from the eyes of her implied audience. Nevertheless, in the evolution of a hybrid form based on a system of advancing and retreating self-portraits, emerging from quickening and slowing time-scales, Beatrice Webb develops a mirroring process of special attractive-ness to women who had grown up essentially as 'Victorians' and found it difficult to shed their instincts of modesty and self-doubt. The dialogue between diary and autobiography illuminates the evolution of the private and public selves, supplying an inbuilt process of self-correction and emerging perspective. Discovering, in the diary, the full range of her conflicts and aspirations, Beatrice Webb rehearses the problems she sub-sequently confronts in *My Apprenticeship*. The fact that her first attempt at a full retrospect of her experiences was written in her diary epitomises the fundamentally private nature of the Victorian woman's impulse to write her life.

Notes

1. *Leave the Letters Till We're Dead: The Letters of Virginia Woolf*, vol. VI 1936–1941, ed. Nigel Nicolson and Joanne Trautmann (London: The Hogarth Press, 1980), p. 453.
2. *A Literature of Their Own*, p. 240; cf. Martha Vicinus, *Independent Women*, 'Conclusion'.
3. Elaine Showalter, *The Female Malady: Women, Madness and English Culture, 1830–1980* (London: Virago, 1987), p. 197.
4. Virginia Woolf, *A Room of One's Own* (London: The Hogarth Press, 1929; St Albans: Granada Publishing Ltd., 1977), p. 76.
5. There are about forty women's autobiographies about the First World War according to Philip Dodd, 'The culture of autobiography in England 1820–1940', a paper given at the Higher Education Teachers of English Confer-ence, Liverpool, 1985.
6. Josephine E. Butler, *Personal Reminiscences of a Great Crusade* (London: Horace Marshall & Son, 1896), p. 4.
7. *A Writer's Recollections*, pp. 372–3.
8. Emmeline Pankhurst, *My Own Story* (London: Eveleigh Nash, 1914), 'Foreword'. Jill Craigie's introduction (London: Virago, 1979) gives useful background.
9. Ray Strachey, *Millicent Garrett Fawcett* (London: John Murray, 1931), p. 343.
10. Millicent Garrett Fawcett, *What I Remember* (London: T. Fisher Unwin, 1924), p. 9.
11. Orlo Williams, 'Some feminine autobiographies', *Edinburgh Review* 231 (April 1920), pp. 303–17.
12. 'A great autobiography', *New Statesman* (8 November 1919), pp. 159–60; *Times Literary Supplement* (23 October 1919), p. 587.
13. Ethel Smyth, *Impressions That Remained* (London: Longmans, Green & Co., 2 vols, 1919), I, p. 1.
14. *The Memoirs of Ethel Smyth*, abridged and introduced by Ronald Crichton (London: Viking, 1987), p. 51; p. 356.

15. Ethel Smyth, *Streaks of Life* (London: Longmans, Green & Co., 1921), p. 1.
16. Woolf *Letters*, VI, 453.
17. Smyth, *Memoirs*, p. 42.
18. *Ibid.*, p. 44.
19. *The Diary of Virginia Woolf*, vol. I, 1915–1919, intro. Quentin Bell, ed. Anne Olivier Bell (London: The Hogarth Press, 1977), p. 315.
20. *The Autobiography of Margot Asquith*, with an Introduction by Mark Bonham Carter (London: Methuen, 1985), p. xxviii.
21. 'Mrs. Asquith's autobiography', *New Statesman* (6 November 1920), pp. 135–6.
22. *The Autobiography of Margot Asquith* (1920; 2 vols, London: Penguin Books, 1936), I, pp. 187–93; p. 133.
23. 'Mrs. Asquith's memories', *Times Literary Supplement* (4 November 1920), p. 716; *Nation* (13 November 1920), pp. 226–8.
24. Daphne Bennett, *Margot: A Life of the Countess of Oxford and Asquith* (London: Victor Gollancz, 1984), pp. 313–14.
25. Asquith, *Autobiography*, Preface.
26. *Myself When Young by Famous Women of To-day*, ed. the Countess of Oxford and Asquith (London: Frederick Muller, 1938), p. 24.
27. *The Diary of Beatrice Webb*, vol. II, 1892–1905, 'All the good things of life', ed. Norman and Jeanne MacKenzie (London: Virago/London School of Economics and Political Science, 1983), p. 160.
28. *Myself When Young*, pp. 132–3.
29. W. B. Yeats, *Autobiographies* (London: Macmillan Papermac, 1980), p. 188.
30. Smyth, *Memoirs*, p. 56.
31. *Jung: Selected Writings*, ed. Anthony Storr (London: Fontana Paperbacks, 1983), p. 94.
32. H. G. Wells, *Experiment in Autobiography: Discoveries and Conclusions of A Very Ordinary Brain (since 1866)* (London: Victor Gollancz/The Cresset Press, 2 vols, 1934), I, pp. 26–8.
33. *My Life by Isadora Duncan* (London: Victor Gollancz, 1928), p. 19.
34. Virginia Woolf, *To the Lighthouse* (1927; Harmondsworth: Penguin, 1976), p. 224.
35. *Jane Eyre* (1847; Harmondsworth: Penguin, 1966), pp. 140–1; *Villette* (1853; Harmondsworth: Penguin, 1979), p. 228.
36. *Times Literary Supplement* (24 May 1928), p. 392.
37. 'The craft of a social investigator', *Times Literary Supplement* (4 March 1926), p. 155.
38. 'The industrious apprentice', *New Statesman* (27 February 1926), pp. 616–17.
39. *The Diary of Virginia Woolf*, vol. III, 1925–1930, ed. Anne Olivier Bell, p. 74.
40. *The Diary of Beatrice Webb*, vol. three, 1905–1924, 'The power to alter things', ed. Norman and Jeanne MacKenzie (London: Virago/London School of Economics and Political Science, 1984), p. 327; p. 356.
41. *Ibid.*, p. 412.
42. Beatrice Webb, *My Apprenticeship* (London: Longmans, Green & Co., 1926), p. 1.
43. *The Diary of Beatrice Webb*, vol. four, 1924–1943, 'The wheel of life', ed. Norman and Jeanne MacKenzie (London: Virago/London School of Economics and Political Science, 1985), p. 61.

44. *Ibid.*, pp. 50–2; pp. 48–9.
45. *Ibid.*, p. 236.
46. *The Diary of Beatrice Webb*, vol. one, 1873–1892, 'Glitter around and darkness within', ed. Norman and Jeanne MacKenzie (London: Virago/London School of Economics and Political Science, 1982), p. 25.
47. *Ibid.*, pp. 129–31.
48. *Ibid.*, p. 27; p. 169; p. 172.
49. *Diary*, IV, p. 448; p. 344.
50. 'Women's autobiography in France', *Women and Language in Literature and Society*, p. 270.

Conclusion

One of the earliest modern critics of autobiography as a genre was, unexpectedly perhaps, a woman: Anna Robeson Burr. Her book, *The Autobiography: A Critical and Comparative Study* (1909), offers an exhaustive survey of European self-writing classified according to type and content; but she confesses herself weary of endless discussion about the 'attributes of the sexes':

> How much of woman is in man, and how much of man in in woman, is a discussion perpetually in search of fresh evidence. Once for all, then, these pages can aid it little, for there is no sex to the autobiographer; on this field the writer stands or falls by the performance itself. The great self-student may be either man or woman; it is only required that he be thoroughly the one or the other. Equipment for this task is as much woman's as man's; each has his special candor, each his temperamental reticence.

Yet immediately Burr begins to hedge. 'As regards memory alone,' she continues, 'the woman's is usually more intimate, more personal, more limited and more complete.' She also appears to be 'naturally more secretive and reticent than man'.[1] Irresistibly, the case for absolute parity between male and female autobiographers disintegrates, and Burr is left insisting that Harriet Martineau, George Sand and Margaret Oliphant, at least, cannot be accused of presenting only 'a few scattered points', rather than a 'continuous stream'.

This study has argued that there is an identifiable tradition of Victorian women's autobiography that is distinct and apart from autobiography by Victorian men, although there are places where the two trajectories meet, and the notion of even a male 'tradition' in autobiography is sometimes difficult to substantiate. If I have stressed the similarities rather than the differences between the women's autobiographies I have discussed, that is because the recurrent patterns, rhetorical strategies and images were the most striking things about them; and in some respects, it was a disappointing experience to discover that so few women were able to deviate from the cultural norm. What chiefly emerges from a close study of Victorian women's autobiography is a sense of their fundamental estrangement from the genre. Even those women who had already violated the hidden quality of their lives had partially internalised the values of the dominant patriarchal culture. As Deirdre David has argued in her recent study of Harriet Martineau, Elizabeth Barrett Browning and George Eliot as intellectuals, many achieving Victorian women were 'both complicit with and resistant to the powers generating their authority to speak'. They were not consistently in conflict with the dominant culture: indeed, they actively contributed to its formation, frequently reinforcing images of the feminine ideal, and upholding traditional notions of the domestic and dependent womanly stereotype. As Deirdre David suggests, they were 'both collaborators and saboteurs in the world that enabled their very existence as women intellectuals'.[2] Hence the motif of the 'double life' that haunts so much self-writing by Victorian women. Sarah Bernhardt even called her memoirs *My Double Life* (1907); but most other women reveal their ambivalent commitment to autobiography in the rash of disclaimers, apologies and self-contradictory statements that mark their rhetorical strategy.

Throughout the nineteenth and early twentieth centuries, women can be seen resisting the autobiographical label, evading it, domesticating it, being defeated by it, or reshaping it to suit their priorities. Only a few, such as Harriet Martineau, approximate to the ideal of sustained self-writing established by the tradition of male critical theory. The rest prefer to assemble a collage of viewpoints and identities, mediated through selected diary entries and letter extracts, which instead of presenting a coherent picture of an individual life, stray off into eddies of gossip, incidental allusions to current affairs, and sketches of the great and famous. When these are removed, the connecting thread of narrative, particularly beyond childhood, may become minimal, as in Fanny Kemble's case, or impersonal, as in Emmeline Pankhurst's, or a social, professional and travel memoir, as in Mary Somerville's. Women autobiographers prefer to screen themselves behind a variety of poses: the devoted aunt, the indefatigable mother, the actress who enjoyed the simple things of life. The mirror they hold before their faces is often cracked or distorting, with perhaps the centre missing. The narrative they produce withholds those details the reader most wants to know, and gives instead the kind of information that can be found in any literary memoir.

The critic's task is to decide whether these characteristics of women's autobiography can be given a positive interpretation. Do they imply that women knew they could not match the professional self-portraiture of men (though this, of course, is often patchy and rarely consistent), and fall back on entertaining stories of respectable platitudes? Or is it possible to see women making something significant of their autobiographical difference? Can their use, and sometimes their invention, of alternative forms, such as diaries and letters, or Beatrice Webb's composite picture of herself through combined diary and autobiographical narrative, be seen as an attempt to remake the genre, or smash old moulds?

Unfortunately, Victorian women rarely allude to any theory of autobiography, other than their dislike of excessive egoism in the author, and their appreciation of her triumphant moral rectitude. On the other hand, they were keen readers of one another's works, more moved by them, on the whole, than they were by men's. George Eliot reading Harriet Martineau's *Autobiography*, Margaret Oliphant reading Fanny Kemble's and Mary Somerville's, Geraldine Jewsbury reading Margaret Fuller Ossoli's, Virginia Woolf reading Beatrice Webb's, and Beatrice Webb Harriet Martineau's, Katherine Mansfield reading Margot Asquith's, and Virginia Woolf Ethel Smyth's: the sheer energy of interest and comparison suggests a keen critical awareness, among Victorian and early twentieth-century women, of the range and scope of female self-writing. Nevertheless, it would be difficult to argue that they were conscious innovators, or that they were mounting a systematic critique of the male tradition, though here and there they comment on individual male autobiographers.

Their most important contribution to the genre is probably their reclamation of childhood experience: their sensitive recovery of childhood emotion, and their assemblage of richly suggestive images ranging from Elizabeth Sewell's fantasies of tight-rope walking before a royal duke, to Fanny Kemble's 'lingering desire for the distinction of a public execution by guillotine'.[3] In a post-Freudian age, these images have acquired a depth of significance undreamt of by their creators, which places them alongside Dickens's portrayal of a dense Gothic world of imaginative childhood experience. In describing this period of their lives, many Victorian women are relatively unselfconscious, secure in the comic potential of their narrative, their temporal distance from the events they describe, and the reduced risk of egotistical overtones. They frequently achieve an emotional intensity and coherence, founded on their willingness to probe an area of their lives that for centuries male autobiographers had not considered worth their attention. Few Victorian women employ the more traditional autobiographical myths of childhood as the Garden of Eden, or adolescence as a journey or a broadening river: hence their absence from critical studies based on recurrent hermeneutic structures, but hence, too, their sharp originality and freshness of vision.

They also write powerfully of their years of struggle, and first taste of publicity. This section of a woman's autobiography is often the richest in rhetorical confusion, as she tries to reconcile her pride and her modesty in the celebration of achievement, and may contain a subversive element of direct, or only half-articulated protest against the limitations of her condition. From the process of struggle gradually emerges the autobiographer's discovery of a distinctive and unexpectedly powerful voice, as in the work of Annie Besant, Harriet Martineau, Fanny Kemble, and Louisa Twining, though nearly all women autobiographers profit from a gaining of verbal, if not full economic independence. The moment of breakthrough is filled for most of them with mixed feelings of surprise, guilt and exhilaration, forcing their audience into vigilant acts of interpretation.

In an age where works seem to belong to the reader as much as to the author, and the emphasis is on a shared production of meaning, Victorian women's autobiography exhibits some of the most intriguing characteristics of the elusively authoritative text. In the gap between outward profession and a subtext of dissent, the author plays out her quest for an identity equally acceptable to herself and her audience. When, as frequently happens, only the audience can be overtly satisfied, the autobiographer chooses a form that leaves gates open and doors ajar. She allows her 'family memoir' to demonstrate her superior business sense, or her unshakeable energy, without blaming those who stood in her way or held her back; or she leaves a margin for the pencilling in of pride, success, and self-approbation, implicit in her achievements, but not allowed to be voiced. In other words, women's estrangement from the genre can be productive of multiple meanings. Their writing invites the reader to enter a debate about the equivocal nature of language used by a 'muted' group in a male-dominated genre.

Autobiography took the forms it did, in women's hands, because the demands made on their public personae were more complicated than those required of men. Much of their difficulty stems from the problem of communicating an acceptable personality, in an age (well into the twentieth-century) that condemned any form of exhibitionism by women. 'In short,' Geraldine Jewsbury told Jane Carlyle in 1850, 'whenever a woman gets to be a personage in any shape, it makes her hard and unwomanly in some point or other. . . .'[4] Most of their male contemporaries linger expansively over their self-portraits, as no woman had done since the eighteenth century. In fact, seventeenth- and eighteenth-century women are generally bolder and more innovative in their autobiographical writing than are their Victorian successors, who often prefer to refract a splintered self-image through several media at once:

the quoted letter or diary, the autobiographical narrative, and the novel, in which they may play a transvestite role. In this way, they appear to dilute the egotistical impact of their writing, taking, wherever possible, the most indirect paths towards themselves. H. G. Wells, by contrast, actually boasts of his 'obstinate self-conceit', which helped him survive, adding:

> I shall die, as I have lived, the responsible centre of my world. Occasionally I make inelegant gestures of self-effacement but they deceive nobody, and they do not suit me. I am a typical Cockney without either reverence or a sincere conviction of inferiority to any fellow creature.[5]

Many women were not the 'responsible centre' of their worlds; and even if they were, it was not something they chose to advertise. The forms of their autobiographies comply accordingly with a deflected image of themselves. Even those such as Margaret Oliphant and Elizabeth Sewell, who were the main breadwinners of their families, tend to marginalise their presence in narratives that occasionally stop altogether for a while, until the author has again found both the time and the urge to continue writing.

Some readers may well feel cheated by Victorian women's autobiography. As Estelle Jelinek has argued, autobiography is rarely as genuinely introspective as its name and associations imply, and in fact, the difficulty of representing lived experience in a written format is often seen as being insuperable.[6] Instead of helping them to dominate their experiences, autobiography seems to tangle women still further in the dilemmas that disturbed them when they were younger, pushing them back into an inaccessible personal past. An alternative way of reading women's autobiography, however, is to notice what is *not* said, to observe the places where initiative is downplayed, success denied, emotion dismissed, and ambition merely latent. It is this that makes the literary study of Victorian women's autobiography ultimately rewarding, and the texts themselves a significant contribution to the history of women's writing. If the retreating image cannot finally be caught, it can at least be pursued and its inconsistencies explored. Admittedly, this argument may be a way of saying that Victorian women's autobiography has *become* interesting because of new approaches to reading and interpretation. It may also belittle the consciousness of the writers, suggesting that their works have become hermeneutic curiosities. But after all, perhaps no author, whether man or woman, has ever satisfactorily resolved the contradictions, paradoxes, and sheer impossibility of writing a fully self-revelatory and accurate autobiography, and our definition of the genre ought to take account of the fact. The attraction of Victorian women's autobiography is chiefly its fruitfulness as a response to the social and linguistic strains experienced by literary women in the nineteenth century. Consideration of their special difficulties should remind us that if Benvenuto Cellini had been a woman living in Craigenputtoch with a dyspeptic husband, sixteen miles from a baker, '*and he a bad one*', he might not have fashioned his statue of Perseus, still less the story of his life.

Notes

1. Anna Robeson Burr, *The Autobiography: A Critical and Comparative Study* (London: Constable & Co. Ltd; Boston and New York: Houghton Mifflin Company, 1909), pp. 224–5.
2. Deirdre David, *Intellectual Woman and Victorian Patriarchy: Harriet Martineau, Elizabeth Barrett Browning, George Eliot* (London: Macmillan, 1987), p. 225; p. 230.
3. Kemble, *Record of a Girlhood*, I, 69.
4. *Selections from the Letters of Geraldine Endsor Jewsbury to Jane Welsh Carlyle*, ed. Mrs Alexander Ireland (London: Longmans, Green & Co., 1892), p. 368.
5. Wells, *Experiment*, I, 291.
6. Jelinek, p. 10.

Bibliography

I: Autobiographies by Victorian Women

Asquith, Margot, *The Autobiography of Margot Asquith* (London: Thornton Butterworth, 2 vols, 1920, 1922; Harmondsworth: Penguin, 1936; abridged, ed. Mark Bonham Carter, London: Methuen, 1985).

Barrett, Elizabeth, 'My own character' (1818) and 'Glimpses into my own life and literary character' (1820), in *Two Autobiographical Essays by Elizabeth Barrett*, ed. William S. Peterson, *Browning Institute Studies* II (New York, 1974).

Besant, Annie, *An Autobiography* (London: T. Fisher Unwin, 1893).

Bray, Anna Eliza, *Autobiography of Anna Eliza Bray*, ed. John A. Kempe (London: Chapman and Hall Ltd, 1884).

Butler, Josephine E., *Personal Reminiscences of a Great Crusade* (London: Horace Marshall & Sons, 1896).

'Charlotte Elizabeth', *Personal Recollections* (London: R. B. Seeley & W. Burnside, 1841).

Charlton, Barbara, *The Recollections of a Northumbrian Lady 1815–1866*, ed. L. E. O. Charlton (London: Jonathan Cape, 1949).

Cobbe, Frances Power, *Life of Frances Power Cobbe* (London: Richard Bentley & Son Ltd, 2 vols, 1894).

Coleridge, Sara, 'Recollections of the early life of Sara Coleridge. Written by herself', in *Memoir and Letters of Sara Coleridge edited by Her daughter* (London: Henry S. King & Co, 2 vols, 1873).

Cowden-Clarke, Mary, *My Long Life: An Autobiographic Sketch*, 2nd edition (London: T. Fisher Unwin, 1896).

Duncan, Isadora, *My Life by Isadora Duncan* (London: Victor Gollancz, 1928).

Eliot, George, *Impressions of Theophrastus Such*, 1879. Illustrated Copyright Edition (London: Virtue & Co, 1913).

Eliot, George, *The Lifted Veil*, 1859. Ed. Beryl Gray (London: Virago, 1985).

Fawcett, Mrs Henry, *What I Remember* (London: T. Fisher Unwin, 1924).

Howitt, Mary, *Mary Howitt: An Autobiography*, ed. Margaret Howitt, (London: William Isbister Ltd, 2 vols, 1889).

Jameson, Anna, 'A revelation of childhood', in *A Commonplace Book of Thoughts, Memories, and Fancies, Original and Selected* (London: Longman, Brown, Green & Longmans, 1854).

Jameson, Anna, *Diary of an Ennuyée* (London: H. Colburn, 1826; repr. Philadelphia: E. Littell, 1826).

Jameson, Anna, *Winter Studies and Summer Rambles in Canada*, 1838. Selections, ed. Clara Thomas (Toronto: New Canadian Library, 1965).

Kemble, Frances Anne, *Journal of A Residence on A Georgian Plantation in 1838–1839*, 1863. Ed. John A. Scott (London: Jonathan Cape, 1961).

Kemble, Frances Anne, *Further Records (1848–1883)* (London: Richard Bentley and Son, 2 vols, 1890).

Kemble, Frances, Anne, *Record of a Girlhood* (London: Richard Bentley and Son, 3 vols, 1878). *Records of Later Life* (London: Richard Bentley and Son, 3 vols, 1882).

Linton, Eliza Lynn, *The Autobiography of Christopher Kirkland* (London: Richard Bentley & Son, 3 vols, 1885). *My Literary Life* (London: Hodder and Stoughton, 1899).

Martineau, Harriet, *Harriet Martineau's Autobiography, with Memorials by Maria Weston Chapman* (London: Smith, Elder & Co., 3 vols, 1877). Ed. Gaby Weiner London: Virago, 2 vols, 1983).

Mitford, Mary Russell, *Recollections of A Literary Life; or Books, Places, and People* (London: Richard Bentley & Son, 3 vols, 1852).

Morgan, Lady, *Lady Morgan's Memoirs: Autobiography, Diaries and Correspondence*, ed. W. Hepworth Dixon (London: William H. Allen, 2 vols, 1862).

Morgan, Lady, *Passages from My Autobiography* (London: Richard Bentley & Son, 1859).

Nevill, Lady Dorothy, *The Reminiscences of Lady Dorothy Nevill*, ed. Ralph Nevill (London: Edward Arnold, 1906).

North, Marianne, *Recollections of a Happy Life. Being the Autobiography of Marianne North*, ed. Mrs John Addington Symonds (London: Macmillan, 2 vols, 1892).

Oliphant, Margaret, *The Autobiography and Letters of Mrs. M. O. W. Oliphant*, ed. Mrs Harry Coghill (Edinburgh and London: William Blackwood, 1899).

Ossoli, Margaret Fuller, *Memoirs of Margaret Fuller Ossoli* (London: Richard Bentley & Son, 3 vols, 1852).

Pankhurst, Emmeline, *My Own Story* (London: Eveleigh Nash, 1914). Ed. Jill Craigie (London: Virago, 1979).

Ritchie, Anne Thackeray, *Chapters from Some Memoirs* (London and New York: Macmillan, 1894).

Sellar, E. M., *Recollections and Impressions* (Edinburgh and London: William Blackwood, 1907).

Sewell, Elizabeth M., *The Autobiography of Elizabeth M. Sewell*, edited by her niece Eleanor L. Sewell (London: Longmans, 1907).

Sewell, Mary, *The Life and Letters of Mrs. Sewell. By Mrs. Bayley*, 4th edition (London: James Nisbet & Co, 1889).

Simcox, Edith, 'Autobiography of a shirt maker', MS Journal kept by Edith Simcox, 1876–1900. Bodleian: Eng. misc. d. 494.

Smyth, Ethel, *Impressions That Remained: Memoirs by Ethel Smyth* (London: Longmans, Green & Co., 2 vols, 1919).

Smyth, Ethel, *Streaks of Life* (London: Longmans, Green & Co., 1921).

Smyth, Ethel, *The Memoirs of Ethel Smyth*, abridged and introduced by Ronald Crichton (London: Viking, 1987).

Somerville, Mary, *Personal Recollections, from Early Life to Old Age, of Mary Somerville*, with Selections from her correspondence. By her daughter, Martha Somerville (London: John Murray, 1873).

Terry, Ellen, *The Story of My Life*, 1908. (Woodbridge, Suffolk: The Boydell Press, 1982).

Twining, Louisa, *Recollections of Life and Work. Being the Autobiography of Louisa Twining* (London: Edward Arnold, 1893).

Ward, Mrs Humphry, *A Writer's Recollections (1856–1900)* (London: W. Collins Sons & Co. Ltd, 1918).

Webb, Beatrice, *My Apprenticeship* (London: Longmans, Green & Co., 1926).

Wilson, Harriette, *Harriette Wilson's Memoirs of Herself and Others*, 1825. Ed. James Laver (London: Peter Davies, 1929).

Winkworth, Susanna and Catherine, *Memorials of Two Sisters Susanna and Catherine Winkworth*, ed. their niece Margaret J. Shaen (London: Longmans, Green & Co., 1908).

Wordsworth, Elizabeth, *Glimpses of the Past* (London and Oxford: A. R. Mowbray & Co. Ltd, 1912).

Yonge, Charlotte Mary, 'Autobiography', 1877, in *Charlotte Mary Yonge: Her Life and Letters*, ed. Christabel Coleridge (London: Macmillan, 1903).

II: Other Autobiographies Referred to in the Text

Asquith, Margot (ed.), *Myself When Young by Famous Women of Today* (London: Frederick Muller Ltd, 1938).

Bain, Alexander, *Autobiography* (London: Longmans, Green & Co., 1904).

Bellamy, George Anne, *An Apology for the Life of George Anne Bellamy, Late of Covent-Garden Theatre. Written by Herself*, 2nd edition (Dublin: Moncrieffe, 2 vols, 1785).

Bernhardt, Sarah, *My Double Life: Memoirs of Sarah Bernhardt* (London: William Heineman, 1907).

Brittain, Vera, *Testament of Youth: An Autobiographical Study of the Years 1900–1925*, 1933 (London: Virago, 1978).

Carlyle, Thomas, *Reminiscences*, ed. Charles Eliot Norton (London and New York: Macmillan & Co., 2 vols, 1887).

Carlyle, Thomas, *Sartor Resartus: the Life and Opinions of Herr Teufelsdröckh*, 1831 (London: Centenary Edition, Chapman and Hall, 1896).

Cavendish, Margaret, Duchess of Newcastle, 'A true relation of my birth, breeding, and life. By Margaret, Duchess of Newcastle', 1667, in *The Life of William Cavendish, Duke of Newcastle*, ed. C. H. Firth (London: John C. Nimmo, 1886).

Charke, Charlotte, *A Narrative of the Life of Mrs. Charlotte Charke, Written by Herself* (London: W. Reeve, 1755).

Darwin, Charles, *The Autobiography of Charles Darwin, 1809–1882*,. ed. Nora Barlow (London: Collins, 1958).

de Beer, Gavin (ed.), *Charles Darwin, Thomas Henry Huxley, Autobiographies* (London and New York: Oxford University Press, 1974).

Delany, Mary, *The Autobiography and Correspondence of Mary Granville, Mrs. Delany: With interesting reminiscences of King George the Third and Queen Charlotte*. ed. Lady Llanover (London: Richard Bentley & Son, 3 vols, 1861).

Dickens, Charles, *Fragment of Autobiography* in John Forster: *The Life of Charles Dickens*, 3 vols, 1872–4. New edition A. J. Hoppé (London: J. M. Dent & Sons Ltd, 2 vols, 1966), I, 20–33 *passim*.

Fanshawe, Ann, Lady, *The Memoirs of Ann, Lady Fanshawe*, ed. John Loftis (Oxford: Clarendon Press, 1979).

Gibbon, Edward, *Memoirs of My Life and Writings*, 1796. Ed. Betty Radice (Harmondsworth: Penguin, 1984).

Gosse, Edmund, *Father and Son: A Study of Two Temperaments*, 1907. Ed. Peter Abbs (Harmondsworth: Penguin, 1983).

Halkett, Anne, Lady, *The Memoirs of Anne, Lady Halkett*, ed. John Loftis (Oxford: Clarendon Press, 1979).

Hume, David, *The Life of David Hume Esq.*, Written by Himself (London: W. Strahan and T. Cadell, 1777).

Hunt, Leigh, *The Autobiography of Leigh Hunt; with Reminiscences of Friends and Contemporaries*, 3 vols, 1850. A new edition, revised by the author (London: Smith, Elder & Co., 1859).

Hutchinson, Lucy, 'The life of Mrs. Lucy Hutchinson, written by herself. A fragment.' in *Memoirs of the Life of Colonel Hutchinson*, ed. James Sutherland (London and New York: Oxford University Press, 1973).

James, Henry, *A Small Boy and Others* (London: Macmillan, 1913).

Jemmat, Catherine, *The Memoirs of Mrs. Catherine Jemmat, Daughter of the late Admiral Yeo of Plymouth. Written by Herself*, 2 vols, 1772.

Julian of Norwich, *A Book of Showings to the Anchoress Julian of Norwich*, ed. Edmund Colledge and James Walsh (Toronto: Pontifical Institute of Medieval Studies, 2 vols, 1978).

Kempe, Margery, *The Book of Margery Kempe*, ed. Sanford Brown Meech and Hope Emily Allen (London: Early English Text Society, 1940).

Kempe, Margery, *The Book of Margery Kempe: A Modern Version*, ed. W. Butler Bowdon (London and New York: Oxford University Press, 1952).

Manley, Mary Delariviere, *Mrs. Manley's History of Her Own Life and Times* (London: E. Curll and J. Pemberton, 1725).

Marlborough, Sarah, Duchess of, *Authentick Memoirs of her Grace, Sarah, Late Dutchess of Marlborough, with An Account of her Conduct from her first coming to Court. In a letter from Herself to a Noble Peer* (London: R. Walker, 1744).

Mill, John Stuart, *Autobiography*, 1873. Ed. Jack Stillinger, (London and Oxford: Oxford University Press, 1971).

Newman, John Henry, *Apologia pro Vita Sua*, 1865. Ed. Maisie Ward (London: Sheed and Ward, 1982).

Pattison, Mark, *Memoirs* (London: Macmillan, 1885).

Phillips, Teresia Constantia, *An Apology for the Conduct of Mrs. Teresia Constantia Phillips*. 3 vols, 1748.

Pilkington, Letitia, *Memoirs of Mrs. Letitia Pilkington, Wife to the Rev. Mr. Matthew Pilkington. Written by Herself*, 3 vols, 1749. Ed. Iris Barry (London: Routledge, 1928).

Piozzi, Hester Thrale, *Autobiography, Letters and Literary Remains of Mrs. Piozzi (Thrale)*, ed. A. Hayward (London: Longman, Green, Longman and Roberts, 2 vols, 1861).

Ruskin, John, *Praeterita*, 1885-9. Ed. Kenneth Clark (Oxford and New York: Oxford University Press, 1949/1978).

Spencer, Herbert, *An Autobiography* (London: Williams & Norgate Ltd, 2 vols, 1904).

Strachey, Lytton and Roger Fulford (ed.), *The Greville Memoirs 1814-1860*. (London: Macmillan and Co., 8 vols, 1938).

Thornton, Alice, *The Autobiography of Mrs. Alice Thornton, of East Newton, Co. York* (Edinburgh: Surtees Society, 1875).

Trollope, Anthony, *An Autobiography*, 1883. Ed. Michael Sadleir and Frederick Page, 1950; intro and notes, P. D. Edwards (Oxford and New York: Oxford University Press, Worlds Classics, 1980).

Warwick, Mary, Countess of, 'Some specialities in the life of M. Warwicke', *Percy Society Publications* XXII, ed. T. Crofton Croker, (London: Percy Society, 1848).

Wells, H. G., *Experiment in Autobiography: Discoveries and Conclusions of a Very Ordinary Brain (Since 1866)* (London: Victor Gollancz Ltd/Cresset Press Ltd, 2 vols, 1934).

Woolf, Virginia, *Moments of Being: Unpublished Autobiographical Writings*, ed. Jeanne Schulkind (London: The Hogarth Press, 1976).

Wordsworth, William, *The Prelude*, 1805 Text, ed. Ernest de Selincourt. New ed. Stephen Gill (London and New York: Oxford University Press, 1970, 1975).

Yeats, W. B., *Autobiographies* (London and Basingstoke: Macmillan, 1955; Papermac, 1980).

III: Books on Victorian Autobiography

Bates, E. Stuart, *Inside Out: An Introduction to Autobiography* (Oxford: Basil Blackwell, 2 vols, 1936–7).

Bruss, Elizabeth, *Autobiographical Acts: The Changing Situation of a Literary Genre* (Baltimore and London: Johns Hopkins University Press, 1976).

Buckley, Jerome Hamilton, *The Turning Key: Autobiography and the Subjective Impulse Since 1800* (Cambridge, Mass., and London: Harvard University Press, 1984).

Burr, Anna Robeson, *The Autobiography: A Critical and Comparative Study* (London: Constable & Co. Ltd; Boston and New York: Houghton, Mifflin Co., 1909.

Coe, Richard N., *When the Grass Was Taller: Autobiography and the Experience of Childhood* (New Haven and London: Yale University Press, 1984).

Egan, Susanna, *Patterns of Experience in Autobiography* (Chapel Hill and London: University of North Carolina Press, 1984).

Fleishman, Avrom, *Figures of Autobiography: the Language of Self-Writing in Victorian and Modern England* (Berkeley, Los Angeles and London: University of California Press, 1983).

Jelinek, Estelle C., *Women's Autobiography: Essays in Criticism* (Bloomington and London: Indiana University Press, 1980).

Landow, George P. (ed), *Approaches to Victorian Autobiography* (Athens: Ohio University Press, 1979).

Morris, John N., *Versions of the Self: Studies in English Autobiography from John Bunyan to J. S. Mill* (New York: Basic Books, 1966).

Nord, Deborah Epstein, *The Apprenticeship of Beatrice Webb* (London: Macmillan, 1985).

Olney, James (ed.), *Autobiography: Essays Theoretical and Critical* (Princeton, NJ: Princeton University Press: 1980).

Pascal, Roy, *Design and Truth in Autobiography* (London: Routledge and Kegan Paul, 1960).

Peterson, Linda H., *Victorian Autobiography: The Tradition of Self-Interpretation* (New Haven and London: Yale University Press, 1986).

Shumaker, Wayne, *English Autobiography: Its Emergence, Materials and Form* (Berkeley and Los Angeles: University of California Press, 1954).

Spengemann, William C., *The Forms of Autobiography: Episodes in the History of a Literary Genre* (New Haven and London: Yale University Press, 1980).

Stanton, Domna C., *The Female Autograph: Theory and Practice of Autobiography from the Tenth to the Twentieth Century* (Chicago and London: University of Chicago Press, 1987).

Weintraub, Karl Joachim, *The Value of the Individual: Self and Circumstance in Autobiography* (Chicago and London: University of Chicago Press, 1978).

IV: Books: General Background

Adams, W. H. Davenport, *Child-life and Girlhood of Remarkable Women* (London: W. Swan Sonnenschein & Co., 1883).

[Astell, Mary], *A Serious Proposal to the Ladies, for the Advancement of their True and Greatest Interest. By a Lover of her Sex* (London: R. Wilkin, 1694).

Atkinson, Clarissa W., *Mystic and Pilgrim: The Book and the World of Margery Kempe* (Ithaca and London: Cornell University Press, 1983).

Baker, Michael, *The Rise of the Victorian Actor* (London: Croom Helm, 1978).

Basch, Françoise, *Relative Creatures: Victorian Women in Society and the Novel* (London: Allen Lane, 1974).

Bennett, Daphne, *Margot: A Life of the Countess of Oxford and Asquith* (London: Victor Gollancz, 1984).

Benstock, Shari (ed.), *The Private Self: Theory and Practice of Women's Autobiographical Writings* (London: Routledge, 1988).

Bottrall, Margaret, *Every Man A Phoenix: Studies in Seventeenth Century Autobiography* (London: John Murray, 1958).

Branca, Patricia, *The Silent Sisterhood: Middle Class Women in the Victorian Home* (London: Croom Helm, 1975).

Brontë, Charlotte, *Jane Eyre: An Autobiography*, ed. Currer Bell. 1847 (Harmondsworth: Penguin, 1966).

Brontë, Charlotte, *Shirley*, 1849 (Harmondsworth: Penguin, 1974).

Brontë, Charlotte, *Villette*, 1853 (Harmondsworth: Penguin, 1979).

Butler, Josephine E. (ed.), *Woman's Work and Woman's Culture: A Series of Essays* (London: Macmillan and Co., 1869).

Chapple, J. A. V. and A. Pollard (ed.), *The Letters of Mrs. Gaskell* (Manchester: Manchester University Press, 1966).

Cobbe, Frances Power, *Essays on the Pursuits of Women* (London: Emily Faithful, 1863).

Colby, Robert A. and Vineta, *The Equivocal Virtue: Mrs. Oliphant and the Literary Marketplace* New York: Archon Books, 1966).

Coveney, Peter, *Poor Monkey: The Child in Literature* (London: Rockcliff, 1957).

Cross, J. W., *George Eliot's Life as Related in Her Letters and Journals* (New York: Harper Bros, 3 vols, 1885).

David, Deirdre, *Intellectual Women and Victorian Patriarchy: Harriet Martineau, Elizabeth Barrett Browning, George Eliot* (London: Macmillan, 1987).

de Beauvoir, Simone, *The Second Sex*, 1949. Trans. H. M. Parshley (Harmondsworth: Penguin, 1985).

Defoe, Daniel, *The Fortunes and Misfortunes of the Famous Moll Flanders*, 1722. Ed. G. A. Starr (London and Oxford: Oxford University Press, 1976).

Defoe, Daniel, *Roxana: The Fortunate Mistress*, 1724. Ed. David Blewett (Harmondsworth: Penguin, 1982).

Delany, Paul, *British Autobiography in the Seventeenth Century* (London: Routledge and Kegan Paul, 1969).

De Quincey, Thomas, *Suspiria De Profundis. The Posthumous Works of Thomas De Quincey*. Ed. Alexander H. Jupp (London: Heinemann, 1891).

Erle, Peter, *The World of Defoe* (Newton Abbot: Readers Union Group of Book Clubs, 1977).

Ebner, Dean, *Autobiography in Seventeenth-Century England: Theology and the Self* (The Hague, Paris: Mouton, 1971).

Eliot, George, *The Mill on the Floss*, 1860 (Harmondsworth: Penguin, 1979, 1987).

Ellis, Annie Raine (ed.). *The Early Diary of Frances Burney 1768–1778* (London: George Bell & Sons, 2 vols, 1907).

Ellis, Sarah Stickney, *The Mothers of England: The Influence and Responsibility* (London: Fisher, Son & Co., 1843).

Ellis, Sarah Stickney, *The Women of England* (London and Paris: Fisher, Son & Co. 1839).

Erskine, Mrs Steuart, ed., *Anna Jameson: Letters and Friendships (1812–1860)* (London: T. Fisher Unwin Ltd, 1915).

Fawcett, Mrs Henry, *Some Eminent Women of Our Times: Short Biographical Sketches* (London: Macmillan, 1889).

Finney, Brian, *'The Inner I': British Literary Autobiography of the Twentieth Century* (London: Faber & Faber, 1985).

Foster, Shirley, *Victorian Women's Fiction: Marriage, Freedom and the Individual.* (London: Croom Helm, 1985).

Frank, Anne, *Anne Frank's Diary*, 1947. Trans. B. M. Mooyaart-Doubleday, with a Foreword by Storm Jameson (London: Valentine, Mitchell & Co. Ltd: 1952).

Freud, Sigmund and Josef Breuer, *Studies on Hysteria*, 1895. *The Standard Edition of the Complete Psychological Works of Sigmund Freud*, trans. James Strachey (London: The Hogarth Press, 1955).

Furnas, J. C., *Fanny Kemble: Leading Lady of the Nineteenth Century Stage* (New York: The Dial Press, 1982).

Gilbert, Sandra M. and Susan Gubar, *The Madwoman in the Attic: The Woman Writer and the Nineteenth-Century Literary Imagination* (New Haven and London: Yale University Press, 1979).

Gorham, Deborah, *The Victorian Girl and the Feminine Ideal.* (London: Croom Helm, 1982).

Haight, Gordon S. (ed.), *The George Eliot Letters* (New Haven and London: Yale University Press, 9 vols, 1954–78).

Hardwick, Elizabeth, *Seduction and Betrayal: Women and Literature* (New York: Random House: 1970).

Holcombe, Lee, *Victorian Ladies at Work: Middle-Class Working Women in England and Wales, 1850–1914* (Newton Abbott: David & Charles, 1973).

Ireland, Mrs Alexander (ed.), *Selections from the Letters of Geraldine Endsor Jewsbury to Jane Welsh Carlyle* (London: Longmans, Green & Co., 1892).

Jameson, Anna, *Memoirs and Essays illustrative of Art, Literature, and Social Morals* (London: Richard Bentley & Son, 1846).

Jung, Carl Gustav, *Selected Writings*, ed., Anthony Storr (London: Fontana Paperbacks, 1983).

Kingsley, Mary, *Travels in West Africa*, 1897 (London: Frank Cass & Co, Ltd, 1965).

Klein, Melanie, *Love, Guilt and Reparation and Other Works 1921–1945*. Intro. R. E. Money-Kyrle (London: The Hogarth Press and Institute of Psycho-Analysis, 1975).

Kristeva, Julia, *About Chinese Women*, 1974. Trans. Anita Barrows (London: Marion Boyars, 1977).

Lamb, Charles, *Essays of Elia and Last Essays of Elia* (1823, 1833; London: Everyman's Library, J. M. Dent & Sons, 1962).

Landels, William, *Woman: Her Position and Power* (London and New York: Cassell, Petter, and Galpin, 1870).

Layard, George Somes, *Mrs. Lynn Linton: Her Life, Letters and Opinions* (London: Methuen, 1901).

Lowe, Gordon R., *The Growth of Personality: From Infancy to Old Age*, 1972. (Harmondsworth: Penguin, 1985).

MacKenzie, Norman and Jeanne (ed.), *The Diary of Beatrice Webb* (London: Virago and the London School of Economics and Political Science, 4 vols, 1982–5).

Marks, Elaine and Isabelle de Courtivron (ed.), *New French Feminisms: An Anthology* (Amherst, Mass.: University of Massachusetts Press, 1980; Hemel Hempstead: Harvester Wheatsheaf, 1981, 1985).

Marshall, Dorothy, *Fanny Kemble* (London: Weidenfeld & Nicolson, 1977).

Martin, Helena, Lady, *On Some of Shakespeare's Female Characters* (London and Edinburgh: William Blackwood & Sons, 1885).

Martineau, Harriet, *Household Education* (London: Edward Moxon, 1849).

Matthews, William, *British Autobiographies: An Annotated Bibliography of British Autobiographies Published or Written Before 1951* Berkeley and Los Angeles: University of California Press, 1955).

Misch, Georg, *A History of Autobiography in Antiquity*, trans. E. W. Dickes (Cambridge, Mass.: Harvard University Press, 2 vols, 1951).

Moi, Toril, *The Kristeva Reader* (Oxford: Basil Blackwell, 1986).

Moi, Toril, *Sexual/Textual Politics: Feminist Literary Theory* (London and New York: Methuen, 1985).

Monteith, Moira (ed.), *Women's Writing: A Challenge to Theory* (Hemel Hempstead: Harvester Wheatsheaf, 1986).

Mulock, Dinah, *A Woman's Thoughts About Women* (London: Hurst & Blackett, 1858).

Murray, Janet Horowitz, *Strong-Minded Women and Other Lost Voices from 19th-Century England* (Harmondsworth: Penguin, 1982, 1984).

Nestor, Pauline, *Female Friendships and Communities: Charlotte Brontë, George Eliot, Elizabeth Gaskell* (Oxford: Clarendon Press, 1985).

Olney, James, *Metaphors of Self: the Meaning of Autobiography*. (Princeton, NJ: Princeton University Press, 1972).

Osborne, Dorothy, *Letters to Sir William Temple*, ed. Kenneth Parker (Harmondsworth: Penguin, 1987).

Perry, Ruth, *Women, Letters, and the Novel* (New York: AMS Press, 1980).

Raverat, Gwen, *Period Piece. A Cambridge Childhood.* (London: Faber & Faber, 1952; Faber Paperbacks, 1977).

St John, Christopher (ed.), *Ellen Terry and Bernard Shaw: A Correspondence* (London: Reinhardt & Evans Ltd, 1931, 1949).

St John, Christopher (ed.), *Ethel Smyth: A Biography* (London and New York: Longmans, Green & Co., 1959).

Sand, George, *Histoire de ma Vie (My Life)*, trans. Dan Hofstadter (London: Victor Gollancz: 1979).

Sanders, Valerie, *Reason Over Passion: Harriet Martineau and the Victorian Novel* (Hemel Hempstead: Harvester Wheatsheaf, 1986).

Segal, Hanna, *Klein*, Fontana Modern Masters (London: Fontana, 1979).

Sewell, Elizabeth Missing, *A Glimpse of the World* (London: Longman, Roberts & Green, 1863).

Sewell, Elizabeth Missing, *Home Life and After Life* (London: Longmans & Co., 1891).

Sewell, Elizabeth Missing, *Note-Book of an Elderly Lady* (London: Walter Smith, 1881).

Sewell, Elizabeth Missing, *The Experience of Life* (London: Longmans & Co., 1853).

Shelley, Mary, *Frankenstein, or the Modern Prometheus*, 1818 (Harmondsworth: Penguin, 1985).

Showalter, Elaine, *A Literature of Their Own: British Women Novelists from Brontë to Lessing* (Princeton, NJ: Princeton University Press, 1977; London: Virago, 1978).

Showalter, Elaine, *The Female Malady: Women, Madness, and English Culture, 1830–1980* (London: Virago, 1985).

Showalter, Elaine (ed.), *The New Feminist Criticism: Essays on Women, Literature, and Theory* (London: Virago, 1986).

Simpson, Alan and Mary McQueen, *I Too Am Here: Selections from the Letters of Jane Welsh Carlyle* (Cambridge: Cambridge University Press, 1977).

Smollett, Tobias, *The Adventures of Peregrine Pickle, in which are included Memoirs of a Lady of Quality*, 1751. Ed. James L. Clifford (London and New York: Oxford University Press, 1964).

Spacks, Patricia Meyer, *Imagining a Self: Autobiography and the Novel in Eighteenth-Century England* (Cambridge, Mass. and London: Harvard University Press, 1976).

Spacks, Patricia Meyer, *The Female Imagination: A Literary and Psychological Investigation of Women's Writing* (London: George Allen & Unwin, 1976).

Spencer, Jane, *The Rise of the Woman Novelist. From Aphra Behn to Jane Austen* (Oxford: Basil Blackwell, 1986).

Stauffer, Donald, *English Biography before 1700* (Cambridge, Mass.: Harvard University Press, 1930).

Steen, Marguerite, *A Pride of Terrys. Family Saga* (London and New York: Longmans, Green & Co. 1962).

Stodart, M. A., *Female Writers: Thoughts on Their Proper Sphere, and on Their Powers of Usefulness* (London: R. B. Seeley & W. Burnside, 1842).

Stone, Lawrence, *The Family, Sex and Marriage in England 1500–1800*, 1977. Abridged edition (Harmondsworth: Penguin, 1985).

Strachey, Ray, *The Cause*, 1928 (London: Virago, 1978).

Thal, Herbert Van, *Eliza Lynn Linton: The Girl of the Period. A Biography* (London: George Allen & Unwin, 1979).

Toynbee, William (ed.), *The Diaries of William Charles Macready* (London: Chapman & Hall, 2 vols, 1912).

Trevelyan, Janet Penrose, *The Life of Mrs. Humphry Ward* (London: Constable, 1932).

Vicinus, Martha (ed.), *A Widening Sphere: Changing Roles of Victorian Women* (London and New York: Methuen, 1980).

Vicinus, Martha (ed.), *Independent Women: Work and Community for Single Women 1850–1920* (London: Virago, 1985).

Williams, Merryn, *Margaret Oliphant: A Critical Biography* (Basingstoke and London: Macmillan, 1986).

Wise, T. J. and J. A. Symington (ed.), *The Brontës: Their Lives, Friendships and Correspondence* (Oxford: Basil Blackwell, 4 vols, 1932).

Woolf, Virginia, *A Room of One's Own* (St Albans: The Hogarth Press: 1929; Granada Publishing Limited, 1977).

Woolf, Virginia, *Leave the Letters Till We're Dead: The Letters of Virginia Woolf*, Vol. VI 1936–1941, ed. Nigel Nicolson and Joanne Trautmann (London: The Hogarth Press, 1980).

Wordsworth, Dorothy, *Journals of Dorothy Wordsworth* 2nd edition, ed. Mary Moorman (Oxford and New York: Oxford University Press, 1958, 1971).

Yonge, Charlotte M. (ed.), *Biographies of Good Women: Chiefly by Contributors to 'The Monthly Packet'* (London: J. & C. Mozley, 1862).

Yonge, Charlotte M. (ed.), *The Clever Woman of the Family*, 1865 (London: Virago, 1985).

V: Articles

Anderson, Linda, 'At the threshold of the self: women and autobiography'. *Women's Writing*, ed. Moira Monteith, pp. 54–71.

Athenaeum, 'Annie Besant', 103 (3 February 1894), p. 146.

Athenaeum, 'Frances Power Cobbe', 104 (29 September 1894), pp. 413–14.

Bloom, Lynn Z., 'Heritages: dimensions of mother-daughter relationships in women's autobiographies', *The Lost Tradition: Mothers and Daughters in Literature*, ed. Cathy N. Davidson and E. M. Broner (New York: Frederick Ungar Publishing Co., 1980).

Carlock, Mary Sue, 'Humpty Dumpty and the autobiography', *Genre* 3 (December 1970). pp. 340–50.

Cobbe, Frances Power, 'Personal recollections of Mrs Somerville. By her daughter, Martha Somerville', *Quarterly Review* 136 (January 1874), pp. 74–103.

[Croker, J. W.], 'Journal of Frances Anne Butler', *Quarterly Review* 54 (July 1835), pp. 39–58.

Frerichs, Sarah C., 'Elizabeth Missing Sewell: concealment and revelation in a Victorian everywoman', *Approaches to Victorian Autobiography*, ed. Landow, pp. 175–99.

Greene, Donald, 'The uses of autobiography in the Eighteenth Century', *Essays in Eighteenth-Century Biography*, ed. Philip B. Daghlian (Bloomington and London: Indiana University Press, 1968) pp. 43–66.

Gusdorf, Georges, 'Conditions and limits of autobiography', *Autobiography: Essays Theoretical and Critical*, ed. Olney, pp. 28–48.

Hart, Francis R., 'Notes for an anatomy of modern autobiography', *New Literary History* I, no. 3 (Spring 1970), pp. 485–511.

Howarth, William L., 'Some principles of autobiography', Olney, pp. 84–114.

Jones, Ann Rosalind, 'Writing the body: l'écriture féminine', *The New Feminist Criticism*, ed. Elaine Showalter, pp. 361–77.

Juhasz, Suzanne, '"Some deep old desk or capacious hold-all": form and women's autobiography', *College English*, 39, no. 6 (February 1978), pp. 663–8.

Kemble, Frances Anne, 'On the stage', *Cornhill Magazine* VIII (December 1863), pp. 733–7.

Kent, Christopher, "Image and reality": the actress and society', *A Widening Sphere*, ed. Martha Vicinus, pp. 94–116.

Lifson, Martha Ronk, 'The myth of the fall: a description of autobiography', *Genre* 12 (1979), pp. 45–67.

Linton, Eliza Lynn, 'A retrospect', *Fortnightly Review* 38 N.S. (44 O.S.) (November 1885), pp. 614–29.

[Martineau, Harriet], 'Doddridge's correspondence and diary', *Monthly Repository* 4 (January 1830), pp. 15–26.

Mason, Mary, G., 'The other voice: autobiographies of women writers', Olney, pp. 207–35.

Matthews, William, 'Seventeenth century autobiography', *Autobiography, Biography and the Novel*, papers read at a Clark Libary Seminar, 13 May, 1972 (Los Angeles: William Andrews Clark Memorial Library, 1973).

Miller, Nancy K., 'Women's autobiography in France: for a dialectics of identification', *Women and Language in Literature and Society*, ed. McConnell-Ginet, Borker and Furman, pp. 258–73.

Myers, Mitzi, 'Harriet Martineau's autobiography: the making of a female philosopher', *Women's Autobiography*, ed. Estelle C. Jelinek, pp. 53–70.

Myers, Mitzi, 'Unmothered daughter and radical reformer: Harriet Martineau's career', *The Lost Tradition*, ed. Davidson and Broner, pp. 70–80.

Oliphant, Margaret, 'Autobiographies': Series in *Blackwood's*, beginning with 'Benvenuto Cellini', 129 (January 1881), pp. 1–30. See especially no. 3, 'Margaret, Duchess of Newcastle', 129 (May 1881). pp. 617–39.

Oliphant, Margaret, 'Harriet Martineau', *Blackwood's* 121 (April 1877, pp. 472–96.

Oliphant, Margaret, 'Mary Russell Mitford', *Blackwood's* 75 (June 1854), pp. 658–70.

Oliphant, Margaret, 'Two ladies', *Blackwood's* 125 (February 1879), pp. 206–24.

Osborn, James M., 'The beginnings of autobiography in England', paper delivered at the 5th Clark Libary Seminar, 8 August 1959 (Los Angeles: University of California, 1960).

Peterson, Linda H., 'Audience and the autobiographer's art: an approach to the autobiography of Mrs. M. O. W. Oliphant', Landow, pp. 158–74.

Pomerleau, Cynthia S., 'The emergence of women's autobiography in England', Jelinek, pp. 21–38.

Sanders, Valerie R., '"Absolutely an act of duty": choice of profession in autobiographies by Victorian women', *Prose Studies* 9 (December 1986), pp. 54–70.

Showalter, Elaine, 'Feminist criticism in the wilderness', *The New Feminist Criticism*, ed. Showalter, pp. 243–70.

[Simcox, Edith], 'Autobiographies', *North British Review* 51 (O.S.) 12 (N.S.) (January 1870), pp. 383–414.

[Simcox, Edith], 'New books' [includes Mrs Somerville's *Personal Recollections*], *Fortnightly Review* 21 (January 1874), pp. 109–20.

[Smith, William Henry], 'Miss Mitford's "Recollections"', *Blackwood's* 71 (March 1852), pp. 259–72.

Spacks, Patricia Meyer, 'Reflecting Women', *Yale Review* LXIII (October 1973), pp. 26–42.

Spacks, Patricia Meyer, 'Selves in Hiding', Jelinek, 112–32.

Spacks, Patricia Meyer, 'Women's stories, women's selves', *The Hudson Review* XXX (Spring 1977), pp. 29–46.

Spectator, 'Mrs. Besant's autobiography' (3 March 1894), pp. 309–10.

Spectator, 'Miss Cobbe's autobiography' (10 November 1894), pp. 645–7.

[Stephen, Leslie], 'Autobiography', *Cornhill Magazine* XLIII (April 1881), pp. 410–29.

Walters, Margaret, 'The rights and wrongs of women: Mary Wollstonecraft, Harriet Martineau, Simone de Beauvoir', *The Rights and Wrongs of Women*, ed. Juliet Mitchell and Ann Oakley, Harmondsworth: Penguin, 1976) pp. 304–78.

Walther, LuAnn, 'The invention of childhood in Victorian autobiography', Landow, pp. 64–83.

Weintraub, Karl J., 'Autobiography and historical consciousness', *Critical Inquiry* I, no. 4 (June 1975), pp. 821–48.

Williams, Orlo, 'Some feminine autobiographies', *Edinburgh Review* 231 (April 1920), pp. 303–17.

Winston, Elizabeth, 'The autobiographer and her readers: from apology to affirmation', Jelinek, pp. 93–111.

Woolf, Virginia, 'Ellen Terry', *Collected Essays* IV (London: The Hogarth Press, 1967), pp. 67–72.

Woolf, Virginia, 'Laetitia Pilkington', *Collected Essays* IV (1967), pp. 129–33.

Woolf, Virginia, 'Sara Coleridge', *Collected Essays* III (London: The Hogarth Press, 1967), pp. 222–6.

Wrigley, E. A., 'The growth of population in eighteenth-century England: a conundrum resolved', *Past and Present* (February 1983), 121–50.

Index